DIETZ ©

FACES OF VICTORY

EUROPE: Liberating a Continent

From the Editors of *VFW Magazine*

Bob Snodgrass
Publisher

Richard K. Kolb
Executive Editor

Gary L. Bloomfield
Senior Editor

Michael McKenzie
Consulting Editor

Robert Widener
Design Consultant

Dan Hill
Research Consultant

Anita Stumbo
Design and Typography

Production Assistance: Sharon Snodgrass, Diana Rose, Steve Van Buskirk, Vern Pall, Pat Brown, Betty Bachand, Peggy Allee, Jamie Montgomery, David Sumner, Jack Smith, Jerry Steely, Kristina Brisendine, Clark Nungester, Laura Bostrom, Lydia Steinberg, Kris-Ann McKenzie, Timothy K. Dyhouse, Jeannie Thompson

Contributing Photographers: Chris Vleisides, Chris Dennis

Original artwork courtesy Norman Rockwell Foundation and Jim Dietz

Gatefold map courtesy of U.S. Military Academy, West Point

Select photos courtesy of National Archives

Remaining photos courtesy the Veterans of Foreign Wars Archives

Published by Addax Publishing Group, Kansas City, Missouri

Library of Congress Catalog Card Number: 95-77870

ISBN: 1-886110-00-X (General)
ISBN: 1-886110-02-6 (Limited)
ISBN: 1-886110-05-0 (Collector's)

ADDAX
PUBLISHING
GROUP

To the millions of Americans who served in the
European Theater of Operations between 1941 and 1945,
and especially those who sacrificed their lives there
in defense of the nation.

Table of contents

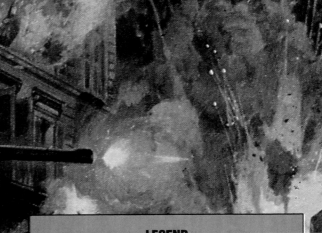

LEGEND

Listed below are some key terms commonly used in military writing. They apply to both unit designations and casualty categories.

UNITS

Term		Abbreviation
Platoon	(25–30 men)	Plt.
Company	(100–130)	Co.
Battalion	(600–900)	Bn.
Regiment	(1,800–2,700)	Regt.
Division	(10,000–15,000)	Div.
Infantry		Inf.
Airborne		Abn.
Armored		Armd.
Regimented Combat Team		RCT
Parachute Infantry Regiment		PIR
Combat Command A or B		CCA or CCB

CASUALTIES

Killed in Action	KIA
Wounded in Action	WIA
Died of Wounds	DOW
Missing in Action	MIA
Prisoner of War	POW

Preface

Capt. Walker "Bud" Mahurin and his Republic P-47 Thunderbolt called *The Spirit of Atlantic City, N.J.*, escort a B-17 of the 1st Bombardment Division, Eighth Air Force, on a bombing raid over Germany in March 1944. Capt. Mahurin flew with the 56th Fighter Group and his 21 shootdowns made him one of the top scoring American fighter aces in the ETO.

"Bud's Jug," by Harley F. Copic, courtesy of
The Air Force Art Collection

PUBLICATION OF *Faces of Victory: Europe — Liberating a Continent* was a project undertaken by the Veterans of Foreign Wars with great enthusiasm. After all, paying homage to America's warriors has been the essence of the VFW's very reason for being for nearly a century.

This volume, like the Pacific volume, is dedicated not only to the more than 1 million VFW members who are WWII vets, but to all 16 million Americans — living and dead — who wore a military uniform during that momentous era.

The idea for such a permanent literary tribute was conceived early on with the launching of *VFW Magazine*'s "50 Years Ago This Month" series, starting in December 1991. The intent of the series, as well as this volume, is twofold: honor those who served and sacrificed, and provide a standard reference for generations to come.

Most other histories focus heavily on the political/diplomatic, strategic/tactical and generalship of the war; this is a chronicle of the average American fighting man. It zeroes in on his experiences, views, hardships and sacrifices. Firsthand accounts provide the heart of the book. Coverage is comprehensive — soldiers, sailors, airmen, Marines and Coast Guardsmen, and specialized unit members, all receive due credit.

Moreover, rather than rehashing the "big battles" exclusively and in great detail, *Faces of Victory* highlights the little-known combats and units rarely spotlighted. It's jam-packed with firsts and lasts. And it is liberally illustrated with photographs, art, sidebars and charts.

The story line is based on geographical theaters of operation, not strict chronological order. This makes for easier reading because of the complexity of recounting simultaneous campaigns.

Release of the book coincided with the 50th anniversary of the end of WWII in Europe because the war was in the headlines and on the minds of

"The Beginning" © Dietz

the American people. It seemed only appropriate that the VFW be in the forefront of recognizing this most important event.

Liberating a Continent is the mutual effort of the editorial staff of *VFW Magazine*, Addax Publishing Group and a half dozen free-lance authors. All combined considerable research and writing talents to produce a work that the venerable VFW is proud to promote. Years of research went into its development; painstaking attention was paid to detail to ensure an authentic account.

Nonetheless, a single volume can cover only so much history. We used our best judgment, based on letters received from WWII veterans over the years, and the desire to offer a fresh perspective, to guide the book's contents. Still, any factual errors or omissions fall squarely at my doorstep.

— RICHARD K. KOLB
Editor-in-Chief
VFW Magazine
Kansas City, Missouri
September 1995

Foreword

Gen. William C. Westmoreland

ORLD WAR II — more specifically, the European Theater of Operations (ETO) — was my crucible. As a young officer, I had the distinct honor of serving with the proud 9th Infantry Division. It was that all-important experience that guided my career and imbued me with a life-long admiration for the American fighting man.

As a lieutenant colonel commanding the 34th Field Artillery Battalion, I arrived at Casablanca, Morocco, on Christmas eve, 1942. For the next 2½ years, my life was intertwined with fighting Hitler's armies. For four months my battalion traversed Morocco, Algeria and Tunisia. At Thala in Tunisia, the men of the 34th earned a Presidential Unit Citation and my abiding respect.

On Sicily, the battalion had the privilege of supporting the 82nd Airborne Division. After my unit moved to England and then across the English Channel, we landed at Utah Beach and fought at Cherbourg. We fought across northern France all the way to the Siegfried Line.

Later, as chief of staff of the division, I played a role in the multiple battles for control of the Huertgen Forest and battled on the Elbe River in eastern Germany.

(In 30 months of combat, the 9th Division lost 4,504 killed in action and 17,416 wounded in action.)

Service in Europe earned me the right to join the Veterans of Foreign Wars, of which I have been a proud life member since 1966. No organization is better qualified to tell the story of the American fighting man than the VFW. My whole-hearted enthusiasm is behind this publication, *Faces*

of Victory: Europe — Liberating a Continent. It is an excellent tribute to the men who served and sacrificed so much for their country. With *VFW Magazine*'s editorial staff at the helm, combined with the historians who have contributed to the magazine over the years, there is no doubt readers will be pleased with this work.

This fast-paced and meticulously researched volume will be a wonderful keepsake for any veteran of WWII to pass on to his children and grandchildren. In capsulizing the essence of the GI's war, *Liberating a Continent* is second to none and I am pleased to introduce it.

— WILLIAM C. WESTMORELAND
General, U.S. Army (Ret.)
Charleston, South Carolina
September 1995

Acknowledgments

"B-17 Nose" © Dietz

TACKLING A PROJECT as monumental as summing up America's fighting man during World War II in Europe in one volume is difficult at best. Fortunately, a wealth of information has been compiled and distilled by historians — both amateur and professional — over the past 50 years.

Consequently, we at *VFW Magazine* are indebted to all those who came before us for painstakingly putting the pieces of the European Theater puzzle together. Without the standard references that have been handed down, no history of GIs in the ETO would have been possible.

Of course, the contributing authors — Dominic Caraccilo, Ken Hechler and David Colley — must be singled out for providing the primary story lines. All three have invested their considerable research and writing talents to make *Faces of Victory: Europe — Liberating a Continent* a reality. Also, Gen. William Westmoreland was kind enough to write the preface. And he, Adm. Chester Nimitz Jr. and President Gerald Ford lent their names to the special collector's edition.

The Veterans of Foreign Wars has a unique reservoir on which to draw. The most valuable contributors to this work are the former fighting men themselves — individual VFW members. It was their personal stories and experiences that made the pages come alive with realism.

Over the past four years, the magazine series on WWII has rekindled fading memories and revived the interest of countless members. Many took the time to write — offering constructive criticism, correcting the editors when we went astray and filling in the historical blanks.

For the hundreds of VFW members who have donated immeasurably to the magazine's archives, I say thank you. It was the insight of those who were actually there on the battlefields, at sea and in the air who inspired this book.

Acquiring photographs and artwork is always a major undertaking, and this project was no exception. Here again, members sent their personal snapshots to use in the book. Most pictures, though, were culled from VFW archives.

The National Archives, U.S. Army Military History Institute, Naval Historical Center, U.S. Naval Institute, U.S. Marine Corps Historical Center, West Point Museum, U.S. Air Force Art Collection and the Smithsonian Air and Space Museum provided the original photographs. Combat artists and photographers deserve the credit for capturing on film and canvas the life and death struggles endured by Americans in WWII.

"Darby's Rangers" © Dietz

Famed WWII artist James Dietz and the Norman Rockwell Museum in Stockbridge, Mass., supplied many of the action-packed prints that open each section of the book.

Everyone in the VFW's Publications and Public Affairs Department played a role in completing this book, too. Gary Bloomfield, Timothy K. Dyhouse, Robert Widener, Betty Bachand, Pat Brown, Peggy Allee, Vern Pall and Steve Van Buskirk contributed their time and efforts. When we panicked about deadlines, they were there to pitch in and bail us out. Both Pat and Robert, no doubt, are grateful for the opportunity to have become WWII experts in their own right.

Outside the Publications Department, several individuals at the VFW provided indispensable assistance. Ron Browning of Marketing Services and Walt Bates of the Information Technology Department helped make the book available to members across the country.

The editors can honestly say our greatest debt is owed to our families. On weekends and in the evening, wives and children must have wondered who that stranger was intruding into their lives; replacing their husband and father in the den.

This is one case where the final acknowledgment is by far the most important. A special thanks to Bob Snodgrass of Addax Publishing for seeing the value in producing *Faces of Victory*. Only his belief in the worthiness of this project allowed it to happen. Undoubtedly, he has aged considerably during the past year in coordinating its production.

As an organization, the VFW was wholeheartedly behind this venture. From Commander-in-Chief Allen "Gunner" Kent to Adjutant General Larry Rivers to Quartermaster General Joe Ridgley, all of the leaders understood the importance of paying tribute to World War II veterans on the 50th anniversary of the war's end. As the publisher's special certificate says, acknowledging service and sacrifice has been a fundamental VFW mission for nearly a century.

ROAD TO WAR

"Goodbye Dear, I'll Be Back in a Year . . ." — As the urgent need for preparedness swept the country in the autumn of 1940, Battery C, 2nd Battalion, 189th Field Artillery leaves Blackwell, Okla., on Sept. 23, 1940, to a waving send-off as part of the nation's greatest peacetime mobilization. Activation of the National Guard doubled the size of the Army, and nearly all the reserve units served five years or more. The Oklahoma unit joined the 45th Infantry Division (Thunderbird), which became one of the most decorated Army divisions while fighting in eight major campaigns. National Guard Heritage painting

Mobilizing for the
War Against the Axis

Causes

"

The campaigns in the Mediterranean and in Europe had no prior parallel in the history of warfare; throughout them, the United States Army had engaged in operations without comparable precedent since its establishement in 1775.

"

— GEN. DWIGHT D. EISENHOWER

WHEN WORLD WAR II began in Europe in 1939 with Nazi Germany's invasion of Poland, most Americans hoped Hitler would be defeated swiftly. Most also favored the U.S. staying out of the European conflict by limiting its involvement to assisting the Allies with war materials and supplies.

After Hitler conquered Norway, France and the Low Countries in 1940 and threatened to invade Great Britain, any hope of indefinite U.S. neutrality vanished. In December 1940, President Franklin D. Roosevelt proposed that the U.S. become the "arsenal of democracy," definitively linking the U.S. to the cause of the Allies.

In March 1941, in response to Nazi propaganda and threats of sabotage by Nazi agents, the U.S. seized German and Italian ships in American ports and interned their crews. The next month the U.S. guaranteed the defense of Greenland, and American vessels began delivering arms and supplies to beleaguered British forces in the Near East by way of the Red Sea.

When a German submarine sank the destroyer *USS Robin Moor* in the South Atlantic outside the war zone in May, the U.S. froze all German and Italian assets in the U.S. German and Italian consulates and propaganda agencies were closed, and their staffs forced to leave the country.

American merchant ships were armed, and in July the U.S. Navy extended its patrol of the inter-American "safety zone" for shipping eastward to the middle of the Atlantic. In September, to keep the sealanes open,

Troops aboard a U.S. Army transport at the New York City Port of Embarkation in 1944 cram into every bit of available compartment space as they prepare to ship out to England and on to battle in the European Theater of Operations. Signal Corps

the Navy began convoying Allied ships to as far as Iceland. Encounters increased between U.S. destroyers and U-boats.

An incident involving the *USS Greer* in September resulted in a U.S. "shoot-on-sight" policy aimed at German U-boats. In October, *USS Kearny* was badly damaged, suffering 11 casualties. Two weeks later, *USS Reuben James* was sunk, with 115 dead. By then, the U.S. had moved from neutrality to playing an important part in support of the war.

Then on Dec. 7, 1941, the Japanese attacked Pearl Harbor. The next day Congress declared war on Japan. Three days later, Germany and Italy declared war on the U.S., and Congress responded with declarations of war on those Axis powers.

Strategy

The U.S. and Britain pursued a "Germany first" military policy, with the most necessary U.S. men and materiel earmarked for Europe and the Atlantic Theater of Operations.

A cross-Channel attack, designed to gain a foothold in France followed

"May Effort" © Dietz

by a build-up of strong forces and a massive thrust into Germany, required:

- At the chosen moment, air forces of overwhelming strength, to sweep the German *Luftwaffe* from the skies so that Allied bombers could isolate the attack area.
- Ground forces vastly superior in numbers and material.
- The U-boat scourge countered so that convoys could count on a safe Atlantic crossing.
- Supporting naval forces strong enough to batter down local coast defenses, and landing craft available in sufficient numbers to pour ashore great armies through an initial breach.

Leadership

The top U.S. planning officer and eventual supreme Allied commander in the Mediterranean and later western Europe was Gen. Dwight D. Eisenhower, probably the war's most important military leader. As commander of Supreme Headquarters, Allied Expeditionary Forces (SHAEF), Eisenhower's principal lieutenants in the field included: British Field Marshal Sir Bernard L. Montgomery, commander, 21st (British-Canadian)

THE SATURDAY EVENING
POST
27, 1943
10¢
BILLION-DOLLAR
PLANE BUILDER
By ALVA JOHNSTON
A Gay Short Story
By ROBERT CARSON
U.S.
Norman
Rockwell
THANKSGIVING

An American unit about to join the war in Europe waits to board a train in a railway station in England.

"

Many young boys became men before their time and became unsung heroes by necessity, and not by choice.

"

— HAROLD TAYLOR
15th Inf., 3rd Inf. Div.

Army Group; Gen. Omar N. Bradley, 12th Army Group, and Gen. Jacob L. Devers, 6th Army Group, in the European Theater, and Gen. Mark W. Clark with the 15th Army Group in the Mediterranean.

Gen. Carl A. Spaatz, of the U.S. Army Air Forces (USAAF), commanded the U.S. Strategic Air Forces. Commander of U.S. naval forces in Europe was Adm. Harold R. Stark; Adm. Royal E. Ingersoll directed the U.S. Atlantic Fleet; and Admirals Henry K. Hewitt and John L. Hall Jr., commanded respectively the naval amphibious forces in the Mediterranean and European theaters.

Battleground

Terrain and climate varied greatly from one war zone to the next, figuring prominently in strategy and tactics and working more often than not to the advantage of the defender — usually the enemy, because U.S. forces were almost always on the offensive. In hot, barren North Africa, the U.S. lifeline was a long, rickety, winding railroad through the Atlas Mountains and across rocky, desert lands. The line was vulnerable everywhere to scavenging, warlike tribes. In Tunisia, small forces could ambush and hold up an army in the hills. Heavy rains turned trails and tracks into seas of mud.

In mountainous Sicily, Allied troops mounted one of the most difficult army-sized amphibious campaigns ever. In the shadow cast by the 10,740-foot earthquake-prone volcano Mount Etna, the dust-driving *sirocco* — the hot, damp wind which blows from Africa — made life miserable in the south three days out of five. Rain made the highlands insurmountable.

However, Italy presented the most inescapably bad terrain over which GIs had to fight in Europe, as Lee Kennett in *GI: The American Soldier in World War II* and others have noted. The land was cut up by mountains and rivers that impeded routes of advance and often required several crossings. Wretched weather occurred so often that GIs referred in sarcastic disgust to "sunny Italy."

The hedgerows of France — earthen walls up to five feet high surrounding fields and farm land — were virtually impassable. These barriers were covered with vines and trees called *bocage*, and bramble bushes. A further impediment were vast expanses of spongy lowlands, known as *prairies marecageuses*, created by canals and streams.

Fighting in France and across western Europe was further complicated by extremes in climate. In autumn 1944, heavy rain turned the battlefield into a muddy quagmire. Then the worst winter in decades greatly assisted the

Germans during the Battle of the Bulge and the Allied drive into rugged Central Europe.

The North Atlantic, presented soldiers and sailors with a bleak realm. In winter, daylight lasted only four hours. Gale force winds buffeted planes and ships, that otherwise routinely bucked rain squalls and dodged deadly icebergs. Off Normandy, ferocious storms swept over the English Channel, sinking or beaching scores of Allied vessels.

Air crews operated over Europe in wicked weather. Missions were frequently made more dangerous by harsh weather: cold winds that pushed in from the sea, driving before them thick thunderheads, impenetrable fog that blotted out targets, coastlines, and other geographical reference points, and scuds of rain and storms.

With average annual rates of more than 840 hospital admissions per 1,000 men, the Mediterranean approached the Southwest Pacific and China, Burma, India theaters as a pesthole of disease and sickness — especially in Sicily, where malaria took a great toll.

On the continent, trenchfoot and more serious illnesses knocked men out of action as much as German resistance. "The most serious menace confronting us today," wrote Gen. George Patton on Nov. 21, 1944, "is not the German Army, which we have practically destroyed, but the weather, which, if we do not exert ourselves, may well destroy us through the incidence of trench foot. To win the war we must conquer trench foot."

U.S. infantrymen trudge off to war in the European Theater.

Order of Battle

At the close of World War II, as Russell F. Weigley, author of *History of the U.S. Army*, put it, the U.S. armed forces were the mightiest in the world. Only the Russian army exceeded the U.S. in numbers; but in weaponry (except tanks), strategic mobility, and logistic capacities the Americans were greatly superior.

Ground Forces

Among Allied nations the U.S. ranked second to the Soviet Union in the total number of men and women mobilized (22 million vs. 16 million). Of the U.S. total, 10,420,000 served in the Army — 3.6 million served in Europe at peak strength. "Our ground strength was, for the size of our population, proportionately much smaller than that of the other belligerents," Army Chief of Staff Gen. George C. Marshall wrote.

Nonetheless, U.S. forces arrayed against Germany were tremendous. About two-thirds of U.S. military resources overall were sent across the Atlantic. The bulk of U.S. strength committed against Germany comprised Army ground forces, which by V-E Day had been built into a vast organization.

"Into Germany" © Dietz

These forces included 47 infantry divisions and their artillery, 16 armored divisions and four airborne divisions, a mountain division, four landing craft brigades, besides amphibious and engineer units, battalions of anti-aircraft units, artillery and tank destroyer battalions by the score, and a multitude of logistics and supporting units. In addition to providing Atlantic Fleet ships' detachments, the U.S. Marine Corps contributed ground troops when soldiers were not available. The Corps deployed the 6th Marine Regiment and 5th Defense Battalion to garrison and defend Iceland in 1941, and sent the 4th Defense Battalion to the Caribbean to guard Guantanamo Bay, Cuba.

In the field, as Weigley explains in *Eisenhower's Lieutenants*, GIs relied on close artillery, infantry, and tank coordination to break strongly defended enemy positions, usually followed by swift mobility to exploit the breakthrough. Artillery almost always preceded major attacks — frequently leaving the defenders stunned — and then moved forward to provide heavy firepower throughout the advance.

When the assault began, tanks usually went first, but sometimes they teamed up with an infantry skirmish line or sometimes the infantry rode them. Tanks typically engaged centers of resistance, while infantry worked to knock out anti-tank weapons and supporting positions. Then tanks, self-propelled guns and motorized infantry exploited the breakthrough.

Tactical air forces flying in close support added their firepower as a sort of "super artillery." Ground forces were always trying to seize and hold places from which fighter-bombers could operate close up to the front lines. In several campaigns, Allied planes flew more than 10,000 combat sorties per day as their share of the battle.

Army Air Forces
The USAAF, which peaked at 2.4 million men, won command of the air by deliberately forcing battle with the *Luftwaffe*, flying deep into Germany and attacking sensitive targets. The bombers met fierce resistance but heavy losses were replaceable. German losses also ran heavy and were not so easily replaced.

Success in the air became apparent when Allied ground forces landed on the continent. Fighters were not needed to form a protective umbrella and could be used as fighter-bombers against enemy troops. Allied armies were thus assured of freedom of movement by day or night, while the German troops were continuously harried.

The Germans had to disperse their industry; and plane losses became so great that they no longer could effectively oppose attack. USAAF efforts included about 1.7 million combat sorties in Europe and the Mediterranean;

Soldiers with their duffel bags in tow create a familiar everyday scene on the gangplank of a transport at the Passenger Pier of the Military Ocean Terminal, the departure site in Brooklyn Army Terminal for GIs headed overseas during WWII. U.S. Army

over 2 million tons of bombs dropped; and 40,259 enemy planes destroyed, at a cost of 22,948 U.S. aircraft lost and 36,320 crew members killed in action.

Key operating components of the USAAF in the war against Germany and Italy were:

- Sixth Air Force, which served in the Caribbean under Maj. Gen. Davenport Johnson, protecting the Panama Canal and providing air cover for Allied shipping in South Atlantic waters.

- Eighth Air Force, Lt. Gen. Carl Spaatz (and later Gen. James H. Doolittle), supplied the strategic air forces that, along with the Royal Air Force, sustained the around-the-clock air offensive against German industry.

- Ninth Air Force, Gen. Lewis H. Brereton, assisted in the defeat of Rommel in North Africa; moved to Great Britain under Lt. Gen. Hoyt S. Vandenberg and supported ground troops in Normandy; and then operated closely with Gen. Patton's drive across France and Germany.

- Twelfth Air Force, Gen. Jimmy Doolittle, flew in the North African and Italian campaigns, and cooperated with RAF units as the U.S. component in the Mediterranean Allied Tactical Air Force during the last two years of the war under Lt. Gen. John K. Cannon.

- Fifteenth Air Force, Lt. Gen. Nathan B. Twining, conducted two-way strategic air operations in coordination with the Eighth Air Force, scoring heavily against targets in southeastern Europe, including the Ploesti oil fields in Romania.

Naval Forces
The U.S. Navy constituted the backbone of Allied naval forces in the Atlantic. Navy Capt. Edward L. Beach, author of *The United States Navy: 200 Years*, called the conflict in the Atlantic "one long gigantic battle with almost unrelieved stress on all participants . . . a long, torturous, weather-traumatized war."

Beach said that fighting "in the inhospitable waters of the North Atlantic against German submarines" was marked by "sheer desperation" and "fantastic convoy battles, in some cases against combinations of submarines, surface warships, and air power — as in the terribly difficult Murmansk runs." U.S. naval forces escorting convoys, patrolled the sea lanes, and hunted U-boats off the East Coast, in the Gulf of Mexico, the Caribbean, and throughout the Atlantic. Deployed forces ran the gamut from planes and blimps in the air to cruisers, escort carriers, destroyers and destroyer escorts, cutters, converted yachts, armed trawlers, special rescue ships, and sub-chasers at sea.

Other U.S. naval action included battle against Vichy French-controlled warships at Casablanca, the amphibious landing in Morocco, armed entry into the Mediterranean, the invasions of Sicily, Italy, southern France and, of course, the greatest amphibious operation ever undertaken: *Overlord*, the landings on the beaches of Normandy.

The Coast Guard manned transports and landing craft and was responsible for convoy escort and air coverage, anti-submarine warfare, search and rescue, aerial mapping and ice flow observation, port management and regulating merchant shipping.

The Naval Armed Guard served aboard Merchant Marine ships, which formed a logistics lifeline to the continent. Before the war ended, NAG swelled to 144,970. Killed in action totalled 1,862.

Unique to the WWII U.S. Navy and the European Theater were a dozen Naval Beach Battalions known as "The Navy's Infantry." Akin to the Army's combat engineers, their job was to get troops ashore on enemy beaches, and keep men and material flowing. More than half the battalions were actually employed during invasions. These included Sicily, Salerno, Anzio, Normandy and southern France (*Operation Dragoon*).

The Enemy

In creating the most formidable fighting force of World War II, the Germans mobilized 17 million men and fielded 313 divisions. The result was qualitatively the best army in the world — possibly the best in history, according to some historians. Germany also launched more than 1,100 U-boats and tens of thousands of planes.

Notwithstanding the size of the armed forces with which they waged war against nearly all the world, the Germans were strengthened in battle by uncommon professional skill among officers, and combat savvy and imposing courage in the ranks. Well-disciplined, well-equipped and battlewise, the German army was to be respected and feared as a foe.

Though it relied on numerous infantry divisions, the German *Wehrmacht* had at its heart its panzer and panzer grenadier divisions. There were also a variety of other formations, most importantly the fanatical Nazi Party SS panzer and *Luftwaffe* paratroop divisions, favored in training and equipment.

German troops were superbly armed. Besides the Panther and Tiger tanks and 88mm dual-purpose artillery, units received support from solid artillery

---

U.S. ARMY ORDER OF BATTLE, MAY 7, 1945

First Army, Germany
Gen. Courtney H. Hodges
VII Corps: 3rd Armd., 9th, 69th, 104th Inf. divisions
VIII Corps: 6th Armd., 76th, 87th, 89th Inf. divisions
Reserve: 78th Inf. Div.

Third Army, Germany, Czechoslovakia and Austria
Gen. George S. Patton Jr.
III Corps: 14th Armd., 99th Inf. divisions
V Corps: 9th, 16th Armd., 1st, 2nd, 97th Inf. divisions
XII Corps: 4th, 11th Armd., 5th, 26th, 90th Inf. divisions
XX Corps: 13th Armd., 65th, 71st, 80th Inf. divisions
Reserve: 4th, 70th Inf. divisions

Fifth Army, Italy
Gen. Mark W. Clark
II Corps: 10th Mountain, 85th, 88th Inf. divisions
IV Corps: 1st Armd., 34th, 92nd Inf. divisions

Seventh Army, Germany and Austria
Lt. Gen. Alexander M. Patch
XXI Corps: 101st Abn., 36th Inf. divisions
XV Corps: 20th Armd., 3rd, 42nd, 86th Inf. divisions
VI Corps: 10th Armd., 44th, 103rd Inf. divisions
Reserve: 12th Armd., 63rd, 45th, 100th Inf. divisions

Ninth Army, Germany
Lt. Gen. William H. Simpson
XIII Corps: 35th, 84rd, 102nd Infantry divisions
XVI Corps: 29th, 75th, 79th, 95th Inf. divisions
XIX Corps: 2nd, 8th Armd., 30th, 83rd Inf. divisions

Fifteenth Army, France and Germany
Lt. Gen. Leonard T. Gerow
XXII Corps: 17th Airborne, 94th Inf. divisions
XXIII Corps: 28th Inf. Div.
Reserve: 66th, 106th Inf. divisions

Other
XVIII Corps (Airborne), Germany, attached to British Second Army: 5th, 7th Armd., 82nd Abn., 8th Inf. divisions; 13th Abn. Div.

IX Troop Carrier Command, part of First Allied Airborne Army, France, Lt. Gen. Louis H. Brereton; 91st Inf. Div., attached to British Eighth Army in Italy

Pvt. Melvin Parker of Pratt, Kan., whiles away idle time reading the comic pages in his bunk aboard a transport carrying him off to war in Europe in 1942. Signal Corps

> 66
>
> *The soldier is the Army. No army is better than its soldiers. The soldier is also a citizen. In fact, the highest obligation and privilege of citizenship is that of bearing arms for one's country. Hence it is a proud privilege to be a soldier — a good soldier.*
>
> 99
>
> — GEN. GEORGE S. PATTON
> Commanding General
> U.S. Third Army

and an abundance of machine guns. Infantry invariably had a high proportion of automatic weapons — especially 9mm Schmeisser MP-38 and MP-40 submachine guns — to their standard Mauser 7.92mm bolt-action rifle.

Col. Trevor Dupuy in *A Genius for War*, wrote that German forces "consistently inflicted casualties at about a 50 percent higher rate than they incurred from the opposing British and American troops. . . . This was true when they were attacking and when they were defending, when they had a local numerical superiority and when, as was usually the case, they were outnumbered, when they had air superiority and when they did not, when they won and when they lost."

The American Fighting Man

In the multi-volume history entitled *Illustrated World War II Encyclopedia*, Lt. Col. Eddy Bauer wrote of the American military: "Surprisingly, this literate, democratic, and well-informed army made war as effectively as many more autocratic forces. One of the chief reasons for this was the feeling that they were fighting a just war."

True enough, at an average age of 26, the typical GI was motivated by patriotism to enter the armed forces. But he fought in combat for very different reasons: When it came to life or death, risking his life hinged on not wanting to let his buddies down.

WWII veteran and former columnist Jeremiah O'Leary summed it up best: "The fire already was burning in most of our hearts. We all knew why. We did it because the American democracy, with all its wends and flows, was worthy of preserving. We fought Japan because we were attacked and we fought Germany because she declared war on us. We fought, of course, for each other, but we also fought for our families, our nation."

Toughened by years of economic depression, the average draftee and volunteer demonstrated a "can do" attitude that allies envied. Adaptable, hardy, aggressive, daring, inventive — all these adjectives applied to the American GI.

Before long, albeit often grudgingly, friend and foe alike admitted the martial qualities that GIs possessed. British Gen. Bernard L. Montgomery concluded: "The American is a brave fighting man, steady under fire, and he has the tenacity in battle which stamps the first-class soldier."

After the Battle of the Bulge, the Germans offered this assessment of their adversary: "First-rate, well-trained, an often physically superior opponent. Often units inside strongpoints had to be wiped out in hand-to-hand fighting. Tough fighters in close quarters."

Many liberated Europeans became convinced of the GI's invincibility. A Czech citizen said of the Americans, "They are free men who fear nothing on this earth."

Earning this reputation had its price. The "devil's helpers" — exposure, disease and fatigue — had to be overcome. The GI's showed the ability to confront the worst conditions of prolonged physical misery time and again. Take one example in the Belgian winter. "The victor in the Ardennes was

THE SATURDAY EVENING
POST
JULY 1, 1944
10¢
UNITED STATES
WAR SAVINGS BOND
EXCLUSIVE
COMMANDO KELLY
TELLS HIS
LIFE STORY
Norman Rockwell

> 66

Following the war I was once chided by a Nazi who said, 'You Americans are the worst possible soldiers. You don't know how to march or even how to salute properly.' He was right, in that we were not professional soldiers, but civilians from all walks of life, hastily mobilized to do a necessary job. The American soldier became personally convinced of the necessity of winning this war, for the freedom of his country and safety of his family, to the point of laying his life on the line. This resolution resulted in a strange phenomenon: a great exhilaration would come over him, to the point of invincibility. The thrill and excitement of war would take over. And the civilian soldier became a very effective soldier, indeed.

> 99

— WALTER KOVAK
World War II veteran

Opposite: Pfc. Thomas W. Gilgore, Macon, Ga., member of Co. A, 1st Bn., 121st Inf. Regt., 8th Inf Div., 1st U.S. Army, relaxes during a lull in the fighting near Huertgen, Germany.

the American soldier," wrote historian and infantry vet Charles MacDonald. "He had met the test when it came, giving his commanders time to bring their mobility and reserve power into play. The American soldier in the Ardennes made the outcome a certainty by his valor and determination."

Beyond the instinct to survive, a higher purpose existed. MacDonald (himself a rifle company commander) wrote in his award-winning account of the ETO, *The Mighty Endeavor:* "Few who fought the fight could question the right of the cause, for the proof of the enemy's depravity, of the awful tyranny that man can practice on his fellow man, was there for all to see at Buchenwald, at Belsen, at Dachau, and at many another place, including little Ohrdruf. Elimination of those cruel monuments to evil was reason enough for the mighty endeavor that it was: from flaming ships in the Atlantic to plummeting aircraft over Germany; from embattled beaches in North Africa, Sicily, and Italy to bloody Omaha; and on to a bridgehead to nowhere over the Elbe."

On a more fundamental level, veteran Jack Belden in *Still Time to Die* summed up an abiding lesson of war — its spirit of self-sacrifice. "It is just those men whose lives are most miserable, the very toughest soldiers, those whose job is to kill, maim and destroy, it is just those men who are the most gentle, considerate and moved by feelings of sympathy for others. War binds men more tightly together than almost any other branch of human activity. . . . To undergo shame, fear, and death with scores of others of your age and mental coloring — who, indeed, would trade these comrades of the battlefield for friends made in time of peace?"

★ ★ ★

NAVAL WAR

U.S. naval escorts shepherded troop convoys across the Atlantic to the European Theater from 1941–1945. Pictured in this artwork are gunners at battle stations aboard the destroyer *USS Champlin.*

Artist Dwight Shepler, Naval Historical Center

Naval War in the Atlantic Ocean

**'First to Fight':
Undeclared Naval War,
Fall 1941**

"

*. . . the clanging call of
the general alarm rasped you to
battle stations, night and day, from
sleep and from meals, always with
the same empty-handedness of
failure in the end . . . you sought
an enemy as shadowy and
untouchable as Nemesis.*

"

— WIRT WILLIAMS
Atlantic Fleet
veteran and novelist

SOON AFTER Nazi forces invaded Poland, the U.S. proclaimed a "limited national emergency" on Sept. 8, 1939. The U.S. Atlantic Squadron launched the Neutrality Patrol to watch for Axis ships and planes along the East Coast and West Indies.

The U.S. Navy's Atlantic Fleet was created Feb. 1, 1941 and the first U.S. convoy protection force — 45 destroyers, 51 patrol planes, one destroyer tender, three aircraft tenders and 10 minecraft — formed to escort convoys and conduct anti-submarine warfare operations.

A network of strategic outposts stretched as far east as Iceland, with way stations on Greenland and a major operating base in the Canadian province of Newfoundland, the "Gibraltar of the North Atlantic." These provided safe haven for the Atlantic convoys. Iceland — "a pistol firmly pointed at England, America and Canada" — had been garrisoned in summer 1941. The 1st Marine Brigade (Provisional), with the 6th Marine Regiment as its nucleus, landed July 7. Adm. Harold Stark considered dispatch of these 4,095 Marines "practically an act of war."

The U.S. built a naval base at Hvalfjordhur that same month, along with a naval air station near Skerjafjordhur. Soon the Army's Iceland Base Command consisted of the 33rd Pursuit Squadron at Meeks and Patterson Fields and the 5,500 soldiers of the 10th Infantry Regiment, 5th Engineers and the 46th Field Artillery Battalion, all of the 5th Infantry Division.

With these North Atlantic bases, the Atlantic Fleet's Support Force was ready to tackle its primary task — escorting

Allied convoys across the cold, vast ocean prowled by the *Unterseebooten*, or German U-boats. Escort duty was physically punishing. One way from Newfoundland to Iceland covered 1,670 miles; a roundtrip took 16 days.

Novelist Wirt Williams later wrote: "Half your life you spent on the bridge; no night passed but that the hard hand on your shoulder and the malevolent light in your face jerked you from sleep made troubled and uneasy by the tossing of that steel shell that encased you and with whose destiny yours was so irrevocably welded."

FDR's undeclared sea war on the Axis took place in measured steps. It started by protecting American merchant ships only, but soon extended to vessels of all nations. America's "first shot in anger" against Germany occurred on April 10, 1941, off Iceland when the destroyer *USS Niblack* rescued the crew of a torpedoed Dutch freighter, then dropped three depth charges on an object detected by sonar.

Patrols were plagued by the elements. "At one time we were 300 miles north of the Arctic Circle," remembered Lt. Cmdr. Russell Miller, captain of the *USS Trippe*. "Ice froze so thick on our deck that we became bow heavy. We fired our 14-inch guns so the concussion would break up the ice."

The inevitable occurred on Sept. 4, 1941. The *USS Greer* came under attack by the *U-652* some 125 miles southwest of Iceland. During the 12-minute clash, the first between Germans and Americans in the battle for the Atlantic, neither side took a hit. A member of the aviation tender *Belknap* wrote prophetically in his diary, "U.S. declares war on Axis."

October proved eventful. On the 17th, *Task Force 4.1.4* became involved in a full-scale convoy battle. SC (Sidney Convoy) 48 was attacked by five German subs south of Greenland on "as black a night as I've ever seen," according to one destroyerman.

> **“**
>
> *The defeat of the U-boat must remain a first charge on the resources of the united nations.*
>
> **”**
>
> — ADMIRAL ERNEST KING

The freighter *Lehigh* sinks after getting hit by a torpedo from a German submarine off the coast of Africa on Oct. 19, 1941, during action that preceded the actual U.S. declaration of war. U.S. Naval Historical Center

Prime Minister Winston Churchill of Great Britain reviews the 6th Marines two miles south of Reykjavik, Iceland, on Aug. 16, 1941. **Marine Corps**

66

The spray from the first bomb completely obscured the ship. The British destroyer that was sitting on our starboard quarter signaled to ask 'What damage?' Just as our signal man prepared to answer 'No damage' a second flight of dive-bombers came heading for us. The bombs fell so near that the concussion lifted the ship and shook her like a dog shakes a rat.

99

— LT. ROBERT B. RICKS
U.S. Navy Armed
Guard, *SS Expositor*

Ricks was the first Armed Guard officer to receive the Silver Star.

Al Ewanchuk, on board the *USS Decatur*, recalled that Squad Dog 27 detected "a U-boat floating upside down after the Oct. 17 engagement. It sank the sub with gunfire. So we had at least one confirmed U-boat sinking during the undeclared war."

A torpedo from a German U-boat nearly cut the destroyer *USS Kearny* in half, killing 11 sailors and wounding 24 — the first American naval casualties of WWII. Ten merchant vessels also were lost, yet not one U-boat was sunk. An even greater loss occurred on Oct. 31.

The *Reuben James*, an old four-piper, was one of five destroyers escorting convoy HX (Halifax Convoy) 156 from Nova Scotia when it was hit by a torpedo from the *U-552*. Blown in two by a torpedo that set off her forward magazine, she went down in five minutes. Some crewmen were killed by the ship's own ordnance. German *Kapitanleutenant* Topp reported, "Wreck atomized by detonation of her own depth charges." To survivors, stunned and exhausted, the sight of fellow sailors sinking below the surface was heart-rending. Of the 159 men aboard "old Reube," 115 perished. The 44 survivors would never forget the terrifying ordeal. For certain, the Atlantic Fleet was in a defacto war, but the country had not yet come to grips with this reality. Adm. Harold Stark underscored the inherent danger in such a situation:

To back into a war, unsupported or only half-heartedly supported by public opinion, is to court losing it. The situation demands that our people be fully informed of the issues involved, the means necessary and available, and the consequences of success or failure. When we go in we must go . . . to the full extent of our resources. To tell our people anything else is to perpetrate a base deception which can only be reflected in lackadaisical and half-hearted prosecution.

Over the next five weeks (Nov. 1–Dec. 7), the Support Force took 14 convoys across the ocean, riding shotgun for 550 ships. Though no other U.S. vessels were damaged in U-boat encounters, loss of life occurred in the harsh northlands and seas.

Early in November, aviators of Patrol Squadron 74 took off from Skerjafjordhur in Iceland to shepherd ships of ON (Westbound Convoy) 30 to a rendezvous point. One of the planes failed to return. What was left of the aircraft was found the next morning on a hillside near Reykjavik; all 12 crew members had died in the crash.

Soon after, the U.S. completed one of the largest U.S. convoy operations of the pre-war era. American warships escorted some 20,000 British troops aboard six transports.

By the time America officially entered the war, the Atlantic Fleet had taken more than 2,500 merchant vessels across the ocean, losing only eight to U-boats. But 126 American sailors paid the price in combat for this success. Many of the Atlantic sailors — "willing, steady, and tough" who "did not doubt or quit" — wondered if their sacrifices were in vain.

"Destroyermen felt a sense of alienation from the nation as a result of their duties; they had the feeling that the country was not backing them, that the risks they took in the Atlantic went unknown and unappreciated," wrote Patrick Abbazia in *Mr. Roosevelt's Navy*, a history of the Atlantic conflict.

Indeed, the undeclared naval war in the North Atlantic was lonely and

The destroyer *USS Reuben James* became the first American warship sunk during WWII when a German U-boat torpedoed it on Oct. 31, 1941. The *Reuben James* was escorting a North Atlantic convoy when it went down, taking the lives of 115 men a full 37 days before the U.S. officially went to war. Lt. Comdr. Griffiths Bailey Coale, Navy Combat Art Collection

'Forgotten Bastards' on 'The Rock'

"Believe me, the war in the European Theater began in 1941 and Iceland was a significant part of that war. From Iceland and in the North Atlantic the Battle of the Atlantic was won against German U-boat wolf packs."

— GEORGE WREN
Iceland veteran

Strategically central during WWII, Iceland was important as a fly route between North America and northern Europe. It hosted the first U.S. troops in the European Theater of Operations (ETO) six months before Dec. 7.

The U.S. Navy's Atlantic Fleet Support Force operated bases there; and the 1st Marine Brigade (Provisional) was stationed on the island from July 7, 1941 until February 1942. The Army's Iceland Base Command was based at Camp Pershing. Army units began arriving as early as Aug. 6, 1941.

"I was with the 256th Station Hospital and remember the Iceland Base Command giving us 3-inch naval guns dredged up from a destroyer sunk in WWI," recalled Dr. Burchard Wright. The hospital also had 5-inch logs painted black and mounted seaward to resemble gun batteries for any enemy reconnaissance planes passing overhead.

"One of the pilots from the 33rd Pursuit Squadron, along with a pilot from the 27th Squadron, 1st Fighter Group, can claim the first U.S. aerial victory in the European Theater of Operations, which took place off Iceland's coast," wrote 33rd Squadron veteran Jack Shotwell. On Aug. 14, 1942, the two American pilots shot down a German plane, each earning the Silver Star.

A few weeks later, VP-84 relieved Squadron 74, flying anti-sub patrols with the British. "VP-84 was later credited with sinking more German U-boats than any other squadron in the U.S. Navy," pointed out James Griffin, a former naval aviator.

"Two battalions of the 10th Infantry Regiment, 46th Field Artillery Battalion and support units of the 5th Infantry Division arrived in Iceland as early as Sept. 16, 1941," notes Julius Ramey. The rest of the 5th Inf. Div. set up shop on May 11, 1942.

Seemingly forsaken as the war passed them by, those stationed there called themselves the "Forgotten Bastards of Iceland." Iceland was called simply "The Rock," and it served as a way station to the continent.

The 5th Inf. Div. left Aug. 5, 1943, destined to fight in the Battle of the Bulge. The 29th Infantry Regiment took over occupation duty on Iceland, eventually joining the fight in northern France and on into the Rhineland.

Above: A silhouette of war: a lookout mans his post, facing a rain squall during a convoy across the North Atlantic in 1943. National Archives

Top: Convoying the frigid North Atlantic was perilous under most circumstances simply because of the hostile environment. But with U-Boat "Wolf Packs" preying on Allied shipping, the journey to Europe was even more treacherous. Here a tanker crew saves a ship by dousing the blaze ignited by a torpedo hit. U.S. Navy

frustrating. As a *Decatur* gunner later recalled: "Nor had we ever seen the enemy. We had steamed . . . miles hunting them, we had bloodied them and they us, and we had never seen them. There seemed no real victory and no real defeat. If either had won anything, we had, because the convoy had made it."

'Wolf Packs' on America's Doorstep

Allied ships and submarines met opposition for control of the North Atlantic from the vaunted "Wolf Packs" of the German navy. During the first half of 1942, and sporadically throughout WWII, the German U-Boat Service waged a deadly undersea war — which it dubbed *Operation Paukenschlag*, or "roll of drums" — against Allied merchant shipping off the U.S. East Coast. It operated virtually unopposed and unstoppable.

The eastern seaboard, especially off the North Carolina coast — the "Graveyard of the Atlantic" dubbed "Torpedo Junction" by sailors — saw plenty of action.

U.S. Navy and Coast Guard ships patroled the Eastern Sea Frontier (ESF), from Maine to Georgia, to provide protection to Atlantic convoys entering America's territorial waters.

Most available naval vessels were committed as convoy escorts to Britain and the Soviet Union, leaving the coastal waters undefended. U-boat skippers didn't even have to search for vulnerable targets. They simply waited along known shipping lanes for their prey to slip out of safe harbor in the dark of night.

With East Coast cities all lit up, U.S. ships were clearly silhouetted for the waiting Wolf Packs.

On March 27, the USS *Atik* (Q-ship or submarine decoy) was torpedoed by the *U-123*: 141 U.S. sailors died either in the explosion, or in the gale that blew up a few hours later.

Eventually, the hunter became the hunted. The USS *Roper* (destroyer) sank the *U-85* off Nags Head, N.C., on April 14 — the first offensive success against the U-boat campaign in the ESF.

Also in April, East Coast cities imposed black out restrictions that stood throughout the war.

Until destroyer escorts and escort carriers could be built, WWI sub chasers, private yachts and Coast Guard cutters served on inshore protective duty. Even blimps and spotter planes were sent aloft to watch for the menacing U-boats.

On May 9, the Coast Guard cutter *Icarus* sank the *U-352* off Cape Hatteras, N.C., entombing 13 Germans.

Later that month, Germany declared unrestricted submarine warfare against U.S. shipping off the East Coast.

In mid-June, U-boats began mining U.S. waters, planting them off

The U.S. Coast Guard cutter *BIBB* rescues survivors of the transport *Henry R. Mallory* in a North Atlantic storm after it was sunk in early 1943 while on its way to Iceland. More than 300 soldiers, sailors and Marines died as they struggled to keep their grip on lifelines tossed to them in the freezing waters. Survivors were exhausted and in shock, clinging with their last strength to life rafts and bits of wreckage when they were rescued. U.S. Coast Guard and National Archives

Boston Harbor, Delaware Bay, the Chesapeake Capes and the waters off Charleston S.C., making it treacherous to navigate the Eastern shores. One ship that fell prey to the mines was the tanker SS *Robert C. Tuttle*, which exploded and ran ashore at Virginia Beach on June 15.

Two days earlier, the cutter *Thetis* sank the *U-157* near the Florida Straits as part of the "hunter-killer" forces' ocean campaign. But the score evened when the patrol craft USS YP-389 was shelled and sunk by the *U-701* off the Carolinas. Six sailors died; 18 survived.

The next day, the FBI announced the arrest of eight German saboteurs who landed by submarine at Amagansett Beach on Long Island and at Jacksonville, Fla. The latter group made it all the way to Chicago.

Several Army bombers claimed the honor of the first U-boat kills off the East Coast in 1942. It appears that the first confirmed enemy submarine sinking was made by a B-18 crew on April 2. That was followed by another score on May 1. Surface oil and wreckage was sighted, according to the Sea Search Command.

Gunnery operations on the *USS Greer* light up the night during a perilous Atlantic crossing in June 1943.
National Archives

66

We Aim — To Deliver.

99

— Armed Guard motto

An A-29 Hudson bomber from the U.S. Army's 396th Bombardment Squadron sank the *U-701* with three depth charges off Cape Hatteras, N.C. on July 7, scoring the first major enemy sub "kill" in the Atlantic by the Army Air Forces. Of the 43-man German crew, seven survived.

A week later, two U.S. Navy planes sank the *U-576*. The gun crew of the steamship *Unicoi* also pummeled the sub before the U.S. destroyer *Ellis* administered the *coup de grace* with depth charges.

U-boats returned to the Chesapeake Capes Sept. 10 to plant 12 mines. But minesweepers cleared the channel within two days and it was the last mine threat off Virginia. Also on Sept. 10, another 18 German submarines planted 12 mines in the channel leading into Charleston. Two months later a U-boat mined the approaches to New York harbor, planting 10 mines about five miles east of Ambrose Light. All traffic in and out of New York halted for 48 hours while the channel was swept.

In a fight to the death July 18, 1943, the U.S. lighter-than-air craft — the airship *K-74* — spotted *U-134* off the Florida Keys, and attempted to drop depth charges on the enemy sub. But deck crews on the U-boat fired their guns, slicing open the blimp, which lost helium and plunged into the ocean — the only U.S. airship shot down during the war. British planes later spotted *U-134* and sank it.

But the Germans scored victories, too. The USS *Captor* (Q-ship) was hit on July 24, but stayed afloat. The gunboat *Plymouth* was torpedoed and sunk on Aug. 5; 91 men went down with the ship.

A German submarine returned to the waters off Charleston to lay more mines, but by October the threat of mines along the East Coast had passed. In two years, the subs had laid 338 mines in U.S. and Canadian waters, accounting for seven Allied ship sinkings and three others damaged. At the height of the war, 125 U.S. minesweepers were occupied with clearing mines in the ESF.

By 1943, East Coast shipyards were launching transports and oilers at breakneck speed, easily outpacing the U-boats. Also, cryptographers in England had broken the Nazis' Enigma naval codes, allowing Allied naval forces to track wolf pack movements and hunt them down.

After 41 U-boats were lost during "Black May" in 1943, operations in the North Atlantic and along the eastern seaboard tapered off.

USS Gandy, *USS Joyce* and *USS Peterson* stalked and sank the *U-550* during a convoy operation in the ESF on April 16, 1944.

Even as WWII drew to a close, waters off the East Coast remained dangerous. In April 1945, the *USS Gustafson* sank *U-857* north of Cape Cod.

A boarding party from the *USS Pillsbury* (DE-133) works to secure a tow line to the captured U-505 after flying U.S. colors from its periscope on June 4, 1944. U-boats presented a peril to ships moving troops and supplies into the European Theater.
National Archives

"Tossing the Cans" depicts sailors on the destroyer *Gleaves* as they fire depth charges at German U-boats lurking in the Atlantic. Often working together in "wolf packs," the U-boats harassed Allied shipping throughout WWII, especially from 1941–43.

Tom Lea, Navy combat artist

66

There were men in the water and men in lifeboats. Some of them swearing, some praying, and some mockingly sticking out their thumbs and calling 'Going my way, mister?' as we slid by not a hundred feet from them.

99

— NAVY LT. ALBERT MAYNARD Naval Armed Guard on board the *SS Schoharie* on convoy to Murmansk, September 1942.

On April 19, the *USS Buckley* and *USS Reuben James* sank *U-879* 200 miles east of Cape Cod. On April 23, the anti-submarine patrolcraft *USS Eagle 56* took a torpedo near Portland, Maine, and sunk with the loss of 54 lives. One week before the war's end, *USS Natchez, USS Coffman, USS Bostwick* and *USS Thomas* sank the *U-548.*

Finally, on May 6, *USS Atherton* and Coast Guard frigate *Moberly* sank the *U-853* off Block Island, R.I., in the last action of the U-boat war waged by Germany off the East Coast.

Over the course of the war, more than 170 (nearly 90 U.S.) Allied ships suffered attacks by 40 different U-boats. Some 120 ships sank with the loss of 2,409 lives, mostly civilian. Included in these figures are six Navy ships and 426 sailors. Ten U-boats went down — six with all hands aboard. Mine warfare accounted for other casualties, too.

Duel in the North Atlantic

In early 1942, German U-boats were prowling the North Atlantic, forming a picket line of sentries waiting to pounce on Allied convoys bound for England. Additional German subs were being built and would soon be joining the wolf packs that had plagued the East Coast.

Lt. Cmdr. Thomas McWhorter, aboard the *USS Sterett*, wrote about the perilous convoy crossings in those early months of '42: ". . . the long days and nights in the Atlantic when there was no respite from the U-boat alarms in the middle of the night; that sent us running to our battle stations as we fastened up our life jackets — with a subconscious thought of that cold, black water." From January to May, 354 Allied ships had been sunk in the Atlantic. Half of those were carrying oil — lifeblood of any air, sea or land operation against the Axis.

The British had been successful in providing protection to the Lend-Lease convoys during the undeclared war, creating a perimeter of warships to surround the unarmed vessels.

The U.S. Navy preferred a "bucket brigade," known as the Interlocking Convoy System, to protect merchant ships. As each convoy departed the East Coast it would be "passed" from the Western Local Escort Group to warships of the Mid-Ocean Escort Group, guarding them until they reached Iceland and Greenland. From there the convoy would be picked up by the Eastern Local Escort Group for passage to Great Britain.

Initially, escort ships fought defensively rather than going on the attack. After Cmdr. Albert Murdaugh deployed his escort ships farther away from the transports of convoy ON67 to drive off the enemy subs in late February 1942, more naval commanders went on the offensive.

Still, the U-boats were menacing the convoys almost at will with little danger to themselves. From July to December 1942, the Allies could claim only 66 U-boats sunk.

Allied convoys were most vulnerable in the Atlantic sector known as the Greenland Air Gap. Destroyers joined the Atlantic Fleet in January 1943 to hunt down or chase off the 45 U-boats then roaming the North Atlantic. "In every convoy there was also at least one Coast Guard ship on escort duty," said Jeremiah Greeley, U.S. Coast Guardsman.

From March 6 to 9, destroyer escorts of ON.166 fought their way through three separate wolf pack attacks, with a loss of six freighters and tankers. But nine days later, 40 U-boats swarmed over convoys SC.122 and HX.229, sinking 21 Allied transports while losing just one U-boat. According to Capt. Kenneth Knowles, German radio intelligence "probably cost us the worst convoy defeat" of the war.

But advances in radar and sonar equipment, breaking the U-boat Enigma cipher codes and use of torpedo-bombers to strafe and hit surfaced U-boats began to turn the tide in March, with 38 U-boats lost that month alone.

From April 28 to May 5, Convoy ONS.5 repelled 51 U-boat attacks — the largest multi-wolf pack concentration of the war. Though 13 of 42 ships were sunk, the convoy escort ships sank five enemy subs and PBY Catalina patrol planes accounted for two more.

"By April 1943, the average kill per U-boat at sea had sunk to 2,000 tons. This might be interesting as a sort of sporting score, but the number of U-boats operating had so greatly increased that it was of little significance in solving the problem. When Daniel Boone, who shot 50 bears a year, was replaced by 50 hunters who averaged one each, the bears saw no occasion to celebrate the decline in human marksmanship," wrote Adm. Samuel Eliot Morison.

On May 20, 1943, the U.S. 10th Fleet was established, and an aggressive anti-submarine campaign using escort carrier hunter-killer formations

Legendary Four Chaplains

On Jan. 30, 1943, the Army troopship *Dorchester*, two merchant ships and three Coast Guard cutters left Newfoundland for the perilous journey to Greenland. The notorious German U-boats lurked beneath the vast unknown, just waiting to pounce on the vulnerable Allied ships. On the night of Feb. 2, 150 miles from Greenland, a torpedo fired from *U-456* hit the *Dorchester* amidships. The 902 troops on board scrambled topside, many only partially clothed, suddenly exposed to the freezing wind and water.

The *Dorchester* listed badly to starboard and the order came to abandon ship. Amid the chaos of scrambling to lifeboats or jumping overboard, four Army chaplains — Lt. Clarke Poling, a Dutch Reformed minister, Lt. Alexander Goode, a Jewish rabbi; Lt. John Washington, a Catholic priest; and Lt. George Fox, a Methodist minister — remained calm, passing out life vests to those without. Even as the ship began to sink, the four chaplains ensured that as many survivors as possible made it off safely.

"I could hear men crying, pleading, praying, swearing," Pvt. William Bednar recalled. "I could also hear the chaplains preaching courage. Their voices kept me going."

As a final act of compassion, the four chaplains gave their own life vests to others. Then, linked arm-in-arm, each of the chaplains prayed as the *Dorchester* slipped beneath the unforgiving seas, taking 672 brave men with it — the third largest single loss of life aboard a troopship during WWII.

L–R: George L. Fox, Alexander D. Goode, Clark V. Poling and John E. Washington

SPECIAL MEDAL FOR VALOR
July 14, 1960
STRUCK BY THE CONGRESS OF THE UNITED STATES OF AMERICA IN HONOR OF THE FOUR CHAPLAINS.
(obverse and reverse displayed)

This special medal for valor, shown front and back, was struck by Congress in honor of the famous Four Chaplains who died aboard the ill-fated *SS Dorchester* in the North Atlantic on Feb. 2, 1943.

was launched. Four days later, German Adm. Karl Donitz ordered a general withdrawal from the North Atlantic because of the "superiority of enemy location instruments" and their ability to achieve "surprise from the air . . . now forces a temporary shift of operations."

Losing 41 U-boats in May directly influenced the admiral's decision. This turnabout allowed the Allies to increase the movement of men and materiel to England and North Africa for the impending assault on mainland Europe.

With hunter-killer task groups formed around the escort carriers *Card*, *Bogue*, *Core* and *Santee*, the Atlantic Fleet sank 16 U-boats and 8 tanker subs (called "Milk Cows") from May to July. A total of 27 U-boats were sunk in the central Atlantic between May and December 1943.

As it became more perilous to attack without being attacked, the German U-boat offensive was shifted to the Russian convoy route, referred to as "hell below zero" by Allied sailors and merchant mariners. Other U-boats took up station farther south in the Atlantic along the North Africa crossing route or in the Mediterranean. The U.S. Fourth Fleet was formed to patrol the South Atlantic in response.

U.S. *Task Group 22.3* was operating 150 miles off French West Africa when, on June 4, 1944, it sighted *U-505*, used depth charges to force it to surface, then boarded it before it could be scuttled by the crew. "They (three admirals, including four-star Ernest J. King, chief of naval operations) were almost in shock to believe we had actually captured a submarine. They wanted all the details," said Lt. Jack Dumford, the communications officer on the *Guadalcanal*. The last time an American warship had captured an enemy vessel on the high seas was during the War of 1812.

U-boats still prowling the North Atlantic concentrated on the European-bound convoys loaded with fuel and supplies, and ignored those returning to the states.

Among the U.S. ships lost in the North Atlantic were the destroyer *USS Leary*, torpedoed on Christmas Eve 1943, losing 97 men; the destroyer escort *Leopold*, hit by a torpedo near Iceland on March 10, 1944, killing 171; and another destroyer escort, the *Frederick C. Davis*, torpedoed in the North Atlantic on April 24, 1945, taking 119 lives.

Bombing missions over mainland Europe targeted U-boat pens along the French coast, and naval ship yards in Germany. This limited the deployment of more submarines to replace those being lost at an alarming rate. Though Donitz had waged a "guerrilla war" at sea in 1944, the entire U-boat campaign ground to a virtual halt in August when the U.S. Third Army isolated German bases on the Brittany coast. By the end of 1944, 51 U-boats were destroyed.

Through the end of the war, 115 U-boats were sunk by the U.S. Atlantic Fleet while losing an escort carrier, four destroyer-escorts, five cutters and six destroyers. Merchant losses totalled 2,775 Allied ships.

★ ★ ★

Opposite: Rear Adm. Daniel V. Gallery poses on the coning tower of captured German U-boat 505, symbolically bearing the Stars and Stripes over and above the Nazi emblem. This marked the first time since the War of 1812 that U.S. troops boarded and captured an enemy vessel on the high seas. The *USS Pillsbury* captured the sub 100 miles off the Cape Verde Islands in June 1944.

AIR WAR

"B-17s Over Germany" — American B-17s on missions over Germany carried a major payload throughout the air war across the European Theater. Combat artist Jim Dietz, Seattle

Air War Over Europe

First Raids from Egypt

"

Although the U.S. Army provided no ground combat troops to the Egypt-Libya Campaign, the close cooperation between American and British staffs set the tone for Anglo-American cooperation for the rest of the war in the Mediterranean and Europe Theaters of Operations.

"

— Official Army History

THE ARMY AIR FORCES' war against the Axis began in an unlikely theater of the war zone, and had inconspicuous origins. It all began some three weeks before the American air offensive from England was launched against northwestern Europe.

By mid-1942, the North Africa campaign taxed British ground forces to the breaking point. The Axis powers — Germany and Italy — had captured the British stronghold at Tobruk and continued the pursuit to El Alamein, just 200 miles from the Suez Canal.

Great Britain desperately asked the United States for B-24 bomber support. Based in Cairo, Egypt, the U.S. Army pulled in B-17 bombers from the 10th Air Force in India to complement the B-24s already in the theatre.

On June 11, 1942, 13 USAAF heavy bombers of the Halpro Mission took off from Fayid near the Suez Canal and hit the oil refineries at Ploesti, Romania, marking the first combat mission against a strategic target in Europe by American pilots.

While inflicting little damage on the ground, this mission was a huge morale-booster that showed the Allies that America was finally ready to get into the fray. Four days later, the first Mediterranean mission was flown by American bombers, crippling Italian shipping near Malta.

The U.S. Army Middle East Air Force was created on June 28, 1942. By then, U.S. air units stationed in England were gearing up for the offensive against German targets in occupied West Europe.

Initial Targets Hit in France and Germany

The 15th Bomb Squadron arrived in England in May 1942 among the first U.S. bomber units deployed to Europe. Absorbed into the Royal Air Force's 226 Squadron, the U.S. bomber crews flew twin-engine Douglas A-20s, a plane never intended for strategic bombing missions.

With just a 1,200-pound payload, the A-20s required low level approaches to ensure that each bomb had maximum effect. But it also meant flying right into the teeth of intense enemy anti-aircraft batteries.

Still, on July 4, 1942, six American A-20 crews teamed up with six British crews for an attack on *Luftwaffe* bases in Holland — the first sortie by U.S. bombers.

The planes skimmed the waters of the North Sea, then split into four groups for their runs. Two of the American pilots were Capt. Charles Kegelman and 2nd Lt. F.A. Loehrl, both targetting the De Kooy Airfield.

Loehrl's plane was hit by enemy fire and burst into flames. Kegelman's A-20 also absorbed a devastating hit, taking out the right engine. He fought the controls to keep it airborne, even skimming the ground and shearing off part of the underbelly, but somehow managed to limp home.

For his efforts, Kegelman received the Distinguished Service Cross and

each of his crew members received the Distinguished Flying Cross. Kegelman would later be killed flying in the Philippines.

On Aug. 17, 1942, U.S. B-17s from the 97th Bombardment Group hit Rouen-Scottville, France — the first mission against enemy targets there. Within five months, on Jan. 27, 1943, Flying Fortresses from the 1st Bombardment Wing pounded Germany for the first time, hitting Emden and Wilhelmshaven.

America's full military might from the air by then targeted the heart of occupied Europe. Selected targets, when destroyed, would severely undermine Germany's ability to make war.

'Tidal Wave' Over Ploesti

In assessing key industrial centers in Europe that, if ruined, would cripple the German war machine, Allied military commanders drew up a hit list of targets. The oil fields at Ploesti, Romania — the Third Reich's source of one-third of its fuel during WWII — ranked high on that list.

On Aug. 1, 1943, a bomber force consisting of 177 B-24s of the Ninth Air Force (376th, 93rd, 98th, 44th and 389th Bomb Groups) — about 2,000 airmen under Brig. Gen. Uzal Ent — attacked Ploesti.

Code-named *Operation Tidal Wave*, the mission was launched from five airbases around Benghazi, Libya. Planes and air crews received special preparation for the mission. To cover the 2,700-mile round-trip flight, the B-24s were fitted with auxiliary fuel tanks. Norden bomb-sights were removed and replaced with special low-level sights for the planned 100–300 foot bombing runs.

For aircrews, there was a stand-down from regular missions and a training program that had them flying low-level missions over North Africa with bombing runs over a simulated Ploesti site. Elaborate relief models of the target area were made for aircrews to study.

Maintaining radio silence, the bomber force flew north across the Mediterranean. But the secrecy of the mission had already been compromised. A U.S. ground station broadcast a routine signal alerting Allied commands in the theater that an operation was on. German listening posts picked it up and sought out the bombers.

The Greek island of Corfu, between Greece and Italy, was chosen as a turning point because it was easy to identify and it lay on a course that would keep the bombers out of range of German radars in Greece. But to keep from being seen by residents of the island, the bombers had to climb to 10,000 feet.

Many problems occurred. First, as the bombers began to climb, the lead plane went out of control and crashed. The backup lead then aborted and returned to Libya. General Ent was farther back in the formation and was spared.

Ahead lay the cloud-covered Pindos Mountain range in Greece. Some pilots elected to climb over the clouds. Planes not equipped with oxygen were forced to fly through them. Immediately, the force was split into two

> "
>
> *Fires were started with the first bombs to hit the refinery at Ploesti and so we had to fly through the flames in order to drop our bombs on the target.*
>
> "
>
> — GEORGE HAMMOND
> 389th Bomb Group

Opposite: Airmen in WWII took great pride in naming their aircraft. Staff Sgt. Frank T. Lusic stands beside the colorful B-17 Flying Fortress *Meathound*, which was attached to the U.S. Eighth Air Force in England in May 1943. British War Museum

Bridgehead in Ulster

It was an unlikely place to start WWII, but Northern Ireland, otherwise known as Ulster, was the jumping off point for tens of thousands of GIs. They arrived in two waves: one in early 1942, and the other in preparation for the invasion of Normandy in mid-1944.

Londonderry soon became the heart of the American naval presence in Europe, and a popular port of call. The Naval Operating Base at Londonderry was established Feb. 5, 1942, and remained active until July 15, 1944. U.S. Navy ships based there peaked at 149, and the number of sailors reached 20,000.

On a misty Jan. 26, 1942 at the nadir of WWII, elements of the U.S. 34th Infantry Division lurched ashore at Pollack Docks in Dufferin Quay, Belfast. The first 3,900 GIs, led by Pfc. Milburn H. Henke of Hutchinson, Minn., disembarked to the tune of the "Star-Spangled Banner," played by the band of the Royal Ulster Rifles.

After 12 days at sea, the landlubbers from the Midwest welcomed the sight of land. Close on the heels of the 34th, based at Omagh, the 1st Armored Division (Castlewellan) and the V Corps came and headquartered at Lurgan. By the end of May 1942, 38,000 soldiers had arrived. Large-scale maneuvers took place that summer.

The coming of the Yanks was a well-kept secret in the Irish countryside. "In town after town, the inhabitants found their streets full of young men in strange uniforms, who had materialized like a regiment of ghosts," wrote Norman Longmate in *The G.I.'s: The Americans in Britain, 1942–45*.

A warm relationship developed between the easygoing GIs and the local children. As one remembered, "The Yank's passport to fame was the 'candy hand-out.'" Kids also relished the opportunity to see movies shown on U.S. military bases.

Beginning in October 1943, another wave of Americans hit the beaches in preparation for the invasion of Europe. The 2nd Infantry Division set up in Armagh and Newry; the 5th Infantry Division in Newcastle; the 82nd Airborne at Cookstown and Castledawson; and the 8th Infantry Division at Omagh. XV Corps established headquarters in Lurgan. In February 1944, U.S. troop strength peaked at 120,000, which included 20,000 airmen of the Army Air Forces.

"To the people of Northern Ireland the Americans appeared to be everywhere," a historian wrote. "Every inch of accommodation in camps, barracks and hotels was taken up by them."

But by June, most GIs were sent to England for the big invasion.

Romanian oil refineries were strategic targets of the U.S. Ninth and Fifteenth Air Forces. *Operation Soapsuds/Tidal Wave* created fiery scenes over Ploesti on Aug. 1, 1943.

U.S. Air Force painting by Galloway

sections. The two groups above picked up a tailwind and sped ahead of the three lower groups. Out of sight of each other and maintaining radio silence, the two sections made their separate ways toward Ploesti.

Their perilous route took them over Albania, Greece, Yugoslavia, Bulgaria, and into Romania. German radar detected the high groups and some old Bulgarian biplanes were sent to intercept. They sighted the B-24s, but could not match the 160-mile-an-hour speed of the bombers. Then Ploesti appeared, one of the three most heavily defended targets in Nazi-held Europe (along with Berlin and Vienna).

As the bombers approached the target area they were no longer a single force. The 376th and 93rd flew together while the 98th, 44th and 389th followed 30 minutes behind.

"I was in the second group so when we got over the target, the Germans were ready for us," recalled George Hammond, group staff bombing officer of the 389th. "We were to bomb at an altitude of 250 feet. The concentration of anti-aircraft fire and engine exhaust seemed to make the air difficult to breath; or perhaps it was the excitement of the mission and I was holding my breath all during the attack! Fires were started with the first bombs to hit the refinery and so we had to fly through the flames in order to drop our bombs on the target."

The first initial point was Pitesti, and each force identified it correctly. Someone on General Ent's crew mistakenly identified the second initial point, and disaster followed. Mistaking the town of Targoviste for Floresti,

Ent broke radio silence and told those in his force to follow him. Confusion reigned.

The aerial tumult which followed was described by a pilot: "Flights of three or four, or single planes, were flying in different directions, streaking smoke and flames, striking the ground, wings, tails and fuselages breaking up, big balls of smoke rolling out of the wrecks before they stopped shuddering."

The bombers destroyed two target facilities completely — the Steaua Romana and Credituel Minier refineries. These hits accounted for a large part of the 40 percent reduction that the raid inflicted.

But 54 U.S. aircraft were lost and many more damaged. Among the crew members, 310 were killed, 54 wounded, 150 taken prisoner and 79 interned in Turkey. Five fliers received the Medal of Honor.

Operation Pointblank

Code-named *Operation Pointblank,* the Anglo-American Combined Bomber Offensive against Germany was launched in the summer of 1943. It was designed "to accomplish the progressive destruction and dislocation of the German military, industrial and economic system, and the undermining of the morale of the German people to a point where the capacity for armed resistance is fatally weakened . . . so as to permit initiation of final combined operations on the continent."

The enemy aircraft industry was a prime target. *Pointblank* began with "Blitz Week" from July 24–30. Targets ranged from U-boat facilities in Norway to an FW-190 plant in Oschersleben, the longest penetration of the war so far. Deep raids also were made against plants in Regensburg,

This trusty "Flying Fortress" unleashed its bombing fury on an aircraft plant in Germany. Strategic raids on sites such as Schweinfurt, Berlin and Dresden wreaked havoc on Nazi materials and supplies throughout Hitler's homeland. National Archives

Schweinfurt, Stuttgart, Bremen, Marienbad and Munster from August through October, with unacceptable casualty rates.

U.S. Strategic Air Forces, Europe, eventually coordinated missions. "Big Week" or *Operation Argument*, in February 1944 was another concentrated attack on Germany's industrial might. By then, the German war machine was virtually at a standstill.

Dual Disaster: Schweinfurt and Regensburg

To protect important defense plants, the Germans set up lines of anti-aircraft guns along approach lanes; enabling the guns to throw a barrage of flak at incoming bombers. The Nazi gauntlet also included *Luftwaffe* fighters, alerted in plenty of time to meet attacking bomber squadrons. Despite the enormous odds, Allied missions had to be flown.

On Aug. 17, 1943, the Eighth Air Force launched a two-pronged attack, sending 376 aircraft against Messerschmitt aircraft manufacturing plants at Regensburg and ball-bearing production plants at Schweinfurt.

But problems developed before the combined forces ever left the ground. The first was weather. Low clouds covered the airbases. The Regensburg attack group, assigned to the 4th Bombardment Wing, commanded by

Shuttles to the Ukraine

By October 1943, Josef Stalin agreed, in theory, to allow Allied bombers to "shuttle" to bases in the Soviet Union to refuel and rearm, then take off on more bombing runs on the return flights. But the Russians were reluctant hosts, allowing the use of only three ramshackle airdromes — Mirgorod, Poltava and Piryatin — in the Ukraine.

Everything to support flight operations had to be brought across the North Atlantic by ships docking at Murmansk, railway from Iran or transport planes out of North Africa.

On June 2, 1944, the marshalling yards at Debrecen, Hungary were hit by Fifteenth Air Force bombers flying out of Italy, launching *Operation Frantic*. Af-

ter refueling and rearming in the Ukraine, the planes returned for another pass.

Russians manned the anti-aircraft batteries at the airdromes, which were ineffective against German planes. This proved especially disastrous after Eighth Air Force bombers hit the Ruhland oil refinery in June 1944.

German planes pursued them that same night to the poorly defended Poltava base and destroyed 53 B-17 bombers, 15 P-51 Mustang escort fighters, numerous Russian planes and 200,000 gallons of precious fuel and munitions. This single raid was among the costliest in aircraft ever for the Eighth Air Force.

Though *Operation Frantic* accomplished 18 missions, with the aid of

1,300 U.S. airmen based in the Soviet Union, it was abandoned within a year — a little-known chapter of the air war in Europe. The Eastern Command, USAAF HQ in Russia, finally shut down with the last evacuation on June 23, 1945. A total of 5,000 U.S. airmen saw duty there.

"Russian soldiers saw the Americans, for the most part, as comrades-in-arms while the political and police officials reflected the deep-seated suspicion of foreigners long nurtured by the Kremlin," wrote Eastern Command veteran Richard C. Lukas. "Nevertheless, the memories of these wartime contacts between young American and Russian soldiers were not forgotten in the postwar years of the Cold War."

Col. Curtis E. LeMay, was to take off first, followed 10 minutes later by Brig. Gen. Robert B. Williams' 1st Bombardment Wing.

LeMay's force planned to draw off some of the German *Luftwaffe* fighter forces from the more heavily defended Schweinfurt area while the 1st Wing slipped in and hit the ball-bearing plants. U.S. fighter aircraft did not yet have the range to escort bomber forces deep inside Germany. Bomber crews had to rely on the protection of the "combat box," which allowed them to concentrate the firepower of each of the 12 B-17's twelve .50 caliber machine guns.

Delayed by the weather, the carefully timed attack fell apart. For LeMay, time was very critical; his force would land in Algeria after the attack, and it had to arrive before dark. When it could wait no longer, the 4th Wing took off on instruments and assembled above the clouds.

The 1st Wing was held on the ground for an hour and a half. Then it flew toward Schweinfurt while the *Luftwaffe* fighters, which had attacked LeMay's force, were back on the ground, refueling and rearming. The 1st Wing was just minutes away from one of the worst battles in aerial warfare.

Royal Air Force Spitfires met them over Holland and fought off the first *Luftwaffe* attacks. The Spitfires then handed the B-17s over to the longer-range U.S. P-47 Thunderbolts, their escort to the German border.

But heavy clouds over the continent forced the 1st Wing to descend to an altitude of 17,000 feet, missing a rendezvous with P-47s from the 4th Fighter Group. So the 78th Fighter Group ultimately provided escort to the German border town of Eupen.

The B-17 pilots soon encountered heavy waves of *Luftwaffe* fighters approaching from the east. At 17,000 feet, the bombers were at an opti-

> ❝
>
> *Plane in flames . . . 'chutes opening. Plane in flames . . . no 'chutes.*
>
> ❞
>
> — ELMER BENDINER
> Navigator
> 379th Bomb Group

Above: A Consolidated B-24 flies a bombing mission over Friedrichshaven, Germany, one of many heavy bombers involved in missions during March 1944.

Top: A lead crew of a 97th Bomb Group B-17G at Amendola, Italy, appears nonchalant in a Jeep before boarding for a bombing run. While the air war raged over Germany, the skies of Italy also hosted U.S. aircraft of the Twelfth and Fifteenth Air Forces.

mum altitude for enemy fighters, and where the anti-aircraft fire — flak — was deadliest.

"Tighten formation! Tighten formation!" Gen. Williams called from his plane *Lady Luck* as the *Luftwaffe* fighter pilots began their lethal work. Since arriving in England in June 1942, Eighth Air Force crews had developed and practiced the tactics necessary to reach their targets through enemy defenses.

As the 1st Wing's nine groups of B-17s, comprising 230 planes, approached Schweinfurt, more than 300 enemy fighters engaged them with machine guns, rockets and air-to-air bombs.

Aboard *Tondelayo*, a B-17 of the 379th Group, navigator Elmer Bendiner listened to the running commentary of the gunners. "Plane in flames . . . 'chutes opening. Plane in flames . . . no 'chutes."

On the ground below, Bendiner saw bright orange fires. "At first I did not understand them. No cities were burning. Then it came to me . . . these were B-17s . . ." Before the first bombs fell on Schweinfurt, 21 B-17s were lost. Fifteen more went down on the way home.

The raid destroyed only one of the three ball-bearing plants. Both raids combined cost 60 planes — a 16 percent loss rate — the highest in a single day at that time. Of the 601 men lost, 102 were killed, 381 taken prisoner, 20 interned and 38 fell into enemy territory but evaded capture.

The 332nd Fighter Group, an all-black P-47 unit that arrived in Italy early in 1944, receives a briefing at its base near Ramitelli before a mission. The 332nd transferred from the Twelfth to the Fifteenth Air Force and flew P-51 Mustangs, receiving a Distinguished Unit Citation for escorting bombers on a 1,600-mile round trip raid against a tank factory in Berlin — the longest mission ever flown by the Fifteenth. U.S. Air Force

U.S. bomber splits the clouds with its payload on a mission over northern France on July 24, 1944, during *Operation Cobra*. In the breakout from Normandy, about 3,000 Allied planes carpet-bombed in bad visibility and accidentally hit U.S. 30th Division troops, killing 89 — including Lt. Gen. Lesley J. McNair, chief of the Army ground forces — and wounding 374. Lt. Col. Don Lhevinne, Army Air Corps

Afterwards, the Germans increased the anti-aircraft defenses around Schweinfurt.

On Oct. 14, 1943, Schweinfurt II was conducted by the 1st and 3rd Bombardment Divisions. Without fighter escort all the way to the target, they incurred devastating losses — 60 planes lost to enemy fighters, 605 men killed or missing and 43 wounded.

'Big Week': *Operation Argument*

The dismal winter of late 1943 and perpetual overcast skies prevented Allied bombers from finding their targets over Germany. From November through late January 1944, American and British bombers were practically grounded. But by February, milder weather allowed bomber crews to prepare for some heavy duty saturation bombing.

For the Eighth Air Force bombers flying out of England and the Fifteenth Air Force planes coming up from Italy, primary targets were the German aircraft factories. The factories produced hundreds of fighters every month; fighters that were knocking Allied bombers out of the sky.

On Feb. 19, 1944, *Operation Argument* kicked off, with all available B-17 Flying Fortresses and B-24 Liberators — more than 1,000 bombers combined, plus an equal number of fighter escorts — converging on targets in central Germany and western Poland.

Allied prognosticators anticipated losing as many as 200 bombers that first day, but miraculously, *Luftwaffe* fighters avoided a fight. As a result, only 21 bombers were lost.

During the next five days, dubbed "Big Week," the Allies flew 3,800 sorties and dropped 10,000 tons of bombs, with the loss of 226 bombers, 28 escorts and 2,600 crewmen killed, missing or wounded.

Above: After taking a hit from enemy fighter planes during a mission over Europe, a U.S. bomber bursts into flames. Courtesy of Lt. Col. Don Lhevinne, Army Air Forces

Right: A pair of U.S. B-26 Marauders, medium bombers, leave a trail of ruins in their raid on a railyard and power station at Charleroi, Belgium. U.S. Air Force

B-24s drop high-explosive bombs on German installations. A large formation could release up to 100 tons of bombs a minute. U.S. Air Force

Though German totals were less, their losses proportionately were more severe because of manpower shortages: 225 pilots dead or missing and another 141 wounded. Aircraft plants that produced the Me-109s at Leipzig, Me-110s at Gotha and Ju-88s at Aschersleben and Bernburg suffered extensive damage. While the Germans were able to salvage machine tools and raw materials from these damaged factories, they were forced to move plant operations to wooded areas, away from aerial reconnaissance.

Even more devastating, though, was the loss of experienced *Luftwaffe* pilots. No longer would they challenge the oncoming waves of bombers and their escorts. The pursuers had become the pursued as Allied fighter pilots frequently broke formation to provoke a confrontation with reluctant Nazi flyers.

"No longer was it a case of their bombers having to run the gauntlet of our fighters, but of our having to run the gauntlet of both their bombers and their fighters," lamented one *Luftwaffe* pilot.

With control of the skies over northern and central Europe, U.S. and British bombers could intensify the attack, looking next toward Berlin, capital of Nazi Germany.

Bombs Over Berlin

Buzz-bombs, which had fallen on civilian populations at Coventry and London, England, changed the rules of warfare. So British bomber crews felt little remorse when told that their bombs had hit civilian populations in Germany. But as much as they wanted to hit Berlin, it remained too risky.

By October 1943, U.S. bomber squadrons in England were ready to test the defenses surrounding Berlin. P-51B Mustang fighter escorts arrived with 75-gallon wing pods, extending their range all the way to the capital of the *Third Reich,* giving the bombers a fiesty sidekick to ward off the enemy's high-flying snipers.

On earlier bombing missions, fighter escorts had to turn back or run out of fuel, leaving the bombers vulnerable to aerial assault deep inside German territory.

By late February 1944, Jimmy Doolittle — who had led the famous bombing raid on Tokyo two years earlier — was commanding the Eighth Air Force and fully intended to lead the first U.S. bombing mission to Berlin. Unfortunately, he knew too much about the impending invasion of Europe and could not take any chances of falling into enemy hands.

On March 4, 500 B-17s from the 1st and 3rd Air divisions took off, but most received orders to turn back because of cloud cover over Germany.

Aiding the Norwegian Resistance

Code-named the *Ball Project,* Allied planes from Scotland dropped supplies, arms and munitions to help Norwegian partisans torment their German occupiers. U.S. bombers also attacked German facilities there, hitting targets at Heroya, Knaben, Bergen, Rjukan and Trondheim. Nearly 70 B-17s were forced to land in neutral Sweden before the war ended, where crews were interned, during such missions.

On Nov. 18, 1943, 82 B-24 Liberators of the 2nd Bombardment Division attacked the Oslo/Kjeller Airdrome, delivering more than 209 tons of bombs. But on the return flight, nine bombers were hit by German fighters; six went down in the North Sea and three were forced to land in Sweden.

On Sept. 9, 1944, another B-24, with 10 American crew members on board, crashed into a Norwegian mountain. The pitch-black Liberator was attempting to drop much-needed weapons and ammo to the Norwegian resistance. For the remainder of the war, the crash site served as a symbol of resolve for the Norwegian underground.

Lasting until March 5, 1945, a total of 41 sorties assisted the resistance in both Norway and Denmark. A U.S. memorial stands in Kjeller in tribute to the 72 Americans killed in action flying over Norway during WWII.

Ground crews in England played an integral part in the air battles over mainland Europe. This pair of Army Air Forces crewmen load a belt of .50 caliber machine gun bullets into the forward gun of a fighter plane.
U.S. Air Force

Above: Mustangs from the 308th Fighter Squadron, 31st Fighter Group, based in England, move in sync into combat positions over the European mainland. U.S. Air Force

Top: The Braunkahle Synthetic Oil Plant at Magdeburg takes a hammering from Liberators of the 392nd Bomber Group in March 1945. U.S. Air Force

66

In that single moment Flakstop *of the 452nd Bomb Group gave up her role as a mighty Flying Fortress and became a flying coffin.*

99

— ALLAN WILLIS
Flakstop's co-pilot

But three squadrons — two from the 95th Bomb Group and another from the 100th — didn't get the message and they pressed on to Berlin. The mission — a psychological blow to Berliners — was a bust, though, with five bombers and four escort fighters shot down by the Germans.

Two days later, 730 bombers and 800 escorts from the 1st, 2nd and 3rd Air divisions tried again. German radar picked up the intruders and dispatched 500 fighter planes to intercept them. It was "like the proverbial swarm of bees," said Allan Willis, copilot of the B-17 bomber *Flakstop* of the 452nd Bomb Group. "The fighters raked our fuselage from nose to tail. The entire starboard wing was, in a flash, a sheet of orange flame! In that single moment *Flakstop* gave up her role as a mighty Flying Fortress and became a flying coffin."

Willis was picked up by the Dutch underground, but many crewmen didn't make it. Of the 21 planes from the 100th Bomb Group that flew the March 6 mission, 15 were shot down. Seventy-five B-17s in all were lost that day, but 1,600 tons of bombs were dropped on Berlin. It was even more costly for the *Luftwaffe*, however, because 82 irreplaceable German fighters had been knocked out of the sky.

Staff Sgt. James McMahon of the 93rd Bombardment Group, Eighth Air Force, flew on those early March missions:

Berlin! The sky was perfect, no clouds, which meant the fighters were going to come up and the flak would be accurate. On this raid I should have been as nervous as hell, but I thought of Thom, Henn, Fred, and all the fellows I had seen go down. I figured if I came back, okay, but if I went down it would be for Thom.

We kept flying through the flak and made two runs on the target. All this time I can see Berlin, and there are 24s and 17s all over the place. I see our bombs hit smack on the target and my heart bleeds for those damned Krauts down there. Well after that for 100 miles I can see the fires and smoke. It looks like all Berlin is on fire.

On March 8, the German air forces lost another 87 fighters trying to ward off the incoming waves of bombers and fighter escorts. From January to April 1944, the *Luftwaffe* had lost 1,684 experienced fighter pilots. Hastily trained rookies were rushed into the cockpits. But they, for the most part, avoided confrontations with the Allied fighters and just wanted to survive the war.

Allied bombers pulverized Berlin throughout the war's last months. Marie Vassilchikov, a citizen of Berlin, remembered the continuous day and night bombing of Berlin in November 1944: "*Luftgefahr* 15 (Air-raid Danger 15). This meant that large (Allied) air formations were on their way. The

planes did not come in waves, as they do usually, but kept on droning ceaselessly overhead for more than an hour. There must have been several hundreds of them."

On Feb. 3, 1945, 1,000 planes struck the city center, killing 3,000 Berliners. Flak from anti-aircraft guns claimed 23 bombers. Charles "Pop" Van Buskirk, a ball turret gunner with the 381st Bomb Group, Eighth Air Force, recalls watching other planes fall from the sky: "Counting chutes was gut-wrenching. As a Fortress was going down, someone would always count the chutes aloud over the interphone as the crew bailed out. If the count was short, a knot would form in your stomach for the rest of the mission. Coming back from the mission, seeing a bunk that hadn't been slept in because that crew member didn't make it . . . that was the hardest part."

On March 18, more than 1,250 U.S. bombers conducted a daylight raid on Berlin, dropping 3,000 tons of bombs, bringing to an end one of the war's costliest air campaigns.

Destruction of Dresden

Allied bombers targetted vital industrial centers such as Ploesti, Romania and Schweinfurt, Germany in hopes of crippling the flow of weapons, munitions and fuel to Hitler's forces waging war on two fronts.

Yet Russia pleaded with its allies to also target transportation hubs in eastern Europe to sever the rail lines and roadways used to send German reinforcements east. Moreover, British strategists felt that further blows to German civilian morale were warranted.

So on the night of Feb. 13, 1945, 244 British Lancaster bombers pounded Dresden in eastern Germany with incendiary bombs. Before dawn, nearly

> **"**
>
> *I have mixed emotions about the Dresden raid. But when you come home from a mission or go off on leave for 36 hours and come back to see half of your barracks empty, you don't worry too much about what you're doing to the enemy.*
>
> **"**
>
> — HERBERT SCHAAF
> B-17 pilot
> 546th Bomb Squadron
> 384th Bomb Group

Col. George Kraigher (left) and his co-pilot prepare for takeoff in their C-47 that will air drop supplies to Tito's partisans in Yugoslavia. **Army Air Corps**

"

Frankfurt, largely roofless.
Looks like Pompeii magnified . . .
Wurzburg. A crumpled mass of
peanut shells. Ludwigshafen.
A vast ruin of rusted iron as far as
the eye can see. Frightful, fantastic
spectacle . . . Worms. Torn to
shreds . . . Munster.
Another ghost . . .

"

— FREDERICK ANDERSON
Eighth Air Force C-54
pilot assessing damage
of strategic bombing
of Germany.

Opposite: A P-51 pilot shows the results of note-taking common at pre-mission briefing sessions — scribbling on the back of the hand for quick reference in the air. At a glance he has the time for starting engines, takeoff, setting course and rendez-vous with bombers, and the compass heading to follow when his plane leaves the target area and heads home. U.S. Air Force

Supplying Partisans in Yugoslavia

Former Sgt. Richard C. Davidson vividly recalled the top-secret missions to supply Tito's guerrilla forces in Yugoslavia during WWII.

"We flew at night in our unarmed C-47s to escape possible detection," Davidson said. "And we didn't fly at too high an altitude, perhaps 2,000 to 3,000 feet, to be sure we hit the drop zone.

"But we had to be very careful as we flew without lights and the terrain was mountainous. A couple times our ships struck mountain tops resulting in complete disaster."

Davidson was a radio operator with the 10th Troop Carrier Squadron, 60th Troop Carrier Group. Other squadrons of the 60th flying these missions were the 11th, 12th and 28th. "We dropped whatever they needed," Davidson recalled. "Munitions, food, clothing. I must have flown about 60 missions over Yugoslavia and one night we even brought a mule and landed it at an airstrip near Tito's headquarters in a farmhouse.

"The entire group received a Presidential Unit Citation for its mission in the summer of 1944."

The 60th flew about 3,000 missions over Yugoslavia, delivering some 7,000 tons of weapons, ammunition, food and medicine. The group lost 10 aircraft and 34 crew members, plus another 15 airmen wounded.

500 more planes struck again, delivering a combined total of 2,700 tons of bombs. A few hours later, U.S. B-17s from the Eighth Air Force dropped an additional 400 tons of high explosives.

The next day, unable to hit their primary target, another 210 bombers swung by Dresden and hit it again for good measure.

An inferno followed, raging out of control for the next week. By then, Dresden — one of the transportation centers on Russia's target list — was little more than rubble. All told, 35,000 civilians died.

"A high price was paid by all," recalled John Hill, a B-17 navigator with the Eighth Air Force. "No one likes to destroy things and kill people, but when you are in a war that is the name of the game."

The Last Missions

Bombing missions were flown to the war's very end. One of the last casualty-producing flights was made by the 12-member crew of the *Black Cat* on April 21, 1945. This B-24 would earn the distinction of being the last U.S. bomber shot down over Germany in WWII — 10 airmen died.

Four days later, on April 25, four squadrons of the 398th Bomb Group earned their niche in history by launching a 10-hour flight that took them over the Skoda Armament Works in Pilsen, Czechoslovakia. To spare civilian lives, the factory was actually forewarned.

On the second pass, anti-aircraft flak brought down two of the bombers with the loss of seven American lives. Still, the last bombing run in the ETO destroyed 70 percent of the factory.

★ ★ ★

NORTH AFRICA

"Kasserine Pass" — The Battle of Kasserine Pass in Tunisia in February 1943 during the North Africa campaign provides the backdrop for an explosive mix of artillery fire.
Combat artist Jim Dietz, Seattle

Desert Warfare in North Africa

Four-Day War with Vichy France: *Operation Torch*

"

The eyes of the world are watching us. The heart of America beats for us. God is with us.

"

— GEN. GEORGE PATTON
Commander of the
Western Task Force
for *Operation Torch*

THE INVASION OF **NORTH AFRICA,** dubbed *Operation Torch,* was set for late 1942. Besides the logistical problems of the landings, commanders had to contend with French regimes controlling Morocco, Algeria and Tunisia. Three factions, in fact, existed in French North Africa, which fielded 200,000 troops combined.

Gen. Charles DeGaulle, along with his Free French refugees, had fled France rather than be subjected to Nazi domination. The underground "French Liberation Movement" in North Africa, led by Gen. Henri Giraud, was suspect and rabidly anti-British. Thrown into this mix were the pro-Vichy French loyal to Marshal Philippe Petain who openly collaborated with the Germans and pledged to resist the Allies.

Lt. Gen. Dwight D. Eisenhower, Allied commander on the European front, was uncomfortable with the invasion plans because of these hostile factions. Also, the invasion diverged from his desire to strike hard at Central Europe. Nonetheless, the invasion unfolded as planned.

Operation Torch consisted of three Anglo-American task forces — Western, Central and Eastern — totaling 107,000 troops (75% U.S.). U.S. units included the 1st and 2nd Armored; and 1st, 3rd, and 9th Infantry divisions; five regimental combat teams; and two elite outfits — the 1st Ranger Battalion and the 509th Parachute Infantry Regiment (PIR). Elements of the U.S. 12th Air Force provided air cover. Their collective objective was to capture five ports — three in Morocco and two in Algeria.

More than 100 ships departed from America's East Coast in early October for Morocco in the first-ever transoceanic

amphibious operation. Aboard were 33,834 men from the 3rd and 9th Infantry divisions, the 2nd Armored Division, plus support elements. Other ships left Britain bound for Algiers and Oran, Algeria.

Along the way a U-boat made a minor hit on the *HMS Panther*. The *USS Thomas Stone*, with more than 700 soldiers of the 2nd Bn., 39th Inf. Regt., 9th Div., aboard, was also disabled. "I was one of the members of the 36th Engineers aboard the *Thomas Stone* when an enemy plane dropped a torpedo on the ship," said John Cummings. "An estimated 30 crewmen were killed."

Rather than miss the invasion, the men on the two ships set out in 24 landing craft unsuited for the lengthy journey. Eventually they crammed on board the escort *Spey* and arrived half a day late for the beach assault.

In the darkness of Nov. 8, hundreds of Free French insurgents in Algiers seized key facilities, knowing they could only resist for a few hours before being overrun. Little did the partisans know that the invasion forces they were counting on would encounter many problems.

The U.S. 34th Infantry Division's 168th RCT led the assault on Algiers with a 650-man raiding party on the harbor's docks. Soon after, jeeps bogged down in the sand, or were lost in shallow water, and tanks sank in the mud. Radios failed, leaving many units dispersed for miles without any idea of which way to go; yet the landing ultimately succeeded.

While the landings plodded along, the first major engagement unfolded in Algiers Harbor. With 662 U.S. and 74 British soldiers on board, the destroyers *HMS Broke* and *Malcolm* plowed into the harbor to secure it before French ships could be scuttled. Coastal batteries were supposedly neutralized by the invading troops. But because of delays, the guns were

> **"**
>
> *Operation Torch was the biggest gamble in world history. I went in at the beach resort of Mehdia at Port Lyautey. The landing was a mass of confusion. We went in on 15-foot waves. All the landing craft were swamped on the beach. None of them could return to the ships for more troops. Sailors even went ashore and fought with us.*
>
> **"**
>
> — SGT. ERNEST WHITEHEAD, SR.
> C Co., 15th Combat
> Engineers, 9th Division

During *Operation Torch*, U.S. troops wade ashore at Oran, Algeria, November 1942. British War Museum

Throughout the war, the North African Coast remained a deadly arena for the Navy. U.S. Navy seaman relaxes as two Coast Guardsmen scrape a thick coating of oil from his body. The survivor's ship, the *USS Lansdale,* was sunk off Cape Bengut, Algeria, by German aircraft with the loss of 47 American lives on April 20, 1944.
Coast Guard

still operational, and they suddenly erupted on the two easy targets. Americans killed in action (KIA) numbered 15 plus 33 wounded in action (WIA). The British counted 9 KIA and 19 WIA.

Another torpedoed ship, the *USS Leedstown,* was hit off Algiers on November 9, losing eight American dead.

Two hundred miles west of Algiers at Oran, two U.S Coast Guard cutters, the *Walney* and *Hartland,* were mustered to sneak into the port and deposit commandos. But the *Walney* took an immediate broadside, killing many of the troops aboard, and disabling its engines. (Most troops — 393 — on both ships were from the 1st Armored Division's 3rd Bn., 6th Armd. Inf. Regt.) The *Hartland* was also hit. This venture proved costly; 189 U.S. and 113 British servicemen KIA; 158 U.S. and 86 Brits WIA. Survivors were taken prisoner.

The soon-famous 1st Ranger Battalion made its debut near Oran. Maj. William O. Darby's men quickly and flawlessly scaled the cliffs overlooking the beach at Arzew and took out the coastal guns. Then the Rangers captured the Foreign Legion garrison at Fort DuNord without firing a shot.

The famed Legionaires didn't quite live up to their fearsome reputation.

Farther south, the 18th Regimental Combat Team went ashore in the dark. Its 1st Battalion ran into a buzzsaw when it battled with the 1st Foreign Legion Bn., 16th Tunisian Regt. and the 68th African Artillery Regt. at St. Cloud. Overhead, British and French fighters engaged in dogfights with enemy planes.

Fledgling paratroopers of the 2nd Bn., 509th Parachute Inf. Regt. also were tossed into the fray. The unit's baptism of fire raised concerns. "The future of the paratroops is on the line," Lt. Col. Edson Raff said to his officers of the 509th. "If we do well, the airborne will be greatly expanded. If we fail, our paratroop units may be disbanded."

Their mission: secure vital airfields at La Senia and Tafaraoui in Algeria. But no one knew, even after takeoff, if the French would remain passive or hostile. "Are we supposed to go over there and fight or kiss our opponents?" joked Army sergeant and paratrooper Ray Cagle.

British Royal Air Force commanders feared being shot down, as well as flying off course. Both fears were realized. Thirty-nine C-47s took off from Britain on the eve of the operation and most became lost.

Some troops parachuted over Spanish Morocco and were taken prisoner. Paratroopers on 12 other transports jumped over Lourmel, a day's march from their objective. Several transports encountered French fighters. Three were forced down by strafing, and Lt. Dave Kunkel from the 509th became the first U.S. paratrooper KIA. The 509th lost six more men killed and 27 WIA in this action..

Meanwhile, on Morocco's coast, landing craft accidentally dumped troops overboard. Weighted down by backpacks and weapons, many discarded everything just to keep from drowning. Vehicles and artillery pieces often ended up in the drink.

The 47th Inf. Regt., 9th Inf. Div., spearheaded the invasion of Morocco, encountering its first resistance from the 2nd Foreign Legion Regiment. French coastal batteries at Safi were taken out by the American warships *New York* and the *Philadelphia*. Likewise at Fedala, U.S. battleships pounded French artillery.

Col. von Wuhlisch, head of the German armistice commission at Fedala, told a French general when the invasion was launched: "This is the greatest setback to German arms since 1918. The Americans will take Rommel in the rear and we shall be expelled from Africa."

Mehdia, the coastal resort near Casablanca, proved more difficult a target. Its artillery, combined with French fighter pilots, devastated the slow-moving landing craft.

In an effort to reduce needless casualties on both sides, two American

Above: Lt. Col. William O. Darby, commander of WWII's famous "Darby's Rangers," leads his men on a "speed march" in North Africa in December 1942. The Ranger battalions performed their first major mission in Algeria during *Operation Torch.* Signal Corps

Top: GIs establish a machine gun position near Oran, Algeria, on Nov. 10, 1942, during America's four-day war with Vichy France. U.S. Army

'First American Women's Expeditionary Force'

When Allied troops stormed onto North Africa's shores on Nov. 8, 1942, six women of the Army Nurse Corps moved in right behind them to care for the wounded.

Two months later, the 149th Women's Army Auxiliary Corps (WAAC) Post Headquarters Company — "the first American women's expeditionary force in history" according to the press — arrived at Algiers. The 149th WAAC had been among the U.S. forces sent to England and Northern Ireland earlier in 1942.

Army nurses were also present at Sicily and Anzio, Italy, first on hospital ships and then, just days later, on the beachhead itself. June Wandrey, a combat surgical nurse, wrote home to her family while on Sicily:

Working in the shock wards, giving transfusions, was a rewarding, but sad experience. I recall one 18-year-old who had just been brought in. I went to him immediately. He looked up at me trustingly, sighed and asked, 'How am I doing, Nurse?' I was standing at the head of the litter. I put my hands around his face, kissed his forehead and said, 'You are doing just fine, soldier.' He smiled sweetly and said, 'I was just checking up.' Then he died.

At Normandy — with German artillery units and aircraft within striking distance — a contingent of Army nurses and Red Cross workers helped set up aid stations and evacuation hospitals.

Whether on the beachhead or on a ship standing just offshore, Army nurses were aware of the imminent danger. But they also knew they couldn't desert the wounded who depended on them.

Of the 200 Army nurses who served at Anzio, Italy, six were killed in action.

A group of GIs socialize with members of the Women's Army Corps in North Africa. Some 17,345 nurses served in Europe; 201 U.S. Army nurses lost their lives — 16 as a result of hostile action.
Women's Army Corps Museum

Making do by the flickering light of a kerosene lamp under a canvas cover, 2nd Lt. Juanita H. Williams of Langley, Okla., prepares a syringe at an evacuation hospital in the British Isles during February 1943. U.S. Army

On Feb. 17, 1944, a German bomber directly hit the 95th Evacuation Hospital surgical section, killing three nurses. Three days later, enemy long-range artillery killed two off-duty nurses in a tent.

2nd Lt. Francis Slanger was assigned to the 45th Field Hospital in Belgium. In a letter written the day before she died in October 1944, Slanger conveyed the devotion and the caring all Army nurses felt for the men they treated in WWII:

Sure we rough it, but in comparison to the way you men are taking it, we can't complain, nor do we feel that bouquets are due us. But you, the men behind the guns, the men driving our tanks, flying our planes, sailing our ships, building bridges and to the men who pave the way and to the men who are left behind — it is to you we doff our helmets. . . .

Yes this time we are handing out the bouquets . . . after taking care of some of your buddies . . . when they are brought in bloody, dirty with the earth, mud and grime, and most of them so tired. . . . Seeing them gradually brought back to life, to consciousness and to see their lips separate into a grin. . . . Usually they kid, hurt as they are. . . . 'How ya, babe,' or 'Holy Mackerel, an American woman!' or most indiscreetly, 'How about a kiss?'

The wounded don't cry. Their buddies come first. The patience and determination they show, the courage and fortitude they have is sometimes awesome to behold. It is we who are proud to be here.

Rough it? No, it is a privilege . . . to receive you, and a great distinction to see you open your eyes and with that swell American grin, say, 'Hi ya, babe.'"

By June 1945, Army nurses in Europe peaked at 17,345. Of the 201 Army nurses who died on foreign shores, 16 were killed as a result of direct enemy action.

officers — Col. Demas Craw and Maj. Pierpoint Hamilton — tried to reach the French commander at Port Lyautey. However, their jeep was ambushed, despite flying a truce flag. Craw was killed. Hamilton reached the French commander, who reluctantly informed him that he had not yet received orders to surrender. So the French fought on. Hamilton was then taken prisoner. (Both men later received the Medal of Honor for their courageous actions.)

Fierce fighting continued against French Foreign Legionnaires and the Moroccan 1st Infantry Regiment. Mehdia fell after Allied fighter planes were called in.

At Casablanca, Gen. George Patton got his force ashore — primarily the 3rd Infantry Division — while under fire from enemy battleships, coastal guns and fighter planes. Weeks before, Patton had written, "We should plan either to conquer or be destroyed at Casablanca." And the night before the attack he recalled his battle cry to all his troops: "The eyes of the world are watching us. The heart of America beats for us. God is with us."

In an attempt to negotiate a truce, Patton dispatched Col. William Wilbur to find the area French commander, who turned Wilbur away. Returning to the Fedala beaches, Wilbur corraled four tanks along with infantrymen. Riding shotgun, he ordered them to take out a gun battery that was firing on the landing craft. After a pitched battle, the French artillerymen agreed to surrender. They relinquished their guns to Col. Wilbur, who later received the Medal of Honor.

The heavily defended fortress at the Casbah, which overlooked the Sebou River and the town of Mehdia, exacted a heavy toll: 225 U.S. killed or wounded. French losses were considerably greater.

Casablanca, though, still held out, so Patton ordered a naval barrage for dawn on Nov. 11.

"We entered the harbor at Casablanca before sunrise and gave the Vichy Frogs a wake-up call with all we had to offer — approximately 1,200 eight-inch projectiles," said E.W. Godwin. "We sank every ship in the harbor, with the exception of one French battleship."

Soon the French caved in and Casablanca was spared. The 3rd Infantry Division rushed to secure the city.

By D-Day plus two most of the French forces had surrendered. Sporadic sniper fire continued from feisty Arabs who picked up discarded weapons and shot at anything that moved.

Enemies for four days, then allies against the Germans for the duration of WWII, both American and French forces suffered heavy losses during

GIs haul an anti-aircraft gun onto a beach in Algeria during *Operation Torch*, November 1942. Vichy French pilots strafed landing sites (many in U.S.-made P-36s sent to France before its fall), but did not stop the steady Allied flow of men and materiel that carried the war to North Africa.

66

Us WACs went in early. I spent a year on the Libyan Desert in Egypt, replacing a man to go into battle. There were a lot of us girls (at) Camp Russell B. Huckstep . . . we did a good, good job. In Italy in a short spell, we could hear the guns of Anzio. Very scary.

99

— MARY ELLEN MCTUCKER
Women's Army Corps

Above: American soldiers interrogate a French prisoner at Oran, Algiers, during *Operation Torch* in 1942. The Allies fought a four-day war with the Vichy French of Algeria and Morocco.

Top: Officers with a tank destroyer battalion at El Guettar, Tunisia, during March 1943 examine a map of enemy-held territory. U.S. units occupied the town on March 18, but heavy fighting in the outlying area over the next five days exacted a heavy Allied casualty toll. U.S. Army Military History Institute

Operation Torch: 479 U.S. Army KIA and 696 WIA. Offshore, the Navy sustained 493 dead in action. French killed numbered 700 (mostly at sea), 1,400 WIA and 400 MIA.

The four-day fight for French North Africa provided a much-needed foothold for the Allies to strike at the Germans and Italians in Tunisia who were led by Erwin Rommel's *Afrika Corps*. It also provided a training ground for the untested American troops. Retired Lt. Gen. Bill Yarborough, a major in 1942 with the 509th Parachute Infantry Regiment, said: "We learned a lot about the art of war, about logistics, about terrain factors, weather conditions and all that kind of thing, in North Africa. It was a damn good proving ground."

Target Tunis

With Morocco and Algeria firmly under Allied control, anxious American units dashed toward Tunis, capital of Tunisia, largely uncontested. By Nov. 16, 1942, they were at Souk el Araba, a railhead 80 miles southwest of Tunis.

At Tebourba, 20 miles outside the city, a U.S. tank battalion destroyed 20 German planes on the airfield at Djedeida. Next day, however, GIs took a beating in the first armored battle with the Germans at Chouigui.

Both sides later scrambled for strategic positions in the mountains. At a place called Longstop Hill, from Dec. 23-25, the 1st Bn., 18th Inf. Regt., 1st Inf. Div., and its British allies fought to retain the hill until ordered to withdraw. But only after sustaining 356 U.S. casualties.

Having lost the race for Tunis, the Americans backed up to the Algerian-Tunisian border to build up reinforcements and supplies for the strike against the *Afrika Corps*.

Heavy downpours curtailed the attack until the end of the rainy season, which allowed the *Afrika Corps* time for refitting with new and powerful Mark VI Tiger tanks.

On Jan. 21, 1943, the U.S. 1st Armored Division began the campaign to rout the Axis forces from the Ousseltia Valley in Tunisia.

Retired Col. Charles Hangsterfer, a company commander with the 16th Inf. Regt., 1st Inf. Div., said: "We gradually gained combat experience, first against the Vichy French in North Africa, who had no real desire to fight, and then against the Italians, who also had no desire to fight. Then, when we finally went up against the German *Afrika Corps,* they were like cornered rats after being pushed so far back by the British 8th Army."

Within a few weeks, GIs would engage in a fateful fight with Germany's battle-tested troops.

President Franklin D. Roosevelt cheerfully greets a soldier at Castle Vetrano during a visit to the battlefields in North Africa.

Kasserine Pass

On St. Valentine's Day 1943, America's first major battle against the Germans began, only to end eight days later in reversal. Members of the U.S. II Corps, mostly untested in combat, "paid in blood the price of battlefield inexperience," concluded one student of the battle.

The series of operations known as the Battle of Kasserine Pass in Tunisia — from the start at Faid through Sidi bou Zid and Sbeitla to the final act at the Kasserine defile — constituted a significant jolt for the U.S. Army, but one from which it recovered quickly.

Led by the controversial Maj. Gen. Lloyd Fredendall, the U.S. II Corps faced 60,000 Germans and 40,000 Italians in northeastern Tunisia. It confronted the "Desert Fox" himself, Gen. Erwin Rommel, and his vaunted *Afrika Korps*, veterans of two years of fighting in the desert.

"Kasserine," Secretary of War Henry Stimson later said, "serves to remind us that there is no easy road to victory and that we must expect setbacks . . . we will not have an easy nor a quick victory."

> 66
>
> *Kasserine serves to remind us*
> *that there is no easy road*
> *to victory.*
>
> 99
>
> — Henry Stimson
> Secretary of War

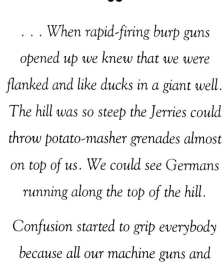

66

. . . When rapid-firing burp guns opened up we knew that we were flanked and like ducks in a giant well. The hill was so steep the Jerries could throw potato-masher grenades almost on top of us. We could see Germans running along the top of the hill.

Confusion started to grip everybody because all our machine guns and mortar emplacements were dug to shoot down the valley; base plates had to be turned to shoot at the Germans on top of the hill. In some cases the machine guns could not be elevated enough to shoot at the ridge and had to be removed from tripods for hand-held shooting.

99

— JOHN F. LEBDA
1st Bn., detached,
26th Regt., 1st Div.

U.S. II Corps GIs move through Kasserine Pass, Tunisia, in February 1943. The U.S. Army met the famed *Afrika Corps* for the first time head-on in the rugged mountains of the French colony.

A troop train carries Allied soldiers closer to the battlefields of North Africa. National Archives

"

We never, never gave up ground in a battle. Once territory was taken by the 1st Infantry Division it was not subject to repossession by any enemy force! That's something the German found hard to understand as he sent his best units against our defenses and always had nothing for his endeavors but enemy dead, burnt out hulks of tanks, destroyed artillery and massed prisoners of war. Maj. Gen. Terry de la Mesa Allen said it best . . . 'Nothing in Hell must stop the First Division.' Nothing ever did!

"

— CPL. WILLIAM M. LEE

Despite warnings of an enemy attack through Fondouk Pass in the Eastern Dorsal (French for fin), little had been done to defend it. Journalist A.B. Austin described the bleak terrain there: "The hills of Tunisia had one thing in common — their curious tortured tops. Their peaks or ridges would either be carved with rocky whorls or curves, or would stick up in knife-edges like the comb of a cock, or would be studded with pinnacles like the jagged spine of a brontosaurus. Soon we understood that the whole future of the Tunisian campaign lay in them."

Small pockets of U.S. troops were dispersed over a very large area — one battalion of the 1st Infantry Division at Gafsa in the south; another blocked the Fondouk Road to Sbeitla, Combat Command A (CCA) of the 1st Armored Division was located forward at Sidi bou Zid near the Faid Pass; and Combat Command B (CCB) remained in the rear near Tebessa.

Other major U.S. units that ultimately played a part in the Tunisian campaign included the 1,200-plane 12th Air Force, 9th and 34th Infantry divisions, 509th Parachute Infantry Battalion and 1st Ranger Battalion.

Recoiling from defeat at El'Alamein, Rommel's 10 divisions, standing at half strength of about 78,000 men and 128 tanks, occupied French fortifications in southern Tunisia. On Feb. 9, he met with his counterpart and nemesis, Gen. Juergen von Arnim, commander of the German Fifth Corps, to plan strategy.

Under the guise of Field Marshall Albert Kesselring, they decided to combine forces to give the Axis the needed strength to resume the offensive. "What counts isn't the ground we gain, but the damage we inflict on the Americans," Rommel believed.

He attacked what he called "those new boys from the Land of Boundless Possibilities" on Feb. 14 not at Fondouk Pass, but 30 miles to the south at Faid Pass. Within five hours his 10th Panzer Division destroyed CCA at Sidi bou Zid and the 168th Regimental Combat Team (RCT) at Lessouda.

The massive 60-ton German Tiger tanks rolled over the forward American positions, causing a panicked withdrawal. "There were notable pockets of gallantry," Gen. Omar Bradley later recorded, "but for the most part, our soldiers abandoned their weapons, including tanks and fled to the rear . . . "

One of these pockets was held by the 1st Bn., 26th Inf., 1st Division. "I was there and I can assure you we did not panic, retreat, or leave any equipment behind," insists veteran John Lebda. "Some was captured, but none abandoned by us."

An American machine gun crew remains on alert at El Guettar, Tunisia, after it was occupied as an Allied stronghold March 18, 1943.

U.S. Army Military History Institute

Another member of the 1st Battalion, William Lee, added, "We acquitted ourselves well in the face of the enemy. I wear my Presidential Unit Citation, as do all veterans of the 1st Battalion, 26th Infantry."

Then the *Afrika Korps* committed a second force in the south at Gafsa. Over the next two days, it swept northwest some 50 miles and overran the quickly abandoned U.S. airfields at Thelepte.

Rommel's intent now was to combine the converging forces and fight his way north to the coast to cut off the British First Army, and then plunge deep into Algeria.

After the setback at Sidi bou Zid, GIs attempted a reprisal attack. Combat Command C of the 1st Armored Division, augmented by a battalion from CCB detached from the British in the north, counterattacked the 10th Panzers at Lessouda.

German dive-bombers initially disorganized the attack, then the defenders enveloped the Americans. Most of the U.S. infantrymen and artillery escaped, but only four tanks in the entire counterattack force left the battlefield intact. The RCT that led the assault was later captured trying to evade by foot across the treeless plateau.

Above: U.S. aircraft make a combat run over the barren expanse of Tunisia in 1943. National Air and Space Museum

Right: A 105mm howitzer crew provides fire support to infantry forces assaulting Kasserine Pass in Tunisia during February 1943. Allied forces at Kasserine would suffer 10,000 casualties, compared to 2,000 Axis losses. National Archives

By Feb. 16, II Corps was pulling in its horns. The 26th Infantry Regiment of the "Big Red One" held the line forward just east of Sbeitla while the battered 1st Armored Division withdrew. The 26th Infantry and the 19th Engineers held out as long as they could and then fell back to Kasserine as ordered. As these units pulled back, the British 26th Armor and 18th U.S. Infantry moved south to reinforce the positions around Kasserine.

The German 10th and 21st Panzers descended upon the Kasserine Pass west from Sbeitla and north from Feriana. Everyone understood there would be no withdrawal from the Western Dorsal and, most important, the pass at Kasserine must be held.

Shaped like a crude X, the pass was one mile across at its narrowest point, flanked by the Hatab River and by heights that reached up to 1,000 feet.

The 19th Engineers mined the entire valley floor, forcing the Germans to stick to the roads where the 26th Infantry, dug in behind a triple belt of anti-tank and anti-personnel mines, could observe them as they approached the pass.

As Feb. 18 ended, discipline among the troops broke down during the cold desert night. As Col. Anderson Moore admitted, "Fear and poor control by officers and non-coms were the root cause." Pfc. James Grimes recalled, "It was one hell of a long night. Everybody was jumpy and nervous."

But with the end of darkness came the moment of truth at Kasserine. Initially withstanding an artillery barrage, Rommel's 10th Panzers gained some ground. Simultaneously, in the north, the British Guard units and the U.S. 18th Infantry held off an attack by the 21st Panzers at Sbiba. But the 26th Infantry was overrun.

"What happened during the night of February 19–20," states the official

A field artillery crew of the U.S. II Corps in Tunisia loads ammo after unleashing a heavy barrage on German defensive positions eight miles south of El Guettar on March 21, 1943.
U.S. Army Military History Institute

U.S. history of the campaign in North Africa, "cannot be clearly reconstructed from the record."

On the main route to Thala the U.S. defenders had scraped together what forces they could to guard from further advances beyond the Kasserine Pass. Just as Rommel's forces were about to overrun the British 26th Armor at Thala, the U.S. 9th Division's artillery arrived. Part of the rescue force was the 34th Field Artillery Battalion — commanded by Lt. Col. William C. Westmoreland — which earned a Presidential Unit Citation for its brilliant actions.

After a four-day, 800-mile forced drive from Oran in Algeria, the artillery effectively halted the advancing Germans. One German colonel said of the 9th's continual bombardment: "Yanks' guns began to hammer us . . . shells seemed to rain on us from all directions."

Other units also distinguished themselves. "Elements of the 1st Armored Division blunted the enemy tank attack and forced them to withdraw," asserts Robert Vaurinek, a veteran of that division. "On Feb. 22, the Axis assault was thrown back. Yet our division received little notice or credit for its work in the campaign."

By morning on Feb. 22, Rommel realized he could not break through to the coast, so he called off the offensive and withdrew his forces to the

Above: Maj. Bernard Muldoon of Springfield, Ill. (center in front of map) synchronizes watches with the pilots of his 49th Fighter Squadron, 14th Fighter Group, under the headquarters tent in War Theater No. 15, North Africa, during the summer of 1943. Smithsonian Institution

Opposite: A pet monkey, obtained from an Arab friend, entertains 1st Lt. H.E. Robinson serving with a glider field artillery battalion in Oujda, Tunisia, during June 1943. Signal Corps

Eastern Dorsal. Next afternoon, the Allies reoccupied Kasserine, and without firing a shot, retook all ground lost to the Germans in the preceding series of battles.

German losses at Kasserine totaled 200 KIA, 550 WIA and 250 MIA. Of the 30,000 Americans engaged at Kasserine, 300 were killed, 3,000 wounded and nearly 3,000 missing. In addition, the 34th Division at Sbiba lost 50 KIA, 200 WIA and 250 MIA.

During March and April, the tide turned in favor of the U.S. Army. In achieving their triumph, GIs demonstrated a remarkable ability to recover. Subsequent operations proved their confidence. The road to Bizerte, with stops along the way at places like Hill 609, was paved with examples of the U.S. Army's competence.

When the Axis force finally surrendered in May 1943, 32,000 of its troops had been killed in Tunisia and 238,000 taken prisoner (two-thirds German). In contrast, the U.S. lost 2,838 killed and 8,279 wounded.

"The Americans made many mistakes in this first large-scale engagement of the war in Europe, but they learned from their errors and made adjustments that enabled them to go on to victory in Tunisia and beyond," wrote Martin Blumenson in *America's First Battles.* "That they quickly became proficient in the warfare of the 1940s confirmed their spirit, their flexibility, their strong sense of purpose — their will to win."

★ ★ ★

Persian Gulf Command Achieves Logistical Triumph

At its peak, more than 30,000 American troops served in the little-known Persian Gulf Command. Among them were members of A Co., 516th Quartermaster Regiment at Avej Pass, Iran, in January 1944. L–R: George Thornton, Urban Moeller, Harris Bryant, Russell McDowell and (kneeling) Martin Sandberg. U.S. Army

"

We were some 45,000 to 50,000 Army personnel in the Persian Gulf, working under the most intolerable heat, disease, and all the other discomforts, yet it seems that no one knows we were even there. It was probably one of the most difficult logistics triumphs of our century.

"

— COL. ROBERT SAWTELLE
Persian Gulf Command

A historic route from the Persian Gulf to Teheran and Kazvin in Iran — once used by Marco Polo and Alexander the Great — conveyed war materiel to the Russians courtesy of the seldom-heralded Persian Gulf Command (PGC) for three years during WWII.

The first sizeable detachment of U.S. troops landed at Khorramshahr, Iran, in December 1942. By August 1943, there were port and railway-operating battalions, road-maintenance groups, truck regiments and engineer battalions there. Other support personnel included military police and medics. A peak strength of nearly 30,000 Americans was reached in February 1944.

PGC had, as journalist Joel Sayre wrote, "no fancy-pants dash whatever."

Relying heavily on the Iranian State Railway, which was operational before WWII, the PGC's biggest contributions were in maintaining and improving the existing tracks, and round-the-clock operation of the railroad.

U.S. engineers also had to lay a roadbed wide and sturdy enough to support the steady flow of trucks carrying Sherman tanks and artillery pieces.

"With few exceptions," wrote Simon Rigge in *War in the Outposts*, "the Americans who served in the PGC considered their tour of duty in Iran a form of cruel and unusual punishment. It was not just that the weather was abominable and the work grueling; there was practically nothing to do in the off-duty hours."

Americans in Iran battled the unbearable desert heat — often curtailing work from mid-morning to late afternoon in July and August — and dealt with blinding sand storms, flooding, malaria, dysentery and sand fly fever.

In their role of providing security along the route, GIs confronted leprous beggars, German-supported nomadic tribesmen who attacked the convoys and trains, and warring Arab leaders who needed weapons and ammunition for their own regional skirmishing. Eventually, Col. H. Norman Schwarzkopf, former superintendent of the New Jersey State Police, molded an effective 20,000-man Iranian security force to confront these threats.

In one instance, PGC personnel provided security, apprehending German paratroopers sent to sabotage the supply routes and to assassinate the "Big Three" — Roosevelt, Churchill and Stalin — during the 1943 Teheran Conference.

The last GIs sailed away from Iran Dec. 30, 1945.

Lend-Lease aid to the Soviet Union sent 5,767,301 tons of supplies — including 184,000 U.S. trucks — through the Persian Corridor, playing a vital role in ending WWII.

U.S. and Russian air crewmen worked side-by-side at Qualeh Morgeh Airport in Tehran, Iran from December 1942 to December 1945. C-47 transports and B-24 bombers were among the many planes arriving with equipment, gasoline, ammunition, etc., bound for Russian troops fighting against Germany on the Eastern Front. U.S. Army

Aside from the raids on our truck convoys, fatal accidents, treacherous mountain roads and sheer exhaustion from pounding the road 16 to 18 hours a day, the biggest problems were in the desert where there were many severe sandstorms and temperatures that averaged 120 degrees in the shade.

On July 27, 1943, the temperature was 132 degrees and the next day it reached 136 degrees. This was two degrees hotter than the then-world record of 134 degrees.

Sun temperatures were as high as 179 degrees and one can only imagine the toll on men and equipment. At times, one could fry an egg on the steel bed of a truck.

On Nov. 23, 1943, this writer was sent to be part of the 'Honor Guard' for Roosevelt, Churchill and Stalin at the Teheran Conference. The Germans dropped a total of 22 commando groups by parachute on various sites. Their goal was to assassinate the "Big Three" and also blow up several tunnels on the railway to put it out of operation and deprive the Russians of critical supplies.

One group of 60 wore Russian army uniforms — but due to good intelligence, their mission was never completed and all were either killed or captured.

—JOSEPH PETERS
516th QM Trucking
Regiment

Above: Army drivers assigned to the Persian Gulf Command arrive at Qazvin in the Soviet zone on March 4, 1943. This convoy consisted of 46 trucks for the 466-mile trip, one way.
U.S. Army

Top: The route from Teheran, Iran to Russia was trecherous. Still, convoys of trucks travelled it daily, which included a suspension bridge at Talehzang, north of Dezful.
Corps of Engineers

ITALY

The Red Bull in the Winter Line. The 168th Infantry Regiment, 34th Infantry Division, engages in hand-to-hand fighting for Mount Pantano in southern Italy from Nov. 29–Dec. 3, 1943. When their ammo ran out, infantrymen threw rocks and C-ration cans at the Germans. The 1st Battalion held out five days against mortar fire, frigid temperatures and limited supplies, earning a Presidential Unit Citation. The 34th was the first Army division to arrive in Europe and is credited with more days in combat than any other Army division. National Guard Heritage painting by Donna Neary

From Sicily to the Po Valley

WITH NORTH AFRICA firmly under control, the Allies planned next to hurdle the Mediterranean and attack Axis forces occupying Europe's southern flanks in the summer of 1943.

In mid-May, Pantelleria and Lampedusa islands in the Strait of Sicily came under Allied naval and air bombardment. These assaults continued through early June, when both islands surrendered. Soon after, Sicily itself was pounded. In just one day — June 25, 1943 — 300 tons of bombs fell on the island stronghold.

While the German High Command braced for an invasion of Sardinia and Corsica, the Allies prepared to invade Sicily.

"There is no way of conveying the enormous size of that fleet. On the horizon it resembled a distant city," reported Ernie Pyle. "It covered half the skyline, and the dull-colored camouflaged ships stood indistinctly against the curve of the dark water, like a solid formation of uncountable structures blending together. Even to be part of it was frightening. I hope no American ever has to see its counterpart sailing against us."

On July 10, 1943, 15 minutes after paratroopers from the U.S. 505th Parachute Combat Team descended upon Sicily's southern coast, U.S. soldiers waded ashore in what was then the largest amphibious assault in modern history. *Operation Husky*, the code-name for the invasion of Sicily, would last more than a month.

The chief of the Mediterranean Fleet, British Adm. Andrew Cunningham, described the Allied invasion as "the most momentous enterprise of the war . . . striking for the first time at the enemy in his own land."

On Sicily, the U.S. established itself as a force to be reckoned with at places like Gela, Palermo, and especially Messina. Lt. Gen. George S. Patton permanently established the Army's reputation when his newly formed Seventh U.S. Army won the race against the British to the strategic port city of Messina to cut off the enemy from retreating to the Italian mainland.

The overall Allied objective was to eliminate fascist Italy from the war and gain control of the Mediterranean Sea. The Allies then could focus their attention on the eventual cross-channel assault from England onto mainland Europe.

The Strait of Messina, the passage to Messina, was so narrow and well fortified that invaders believed the only solution was to land elsewhere and march on Messina by way of the shallow coastal shelves.

The plan called for three U.S. divisions to land between Licata and Scoglitti. The British, in turn, would assault to the right of the U.S. with over four divisions coming ashore between Sampieri and Syracuse.

Troops about to land on the coast of Sicily during Operation Husky on July 10, 1943, receive last-minute instructions about their objectives. Capture of the island by Gen. George Patton's Seventh Army provided center stage for American soldiers for the first time in the European Theater. U.S. Signal Corps

Above: A U.S. Coast Guard-manned transport lies off Sicily in July 1943. The Coast Guard, part of the Navy during wartime, played a vital role in WWII. Thousands of its members served overseas. U.S. Coast Guard

Right: A sign on a building in Gela, Sicily, behind a blown-up Italian tank, says in Italian, "Mussolini's — Do Not Touch" — but troops of the U.S. Seventh Army entering the village paid little attention. On July 11, 1943, Gela became ome of the first Sicilian towns captured, one day after the island invasion began. U.S. Army Military History Institute

"

The Germans withdrew, leaving behind garrisons of Italian soldiers who would fire a few shots to save face and then raise the white flag in surrender.

"

— WILLIAM L. REED
Master Sergeant
C Co., 504th Parachute
Inf. Regt., 82nd
Airborne Div.

Assisting this massive armada ashore were Allied paratroopers and gliders inserted early on the morning July 10. This force consisted of 226 C-47s of the U.S. 52nd Troop Carrier Wing filled with some 3,400 82nd Airborne paratroopers. Some 109 American C-47s and 35 British Albermarles of the 51st Troop Carrier Wing towed 144 Waco and Horsa gliders. The airborne mission aimed at tactical objectives to facilitate the following seaborne assault.

Patton ordered the 505th to seize the high ground behind Gela, and Montgomery chose the Ponte Grande Bridge near Syracuse as the objective for the British 1st Airborne. However, high winds, poor navigation techniques and improperly trained air crews scattered the paratroopers all over southeastern Sicily, placing only one-eighth in their planned drop zones.

It was the first night parachute assault conducted by an organized Army and proved to be very confusing and costly to the Allies. Much was the same for the British in the east.

A massive seaborne invasion coincided with the airborne assault: the 45th, 1st and 3rd Infantry divisions landed respectively at Scoglitti, Gela and Licata. All told, 66,285 personnel, 17,766 tons of equipment and 7,416 vehicles made it ashore. Their objective was to move northward and open successively the ports of Empedocle, Marsala, Trapani and Palermo.

Other major U.S. units involved in the fight for Sicily included the 2nd Armored Division, the 540th Engineer Shore Regiment, Force X of Darby's Ranger Command, the 945-ship Western Naval Task Force (flagship *Monrovia*) and 400 aircraft from the Northwest Africa Air Force.

Sicily was garrisoned by the Italian Sixth Army consisting of eight coastal

divisions, four Italian mobile divisions and two German units, including the elite *Hermann Goering* Division. All told, the island held 240,000 Italian troops and 30,000 Germans. German reserves were designated to repel the invasion because of poor performance by the Italians.

W.G.R. Jackson, in his book *The Battle For Italy*, wrote: "The worthless coastal divisions, comprised of local troops, could be relied on only to report a landing and to fire a few shots before fleeing."

In accordance with Axis defense plans, the *Livorno* and *Goering* divisions counterattacked the American-held beaches, but with little success. Garrisons throughout the island fell on the first day, in many cases without a shot being fired. The only significant opposition came from Axis air elements, which harassed the U.S. beachheads, sinking the destroyer *Maddox* and a minesweeper.

On July 11, the *Livorno* and *Goering* divisions attacked the 82nd Airborne and 1st Infantry divisions at Gela. After six hours of fighting, nearly 100 Mark III and German Tiger tanks moved within 2,000 meters of the beach. But determined resistance and massive naval gunfire forced the Axis units back, destroying one-third of their tanks.

Members of the 504th Parachute Infantry Regiment, 82nd Airborne Division, prepare to make the U.S. Army's first large-scale jump on Sicily on July 9, 1943. Widely scattered during the night operation, they nonetheless fought tenaciously in small groups on the island. Smithsonion Institution

66

I can still see those boys in the doors of the planes. The planes were so low you could have hit them with a stick. The shrapnel felt like rain.

99

— CLARENCE E. MANSELL
105th AAA Airborne Bn.
82nd Airborne Division

Above: During the pre-invasion naval bombardment, an American cruiser shells enemy fortifications at Gela beach, on Sicily, July 10, 1943. Surprisingly little resistance was met during the assault and by the next day, 160,000 Allied soldiers were ashore. U.S. Navy

Opposite: Twelfth Air Force B-25 Mitchell bombers conduct raids on enemy industrial and military installations in northern Italy. Two Mitchells depart the area of destruction they created far below. Smithsonian Institution

"As salvo after salvo of naval gunfire split their armored hulls, the German panzer commanders wisely concluded that a 26-ton Mark IV was no match for a cruiser," said Gen. Omar Bradley. "The enemy turned and ran for the hills where the Navy could not pursue him."

The Army, however, could. During the invasion "there were human bodies hanging from the trees," recalled Army Capt. James B. Lyle, after witnessing a shelling by the USS *Savannah* at Gela.

Two nights after the initial drop, Patton ordered the remainder of the 82nd Airborne to Sicily. This proved to be one of the most tragic mistakes of the war.

As the transport planes approached the beach, they passed over an American flotilla still at battle stations following a German bomber attack. As the 144 troop transports carrying 2,304 men of the 504th Parachute Regimental Combat Team approached, Allied anti-aircraft batteries mistook them for German bombers. Some 318 U.S. paratroopers and scores of air crew members were killed when 23 C-47s were shot down by "friendly fire."

One bomber crewman remembered: "We couldn't hear the bursts over the roar of the engines, but [we] were rocked again and again by explosions, and the gun flashes were visible below."

Meanwhile, the Seventh Army rapidly advanced to the northwest, but by order, delayed its assault on Palermo and Trapani. When Palermo fell on July 22, Patton wrote: "As we approached, the hills on each side were burning. We then started down a long road cut out of the side of a cliff which went through an almost continuous village. The street was full of people shouting, 'Down with Mussolini,' and 'Long live America.'"

The Seventh then turned eastward and drove along the northern coast to Messina. Simultaneously, two additional German divisions arrived on Sicily to reinforce the unreliable minions of Mussolini.

German forces set up a series of defensive lines, ultimately leading to a withdrawal across the Messina Strait onto mainland Italy. "Trying to win a horse race to the last big town," Patton wanted desperately to beat Montgomery's Eighth Army to Messina. So he conducted a series of amphibious "end runs" with *Task Force 88* assisting the U.S. 3rd Division at Sant' Agata and Brolo. Unstable Italian politics soon caused the Germans to begin evacuating Sicily.

Catania fell on Aug. 5 to the British, as did Misterbianco and Paterno. The next day the "Big Red One" assaulted Troina in a long and bloody battle. "These astonishing Americans. They fight all day, attack all night and shoot all the time," a German soldier at Troina wrote in a letter later found on his body.

In Altavilla near Salerno, Italy, in September 1943, combat engineers from the 142nd Inf. Rgt., 36th Inf. Div. patrol the ruins of the village. By Sept. 18, the 191st Tank Battalion, along with American paratroopers, had secured Altavilla. U.S. Army

> 66
>
> *Fight 'em with the*
> *rammer staffs!*
>
> 99
>
> — 132nd Field Artillery
> Battle cry at Salerno

Randazzo fell seven days later. Meanwhile, the 3rd Division progressed rapidly toward Messina, closely supported by the cruiser *Philadelphia*.

On the night of Aug. 16, U.S. troops triumphantly entered Messina. A reinforced platoon from Co. L, 7th Infantry, led by 1st Lt. Ralph Yates, had pushed into the city proper, ending the Anglo-American race for the port city. Except for occasional rifle fire, the GIs met no resistance.

Already evacuated were 62,182 Italian and 39,569 German soldiers — complete with weapons and supplies — across the Messina Strait to mainland Italy. They would fight another day.

U.S. casualties on Sicily totaled 2,572 KIA and 5,746 wounded on the ground and in the air. The Navy counted 522 dead and more than 500 wounded.

Geoffrey Perret, in *There's A War To Be Won*, wrote: "Sicily — ancient battleground, land of the Mafia and the blood orange — added to the Army's core of veteran divisions the 3rd Infantry, 45th Infantry, 2nd Armored and 82nd Airborne, while extending the combat experience of the 1st and 9th Infantry divisions.

"Sicily provided a dramatic setting for [act one of the invasion of Europe], and the show had taken an unscripted turn. The American soldier, cast in a non-speaking walk-on role, had grabbed center stage."

Salerno: *Operation Avalanche*

Next stage was mainland Italy. On Sept. 3, 1943, a secret armistice was signed, ending Italy's partnership with Germany. Five days later, Gen. Eisenhower announced the surrender.

Then Salerno was hit with an Allied avalanche. Well-trained, but untried, the 36th Infantry Division (Texas National Guard) was the first U.S. unit to set foot on Italy's mainland on Sept. 9, 1943. Yet the Texans felt ready for anything. "Hell, there's nothing anybody could do worse than what the Old Man's tossed at us," Pfc. Bill Craig of Co. K, 1st Bn., 141st Regimental Combat Team (RCT) confided to a war correspondent accompanying the landing, known as *Operation Avalanche*.

But as the coxswains dropped boat ramps 12 miles off Salerno, the Germans responded with a hail of fire. It pinned down the British X Corps in the north and the 36th at Paestum in the south, beginning the tug of war for the highlands surrounding the beachheads.

The 85,000 Allied forces attacking the German 16th Panzer Grenadier Division on the Salerno beachhead consisted of Lt. Gen. Mark Clark's

Fifth U.S. Army, divided into Northern and Southern Attack Forces. In the north, was the British X Corps, including the 46th and 56th Infantry divisions, three U.S. Ranger battalions, and two British Commando forces.

Southern Force comprised VI Corps. Its main effort was undertaken by the 36th Division's 141st and 142nd RCTs (the 143rd RCT was held in reserve), which attempted to seize the high ground between Paestum and Agropoli.

Close behind was the 45th, 34th and 3rd Infantry divisions along with the 82nd Airborne. Offshore, *Task Force 81* included the cruisers *Philadelphia*, *Savannah*, *Boise* and *Brooklyn* led by the flagship *Samuel Chase*.

The destroyer *Rowan* guarded transports and supply ships as they offloaded at Paestum, then accompanied the empty ships back to North Africa, where the convoy was attacked by German E-boats. The *Rowan* pursued the attackers, only to be hit by a torpedo. Almost immediately the *Rowan* sank, carrying 202 of her 273 men to their death.

The Allies ashore at Paestum faced the German Tenth Army, consisting of four panzer and two panzer grenadier divisions equal to approximately 50,000 men.

Many acts of heroism took place that September morning. Tech. Sgt. Manuel Gonzoles, a platoon leader in F Co., 2nd Bn., 142 RCT, won the

Above: Pvt. Arnold Groveman, missing his helmet, and three other GIs hugged the beach at Salerno under heavy air attack in September 1943. Groveman sent the photo to his sister, Mrs. Lilyan G. Pell of New York City, along with these comments: "That beach was really hot. Jerry was dropping bombs and strafing. You can see one of his eggs falling in the background. I picked up another helmet later."
U.S. Coast Guard, U.S. Naval Institute

Top: Paratroopers of the 82nd Airborne Division prepare for their jump on Salerno, Italy, during Sept. 13–14, 1943. Smithsonian Institution

Residents of San Pietro, Italy, overflow to greet their liberators from the 36th Division. One soldier receives a special show of emotion from an appreciative Italian woman. San Pietro was captured Dec. 17, 1943.

Distinguished Service Cross (DSC) for single-handedly destroying an 88mm cannon dug into the sand dunes, which was firing point blank at landing craft.

Pvt. John Jones of E Co., after losing contact with his platoon, came across 50 stragglers and personally led them off an already crowded beach, making way for troops and supplies still arriving.

The 36th's sector was divided into four distinct beaches: Red, Green, Yellow and Blue — all jumbled with troops, supplies, wrecked vehicles, and dead and wounded men. Landing craft could not even lower their ramps.

The 143rd added firepower to the embattled 142nd — still hammering away at a German watchtower at Paestum. Also, men of the 531st Shore Engineer Bn., led by Company D, picked up rifles and drove the enemy out at bayonet point, clearing the beaches. Supported by naval gunfire, the 142nd established a position on the slope of Monte Soprano overlooking the beachhead.

On Sept. 10, the "Thunderbird's" 179th and 157th RCTs went ashore. By nightfall, the 45th had moved to a tobacco factory on the Sele River where seven Sherman tanks from B Co., 191st Tank Bn., were destroyed. Fighting raged for days along the Sele-Calore corridor.

In the northern sector, the British 9th Fusiliers battled at Battipaglia. And U.S. Rangers repelled vigorous enemy attacks against Mount Chiunzi in their attempt to control the passes leading to Naples.

By Sept. 12, the Fifth U.S. Army was fighting desperately to hold the beachheads it had won only three days earlier. At the Sele-Calore corridor, the 1st Bn., 142nd RCT, was trapped in a salient on Hill 424. GIs gave it their best, but the battalion was forced to fall back.

The 157th RCT failed to take the tobacco plant, but U.S. naval and field artillery barrages eventually destroyed the factory.

That night, the *Luftwaffe* bombed three hospital ships, sinking the *Newfoundland*. Four American nurses suffered minor wounds for which they later received Purple Hearts. Casualties continued to mount, with the British sustaining 3,000 losses in a single day at Battipaglia.

German attacks battered the VI and X Corps. *Martin Force*, formed from the 36th, attempted to recapture Altavilla, which would allow the Allies to dominate the corridor. But the force was pushed back to last-ditch positions along La Cosa Creek between the Calore River and Monte Soprano, only five miles from the beaches.

At day's end, the 45th had re-entered the fray. After a fierce battle with the 79th Panzer Grenadier Regiment, the Germans inexplicably paused. The break in fighting allowed the 189th and 158th Field Artillery battalions to emplace their guns on the south bank of the Calore River: Advancing German tanks were quickly halted.

"All afternoon the troops along the Sele fought as desperate a battle as Americans had seen since the Alamo," wrote Geoffrey Perret in *There's A War to Be Won*. "Field artillery battalions cut their fuses to next to nothing and fired point-blank over open sights at oncoming tanks and screaming platoons of Germans. When they ran out of ammo or their positions were about to be overrun, the artillerymen deployed as skirmishers and fought like infantry."

The 36th Division's 132nd Field Artillery held its ground and beat off the attackers. "Fight 'em with the rammer staffs!" became the unit's battle cry, a slogan widely seen in Texas newspaper headlines. One editor predicted that the battle slogan would become part of the Texan heritage — along with "Remember the Alamo."

Remember the Rohna

One roaring burst of flame from a *Luftwaffe* bomber on Nov. 26, 1943, killed 1,015 American soldiers aboard the British troopship *Rohna*. The second greatest naval loss of U.S. troops in WWII, it presaged the missile warfare age, yet this sinking in the Mediterranean went largely unreported.

The *Rohna* sailed in convoy off the North Africa coast when a Heinkel 177 pilot released a secret flying bomb. By manipulating a joystick control box connected to a receiver which controlled a gyroscopic autopilot, the pilot guided the missile into the ship's port side. The explosion tore a huge hole in the *Rohna*, flooded the engine room, knocked out power, and started a fire.

The bomb burst in the midst of the 853rd Aviation Engineer Battalion, killing 491 officers and men. In the composite words of several survivors:

All I could see were bodies lying around. . . . Many boys were killed around me by shrapnel. . . . I was knocked unconscious for about 15 minutes. After recovery I managed to crawl through a hole, where the radio-operated bomb had entered, and lower myself to the sea. . . . My men and I gave first aid to approximately 50 injured men. I estimate that perhaps 500 men, in all, were unable to leave the ship. These men were trapped or killed by fire, explosion or falling debris.

Of the 3,604 American soldiers reported killed at sea during the war with Germany and Italy, almost one-third died when the *Rohna* sank.

Above: As Allied cargo ships approach the beach at Anzio on April 27, 1944, a shell from Nazi artillery fire sends a guyser rising above the boats.
National Archives

When Sept. 14 dawned, the situation remained bleak for the Allies. Fearing the possibility of the enemy cutting the bridgehead in two, Gen. Clark decided to prepare for an evacuation. Not everybody agreed with his decision. "Put food and ammunition behind the 45th," Gen. Troy H. Middleton told Clark. "We're staying."

In the nick of time, the 82nd Airborne parachuted 1,300 men of the 504th Parachute Infantry Regiment (followed by 2,100 paratroopers of the 505th PIR) onto the beaches behind the U.S. lines and bolstered the sagging front at Altavilla. This provided the Allies with much-needed reinforcements.

Over the next two days, the Germans hit the VI and X Corps fronts. Their attacks, though, were rendered ineffective by strategic bombers, massive naval gunfire and a determined Allied resistance. On the 16th, the Germans fell back to the Volturno River. Three days later, the British Eighth Army reached Potenza from Calabria to linkup with the Fifth Army. Then the attack resumed north toward Naples, which GIs took on Oct. 1, 1943. But the German's skillful withdrawal northward allowed them to establish a defensive front on the line of the Volturno River.

U.S. Fifth Army elements reached the south bank of the Volturno, just 15 miles northwest of Naples, five days later. The U.S. II and III Corps crossed the Volturno and quickly established bridgeheads on Oct. 13.

The Germans again retreated, this time to the Winter Line, 75 miles south of Rome, along the Garigliano and Sangro rivers. Throughout November, Allied units assaulted the Winter line, with negligible results.

December opened with the U.S. II and X Corps hitting the Germans in the Camino Hills, capturing San Pietro on Dec. 17, followed by San Vittore, Cervaro and Monte Trocchio in January.

A particularly heroic fight featured the 1st Bn., 168th Infantry, 34th Div. on Mt. Pantano between Nov. 29–Dec. 3. Under constant attack and immersed in hand-to-hand combat, the unit held its position for five days until relieved, earning a Presidential Unit Citation.

When the Naples-Foggia Campaign officially ended Jan. 21, 1944, U.S. ground and air units counted 6,266 killed in action and 14,642 wounded in action.

Anzio: *Operation Shingle*

Operation Shingle began Jan. 22, 1944, when the U.S. VI Corps and elements of the British Eighth Army assaulted the Italian coast 30 miles southwest of Rome at Anzio.

Fighter-bombers known as "Thunderbolts" — P-47Ds — fly in formation during an attack over northern Italy. These raids took place in 1944–45.

The landing intended to surprise the German Army's 14th Corps from the rear as it defended the formidable Gustav Line near Cassino. The Allies hoped to force the withdrawal of the German forces holding up their advance. But this original objective was not destined to be met: Highways 6 and 7 and the rail lines were not immediately cut.

By day's end, 36,000 men had gone ashore with minimal casualties (only 13 KIA and 97 WIA mostly from strafing German aircraft). But the Germans cordoned the beachhead, cornering the Allies into a perimeter some 11 miles long and seven miles deep between the Anzio and Nettuno harbors.

For four long months, the Anzio beachhead became the scene of one of the most courageous and bloody dramas of WWII.

"There was no safe place on the Anzio beachhead," recalled Sgt. Reg Clark of the 3rd Bn., 135th Inf. Regt., 34th Infantry Division. "With more than 50,000 men on a plot of real estate less than a hundred square miles, chances were that an enemy bullet, shell or bomb would kill one or more of our men. And the Jerries never let up."

Sgt. Allan Rossel of the 306th Air Service Squadron recalled German propaganda leaflets with a skull drawn on them and the words: "This is going to be the biggest cemetery for the Allied forces in World War II."

The first wave of the assault forces splashed ashore at three separate points. The British 9th, 43rd Commandos and portions of the 1st Division landed at Peter Beach, six miles northwest of Anzio. The center beach, X-ray Yellow, was seized by the three battalions of the U.S. 6615th Ranger Force, the 509th Parachute Infantry Battalion and the 83rd Chemical Mortar Battalion.

Four miles to the southeast, the U.S. 3rd Infantry Division landed three regiments (the 7th, 15th and 30th) at X-ray's Red and Green beaches.

Within hours that morning, all the port facilities at Anzio and Nettuno fell under Allied control.

66

Surely all who have survived the assault on Anzio will go to heaven, since they have already served their time in hell.

99

— CHAPLAIN WILLIAM JOHNSON
1st Special Service Force

A massive German railway gun known as "The Anzio Express" was captured near Leghorn, Italy, after the Anzio beachhead breakout in the spring of 1944. The barrel had an 11-inch diameter and was 64 feet long. It weighed 90 tons and could lob 550-pound shells a tremendous distance. The iron rods along the barrel provided a means for draping camoflage nets.

Other U.S. ground combat forces that ultimately participated in the battle at Anzio included the 1st Armored Division's 6th Armored Infantry Regt., 504th Parachute Infantry Regt., 751st Tank Bn., 1st Special Service Force, 36th and 39th Combat Engineer Regts., and the 34th, 36th and 45th Infantry divisions.

Even though the Allies caught the Germans by surprise in the initial landing, they didn't expand the lodgement until Jan. 30. By then, eight German divisions were in place with another five en route. A two-pronged Allied attack toward Campoleone and Cisterna met strong resistance. The British seized Campoleone, but could go no farther.

The next day, the Americans began their attack toward Cisterna and Highway 7 by infiltrating the 1st, 3rd and 4th Ranger battalions, numbering 767 men, through the German lines and attacking en masse with the 3rd Division and the 504th PIR. All but six of the Rangers were killed or captured. After two days of fierce fighting, the Germans pushed the Brits out of Campoleone, effectively halting the attack.

Artillery played a crucial role at Anzio. For every shell the Germans fired, the Allies fired back 20 to 30. Silver Star recipient Cpl. James Bird of the 45th's 160th Field Artillery Battalion, recalled: "At the end of the battle for Anzio, our 105mm howitzers had fired more shells than the rated tube life of each piece."

Trapped in a fortress running from the Moletta River in the west to the Mussolini Canal in the east, the Allies sat within deadly range and observation of German artillery.

The beachhead, restricted to some 16 miles in breadth, became a horribly crowded place. There were no rear areas at Anzio. Recuperating soldiers, doctors, nurses and orderlies were all on the front line. Along with the dogfaces, they suffered casualties from the German guns.

One of the most destructive German weapons was the Leopold Cannon — a 280mm railway gun capable of firing a 550-pound shell more than 30 miles. Known as the "Anzio Express" and "Anzio Annie" by the troops, these railed guns were concealed in tunnels in the Alban Hills surrounding the beachhead. Belching forth destruction on the crowded beachhead, it immediately disappeared back into the tunnels hidden on the hillside.

The German Fourteenth Army was ordered to remove the "abcess" [Anzio] from the Italian coast. On Feb. 3, the first of many German assaults on the defending Allies commenced, resulting in the capture of the British-held Factory-Carroceto area along the Campoleone salient. The U.S. 45th Infantry Division made several unsuccessful counterattacks over the next six days, leaving the Factory in enemy hands.

VI Corps was now poised for a major confrontation. On Feb. 16, the enemy resumed its attack down the Albano road toward the beach with simultaneous assaults along the Allied front.

The 2nd and 3rd battalions, 179th Infantry and the 157th Infantry of the 45th Division on the night of Feb. 17–18, as well as the 701st Tank Destroyer Battalion on the night of Feb. 19–20, blocked the advance at the cost of 404 KIA and 1,982 WIA. On Feb. 29, the Germans made their last serious attempt to destroy the beachhead. On March 2, the 12th Air Support Command pulverized the German lines. At the end of March, Allied artillery and the 3rd Division crushed the Germans' last major offensive. For the next two months the front line of the beachhead, with its series of trenches and static defenses, had the look of a WWI battlefield.

GIs wallowed in filthy mud holes near Anzio, fighting under circumstances approximating the trench warfare of WWI. "It was just plain hell all through the day, and the nights were worse," wrote an infantry replacement. "The hole got about six inches of water, and you couldn't do anything but try to bail it out with your helmet.

"A lot of the boys went to the medics with a bad case of trench foot, but I wasn't that lucky. 'Jerry' threw in a lot of artillery and mortars. The best thing to do was pull in your head and pray. God help you if you got hit in the daytime."

By mid-May, 105,000 Allied troops occupied Anzio, hemmed in by 120,000 Germans. On May 23, *Operation Buffalo* was launched to break out. As one author put it, "VI

Operation Diadem was launched on May 11, 1944, when VI Corps — bulked up with seven divisions — assaulted enemy fortifications along the Gustav Line. U.S. Army

During a bombing run on enemy forces at Cassino in early 1944, a B-24 Liberator is hit by flak. On March 15, Allied bombers saturated the enemy positions with bombs. **Army Air Forces**

“

Each hillside became a
small but difficult military problem
that could be solved only by careful
preparation and almost inevitably by
the spilling of blood.

”

— GEN. MARK CLARK
U.S. Fifth Army

Corps poured out of the beachhead like water from a bursting Lister bag." As usual, the horror of war brought out the best in many men. Sgt. Reg Clark said: "It was awesome, combat men always protecting their comrades-in-arms, more interested in taking care of their buddies than they were of themselves. Is it any wonder that 22 Medals of Honor were awarded at Anzio [up until then] more than at any other battle in history? These were men, real men of character, honor and attitude. And they never complained."

A fitting expression used at Anzio, uttered to the survivors of the Anzio beachhead by Chaplain William Johnson, a 1st Special Service Force veteran of the battle, went like this: "Surely all who have survived the assault on Anzio will go to heaven, since they have already served their time in hell."

Anzio cost the U.S. Army 5,538 killed in action and 14,838 wounded. Moreover, the Navy sacrificed 819 sailors during the Italian landings.

Rapido River Crossing

While the Allies remained bogged down at Anzio, the Rome-Arno Campaign got under way by the U.S. Fifth Army along the peninsula's spine.

The Italian Alps offered a formidable barrier for the Germans along the Gustav Line, which stretched across the penisula from the Tyrrhenian to the Adriatic seas.

Steep mountains and rushing rivers created numerous problems. Virtually every river crossing proved vulnerable to enemy artillery batteries and mortar crews perched on nearby peaks. And every patch of low ground held a potential killing field. Still, peaks had to be scaled or cleared of German defenses; rivers had to be forded, each at considerable cost.

In January 1944, the battle-weary 36th Infantry Division was tasked with securing the Rapido River, located two miles below Cassino, and just east of the Gustav Line.

"Hell, we didn't hardly even get a patrol down the river the nights before the crossing without it getting shot up," said Staff Sgt. Billy Kirby, with the machine gun section of 3rd Bn., 143rd Inf. Regt.

At the same time, the British 10th Corps would attack across the Garigliano River to the south. Once it secured bridges across both rivers, armor units from the U.S. Fifth Army could punch through the line.

"Tonight the 36th Division will attempt to cross the Rapido River opposite Sant' Angelo . . . We might succeed but I do not see how we can," said Maj. Gen. Fred L. Walker, 36th Division commander, on Jan. 20, 1944.

"The mission assigned is poorly timed. The crossing is dominated by heights on both sides of the valley where German artillery observers are ready to bring down heavy artillery concentrations on our men. The river is the principal obstacle of the German main line of resistance. I do not know of a case in military history where an attempt to cross a river that is incorporated in the main line of resistance has succeeded. So I am prepared for defeat."

Gunners on nearby Mount Cassino loomed over the 36th Division's assault point. On the night of Jan. 20, division artillery opened up on enemy positions on the far side of the Rapido. Then elements of the 3,000-man-strong 141st Inf. Regt. attempted to cross the river north of Sant' Angelo, but soon was decimated by enemy guns. Thirty men from one company of the 1st Bn., 141st Regt., were killed when an enemy artillery shell exploded in their ranks. Only 100 GIs made it across — pinned down, they would not survive the night.

That same day, the 143rd Inf. Regt. attacked south of Sant' Angelo, with only one battalion scrambling across. Under direct fire, it retreated back to safety on the other side of the Rapido.

Staff Sgt. Thomas E. McCall, Co. F, 143rd Inf., led a machine gun section and single-handedly took out a series of enemy positions. He was severely wounded in action and taken prisoner. For his actions, McCall would later receive the Medal of Honor.

The 141st attacked again on the night of Jan. 21, but was cut down by enemy machine guns, mortars and artillery fire.

Bloody fighting along the Rapido River kicked off on Jan. 20, 1944, when elements of 36th Infantry Division — including mortar and artillery crews — opened up on enemy positions on Monte Cassino and adjacent vantage points. U.S. Army

Throughout the campaign across Italy, the local people greeted American soldiers with open arms and homes in appreciation of the liberation from the oppression of war. And, conversely, GIs often took the local children under their wings.

Above: The Luigi Riolo family in San Benedetto entertain two soldiers from the Fifth Army, providing a traditional spaghetti dinner. GIs loved to make dining arrangements with Italian homemakers and provide the rations from which the cooks would improvise hot meals. National Archives

Left: Infantrymen from the Fifth Army, occupying Rome during June 1944, found willing porters to tote some of their gear in the march into the city. National Archives

Inset: Pfc. Raymond Cyr of St. Albans, Vt., watches his "adopted" Italian children among the 200 orphans receiving food and gifts at a Red Cross Christmas party in Monticatini on Dec. 24, 1944. Signal Corps

Below: A soldier with the 1st Armored Division feeds a young girl as he takes a break from his tank during September 1944. National Archives

A medic administers Red Cross blood plasma to a wounded GI at an aid station for the 2nd Bn., 7th Infantry Regiment, 3rd Infantry Division, near Cisterna, Italy, on May 23, 1944. Three divisions of VI Corps attacked the city and sustained heavy casualties against a strong German defense.
Signal Corps

> “
>
> *The air was filled with sound as if every German gun in the valley had fired toward us at the same time.*
>
> ”
>
> — LT. HAROLD BOND
> 3rd Infantry Division

Remembering the Jan. 21 crossing, Kirby recalled: “I had never seen so many bodies — our own guys. I remember this one kid being hit by a machine gun; the bullets hiting him pushed his body along like a tin can.”

Tech. Sgt. Charles R. Rummel said, “We thought it was a losing proposition, but there ain’t no way that you could back out.” He would be severely wounded in the battle, losing both legs.

After all of its officers were killed or wounded, the regiment fell apart. Survivors dashed across the river. This ended the 36th Division’s attempts to secure the Rapido River.

In the two-day offensive, the 36th Division suffered a total of 2,128 casualties: 921 taken prisoner or missing in action, 155 killed and 1,052 wounded. Another four months passed before the Allies finally penetrated the Gustav Line in May 1944. Along the way was another bitterly contested fight at Monte Cassino.

Gen. Mark Clark would later write, “. . . to reach the Liri Valley, we first had to drive the Germans off the Camino hill mass . . . that would lead us into the head of the valley where the Liri was joined by the Rapido River. It also would, unhappily, bring us under the guns of the Germans in the high hills around a little town called Casino.”

Battle of Monte Cassino

GIs had a major role in one of the most publicized and controversial battles of WWII — the largest battle, in fact, fought in Italy — Monte Cassino. Famous for its Benedictine monastery, it and Cassino stood right in the path of the Allies who were attempting to break through the Gustav Line to the beleaguered beachhead at Anzio.

Beginning Jan. 24, 1944, the U.S. 34th Infantry Division and the 142nd Regiment of the 36th Division stormed the monastery. Renewed attacks on Cassino in early February also failed to dislodge the Germans. But it was not for lack of bravery. 2nd Lt. Paul F. Riordan, for instance, was killed inside the town after being cut off and forced into a bitter one-man struggle that earned him the Medal of Honor.

For three weeks, men of the 34th Division fought gallantly, taking Monte Castellone and Hill 445, placing them only 400 yards from the monastery. Then the “devil’s helpers” — pneumonia, dysentery and trench foot — struck with a vengeance. Casualties mounted in horrendous proportions: Some rifle companies lost 75 percent of their strength. Overall, the “Red Bulls” counted 2,200 men out of action.

Enemy artillery belched shells with deadly accuracy. “The air was filled with sound as if every German gun in the valley had fired toward us at the same time,” described Harold L. Bond in his memoir, *Return to Cassino.* “We pushed down as far as we could in terror, and the ground all around us shook with gigantic explosions. Huge showers of earth rained down on our canvas. The air was full of flying dirt and shrapnel.”

A final American drive on the town failed Feb. 10. Still, the GIs had driven a wedge into the German lines. Indian and New Zealand troops relieved GIs in their sector over the next two days. Remarked a British officer, "How the hell your chaps did it, I can't imagine."

A plan was hatched, meantime, to destroy the strategic summit overlooking the Liri Valley. "If you let me use the whole of our bomber force against Cassino we will whip it out like a dead tooth," said Maj. Gen. John Cannon, commander of the U.S. Twelfth Air Force. On Feb. 15, 229 bombers from seven U.S. bomber groups dropped 1,150 tons of high explosive and incendiary bombs on the abbey. Between bomb runs, II Corps artillery pounded the mountain for good measure.

Frank Duncan's watercolor entitled "First Aid," drawn from a countryside scene behind a makeshift shelter in 1944, is a tribute to the work of medics throughout the Italy campaign. Army Art Activity

The entire top of Monte Cassino was reduced to a smoking mass of rubble. "When the top of Monte Cassino erupted in tongues of flame and boiling smoke, soldiers stood and they cheered and they laughed and they wept, wept tears of ecstatic joy," wrote Geoffrey Perret in *There's a War to be Won*. "It was the only time men's spirits soared freely in the mountains."

By mid-March, another assault was under way on the mountain. It coincided with an attack on Cassino, in part, conducted by Combat Command B of the 1st Armored Division. In concert, bombers and artillery pieces blasted the town, yet it still remained in German hands March 23 when the offensive was called off.

Clark's Fifth Army was strengthened in April with the addition of the U.S. 85th and 88th Infantry divisions to its II Corps, which crossed the Garigliano River near its mouth when offensive operations resumed. These divisions would fight their way up the coast along Highway 7. Monte Cassino finally fell to the Polish 2nd Corps on May 18, 1944. Five days later, engineers from Anzio made contact with II Corps GIs advancing north.

Rome was liberated on June 6, 1944. German defensive belts across central Italy were then quickly cracked. Cecina fell to the 34th Division at month's end, after some of the heaviest fighting since before Rome. Cities continued to tumble to advancing GIs.

The U.S. 91st Infantry Division, which arrived from North Africa in June, entered the action in mid-July and helped the 34th and 88th divisions along with the 42nd Regimental Combat Team (RCT) capture the port of Leghorn on July 19. These units reached the banks of the Arno River with the remainder of the Fifth Army four days later. Offensive operations were halted to rest and refit for forthcoming assaults on the Gothic Line.

When German troops used the Monastery of Monte Cassino as a forward observation site to direct artillery fire on approaching Allied soldiers in the Liri Valley in early 1944, the abbey was destroyed by Allied bombers on Feb. 16. U.S. Army

Strangling Supply Lines

When launched on March 11, 1944, the Mediterranean Allied Air Forces' *Operation Strangle* had the objective "to reduce the enemy's flow of supplies to a level which will make it impossible to maintain and operate his forces in central Italy."

XII Bomber Command's medium and fighter-bombers employed bridge-busting tactics to cripple railroad tracks in the Italian Alps. "Post-Holing" — swooping down on train tracks and dropping delayed-action bombs in a line — also became a popular form of strangulation. Mountain convoys and coastal ships were secondary targets.

Despite inclement weather and conducting missions solely during daylight hours, the Allied bombers crippled enemy transportation routes in Italy. Though these roads and railways were eventually repaired, the Germans were restricted in moving troops and supplies to the front.

During *Strangle*, March 15 to May 11, 65,000 sorties dropped 33,000 tons of bombs in support of the Allied ground forces driving hard on Rome.

66

Each day seemed like

an eternity.

99

— CAPT. GEORGE EARLE
87th Inf. Regt.
10th Mountain Div.

Soldiers of the 10th Mountain Division move into position for the "big push" — a major offensive to clear the Po River Valley — set to kick off on April 14, 1945.
U.S. Signal Corps

The Rome-Arno Campaign, which officially concluded on Sept. 9, 1944, cost the lives of 6,585 U.S. soldiers on the ground alone. Another 4,408 men of the Air Forces died during bombing and tactical air support missions. Both combat arms combined counted 28,124 wounded in action.

North Apennines to the Po Valley

By relentless pursuit, the Allies advanced more than 270 miles in 64 days from June through August 1944. Livorno (Leghorn) was taken by the 34th and 91st divisions without opposition. But the city was heavily booby-trapped. "We found over 25,000 of these hideous devices and many of our lads were killed or injured as a result," wrote Gen. Mark Clark.

By summer's end, the Allies had the Germans backed into the great massif of the northern Apennines Mountains where they dug in along the Gothic Line. This 150-mile defensive line extended across Italy from Pesaro on the Adriatic coast to the mountains north of Pisa in the west. Concrete emplacements, embedded steel turrets, tank traps, bunkers, wire and mines formed a barrier to the Po River Valley.

To wage the Po Valley and Northern Apennines campaigns, the Fifteenth Army Group deployed the U.S. Fifth Army comprising II Corps (10th, 85th and 88th divisions) and IV Corps (1st Armored, 34th and 92nd divisions). The 91st Infantry Division also was under IV Corps.

In the Mediterranean Theater of Operations (MTO), Army Air Forces had available the Twelfth (XXII TAC) and the Fifteenth (XV Fighter Command). On Aug. 4, Florence fell, ending the campaign for central Italy. A new bulwark, known as the Arno Line, faced the Allies. This is where the U.S. Fifth Army temporarily halted in summer 1944.

Members of the 91st Reconnaissance Squadron motor through the bomb-damaged Verona Railroad Station during fighting in northern Italy in April 1945. U.S. Army

The U.S. VI Corps, with anti-aircraft batteries employed in a ground role forming *Task Force 45*, along with the 1st Armored Division, crossed the Arno River on Sept. 1 and occupied Pisa, Lucca and Pistoia.

On Sept. 10, the North Apennines Campaign was launched. U.S. II Corps attacked on the right with the 85th Division forming a spearhead up the Firenzuola Road. The 91st Infantry Division advanced along Highway 65, and the 34th Division pushed north from Barberino, which was captured the next day. Within a week the line was broken.

The only natural obstacles on the entire Fifth Army's front were the Futa and Il Giogo passes. Located 20 miles north of Florence, they were strengthened by man-made defenses. Some 200 men of Co. B, 363rd Regt., 91st Inf. Div., assaulted Monticelli massiff, one of the peaks protecting Il Giogo Pass in mid-September. Only 70 men reached the summit to launch a bayonet charge. Quickly reduced to one man holding a flank, Pfc. Oscar G. Johnson killed 40 Germans, earning the Medal of Honor (MOH).

Capture of Futa Pass by the 362nd Infantry, and Il Giogo Pass by the 91st and 85th divisions, entailed a dozen or more battalion-size engagements. U.S. casualties totaled 2,731, including 524 KIA. Staff Sgt. George D. Keathley, 338th RCT, earned his MOH on Mt. Altuzzo.

Col. James Fry, commander of the 350th Regimental Combat Team (RCT), described the land over which GIs fought in the Apennines: "The rugged mountain terrain presented a picture so dismal my spirits sank. A forest of pines that averaged about 10 inches in diameter had been cut by our own artillery preparations. Shattered trees dangled at all angles. Water dripped from the shrubbery and the mud made huge holes in my shoes."

The 15th Army Group held the initiative for the next two weeks, with the Fifth Army advancing up the Imola Road. But then heavy rains came.

Sgt. Leonard Dziabis of Co. H, 2nd Bn., 351st Infantry, 88th Div.,

> **"**
>
> *By chance, my squad billeted in Field Marshall Erwin L. Rommel's house. I'll never forget sleeping in Rommel's bed. The down comforters seemed a foot thick and like heaven. I reprimanded one of the guys for plopping on it with his dirty boots on. We utilized the upstairs patio as a boxing ring. In a small bookstand was Adolf Hitler's* Mein Kampf *in German script with a wicker cover and the initials ELR.*
>
> *The stamp of the Nazi Party (NSDAP) was on the inside cover, and Hitler's signed photograph is on page 4. I liberated this book and still have it.*
>
> **"**
>
> — STAFF SGT. HARRY C. MCGUIRK
> 1st Bn., 141st Inf. Regt., 36th Division

Wounded GIs of the 10th Mountain Division receive care at a first aid station on the front north of the Apennines Mountains, near Bologna, during the Po Valley campaign in April 1945. U.S. Army

described the weather during a fight on Mt. Capello: "My God how it did rain. It rained so hard it was solid water. If a body stretched out his arms and waved them he would be swimming. The mud was so thick and juicy, the soldiers were sliding, slipping, and falling into it."

Roads washed out; all the bridges over the Foglia River swept downstream; artillery could only be towed by bulldozers; and the rain prevented adequate air support. Finally, troops psychologically and physically deteriorated because of the appalling conditions.

On Oct. 27, the Fifth Army's nearly month-long advance along Route 65 halted. With their artillery ammo exhausted, the Allies went on the defensive to wait out the winter. By then, the Fifth Army had suffered 15,700 casualties.

German Army Group C strengthened its front line positions by adding five more lines in depth; the last one on the Adige River just south of Venice. The Allied 15th Army Group was reinforced, in turn, by the U.S. 92nd Infantry and 10th Mountain divisions, and a Brazilian unit.

The winter stalemate ended when the Germans attempted to break through the all-black 92nd Infantry's front on Christmas Day 1944. This surprise counteroffensive in the Serchio Valley, which was stopped two days later, was the German's last in Italy.

In mid-February, the famed 10th Mountain Division took several mountain summits. One 800-man battalion attacked Riva Ridge southwest of Bologna. An astonished German officer remarked, "We didn't believe your troops could climb anything quite that awkward."

Soon a lull in the fighting settled along the Venetian Line, the last defensive barrier in northern Italy. On April 1, 1945, the final Allied offensive in Italy, appropriately code-named *Operation Second Wind,* began with a supporting attack by the 92nd along the west coast. Within five days, the 370th Infantry RCT had driven toward Massa and the Japanese-American 442nd RCT was conducting a flanking attack against the 2,800-foot Mt. Fragolita. With the 100th Battalion in the lead, the sacrifice and teamwork inherent in this bold and successful maneuver was exemplified by Pfc. Sadao Munemori.

After taking command of his squad, he led it in several assaults against machine gun positions and personally silenced two with hand grenades.

Munemori died that day, but only after earning the Medal of Honor for throwing himself onto a grenade, saving the lives of his comrades.

When the Fifth Army attacked in the central zone on April 14, all German reserves were committed. A week later the 3rd Bn., 133rd Infantry, mounted on tanks of the 752nd Tank Bn., entered Bologna.

On April 20, Co. E, 2nd Bn., 442nd RCT, led by 2nd Lt. Daniel K. Inouye, assaulted Colle Musatello Ridge near the village of Aulla. Though terribly wounded, Inouye fought on and earned the Distinguished Service Cross. The village fell five days later. (Inouye became a senator in 1962 from his home state of Hawaii.)

The Po Valley Campaign neared its climax. GIs crossed the river April 25, and in the following two days GIs entered Verona and Genoa. The 1st Armored Division dashed to the Swiss border and Brenner Pass, gateway to Austria. There a recon unit of the 349th Inf. Regt., 88th Div., linked up with GIs advancing south from Bavaria. Meanwhile, other 88th units met fanatical resistance north of Padua.

The last battle in Italy took place on Lake Garda in the Italian Alps from April 28-29. Combat centered around the town of Torbole, which was taken by the 3rd Bn., 86th Inf. Regt., 10th Div. During this operation,

❝

The Germans concentrated their shelling at breakfast, lunch and dinner — times when they knew we were in groups.

❞

— GUY J. CASTELLANI
52nd QM DUKW Bn.
3rd Inf. Div.

'Go For Broke!'

"Their records in battle have been marked by one outstanding achievement after another. They have written a brilliant chapter in the history of American fighting men."

—GEN. MARK CLARK

The Hawaii Territorial Guard's 100th Infantry Battalion, composed of Nisei (second-generation Japanese in America) from the islands, deployed to North Africa in September 1943.

From there it would fight at Salerno, Italy and on to Monte Cassino, where it was badly mauled, but earned a reputation for its courage. The 100th continued the assault at Anzio and didn't stop until it reached Rome, along with other Allied forces.

Fresh replacements from the "Go For Broke" 442nd Regimental Combat Team arrived in May 1944, then quickly linked up with the 100th outside the "Eternal City."

In tandem, the two Nisei units — collectively known as just the 442nd — pursued the Nazis through northern Italy and into southern France. By war's end, 680 had been killed in action and nearly 10,000 wounded in action.

With only a total peak strength of 4,500, the Nisei earned more than 18,000 individual awards: one Medal of Honor, 52 Distinguished Service Crosses, one Distinguished Service Medal, 588 Silver Stars, 5,200 Bronze Stars, 22 Legions of Merit, 15 Soldier's Medals, 9,486 Purple Hearts, seven Presidential Unit Citations and four Distinguished Unit Citations.

Japanese-American mortar crewmen with the 100th Battalion, Fifth Army, fire into the hills near Montenegro, Italy, where sniper fire was heavy. In action during August 1944 are (L–R): Wallace Higa of Paia, Maui, Hawaii; James Ishimoto and Tsuo Kobayashi, both from Honolulu. U.S. Army

Opposite: A bouquet to the weary. On the outskirts of Rome in June 1944, an Italian boy gathers flowers for an injured member of the 1st Armored Division, who had taken a temporary seat along the road to Rome. National Archives

the leader of *Task Force Darby*, Col. William O. Darby, was killed by a single German 88mm shell burst on April 30.

On April 29, the day GIs reached Milan, the Germans unconditionally surrendered at Caserta, effective May 2. The efforts of three months of negotiations finally were sealed in only 17 minutes without so much as a comment or handshake from the defeated Germans.

GIs had won a crucial victory, but the final two campaigns in Italy were costly. Conquering the Apennines cost 8,486 Americans their lives and wounded 20,945. Po Valley fighting claimed another 1,914 men along with 6,160 wounded.

The longest sustained campaign — 570 days — in WWII had ended. "Each day had seemed like an eternity," Capt. George Earle, author of the *History of the 87th Mountain Infantry*, wrote after the war. "Almost at a foot-slogger's pace . . . Allied troops under a broiling sun or in numbing cold, had slowly pushed ahead."

In fact, Allied forces in Italy advanced 1,140 miles from Cape Pessaro in southwest Sicily to the Brenner Pass on Italy's Alpine frontier. Although often regarded as a secondary operation, the Italian campaign in terms of the number of men involved, casualties, ground gained and material consumed was nonetheless a monumental undertaking.

"The men who fought there had eventually conquered some of the worst terrain and the toughest defenses anywhere in WWII. That deserves to be remembered when all else about the Italian campaign has been forgotten," wrote Geoffrey Perrett in *There's A War To Be Won*.

All told, the war in Italy — six distinct campaigns — claimed the lives of 36,169 Americans in action and wounded 90,455 GIs. These deaths amounted to more than one-fifth of all U.S. soldiers killed in Europe.

FRANCE

"Operation Overlord" by Jim Dietz. As part of the massive invasion of Normandy, France, on June 6, 1944, the 4th Infantry Division, reinforced by the 359th Infantry of the 90th Infantry Division, assaulted Utah Beach. Led by the "Ivy's" 8th Infantry Regiment, the division encountered light resistance, sustaining 197 casualties. By late afternoon, the GIs were flooding across the beach and onto the causeways leading into the Cotentin Peninsula. By nightfall, 30,000 men were ashore at Utah.

Fight for France

**Normandy: Omaha and
Utah Beaches to St. Lo**

❝

*Men were floating in the water,
but they did not know they were
in the water, for they were dead.*

❞

— ERNIE PYLE
War Correspondent

ANYBODY HERE from Baltimore?"
Seaman 1st Class Jim Clark was greeted with a "Yeah, man!" from several GIs scrambling up the gangplank of the Liberty Ship *Frederick W. Wood*, as they readied to cross the English Channel toward Omaha Beach at dusk on June 5, 1944.

Over 5,000 vessels from little PT-boats to battleships maneuvered almost "bumper to bumper," loaded with troops, tanks, artillery and all manner of weapons of war as they made their way to the coast of France for D-Day. *Operation Overlord* was in full swing.

Minesweepers paved the way and marked the sea lanes with buoys, but Field Marshal Erwin Rommel and the German forces had millions of mines on the beaches and in the channel. "Up on the bridge, I felt an awful jolt as we were within sight of land," Clark recalls. "Men were thrown into the water with their legs blown off. We transferred the survivors to LSTs, and they stormed ashore."

As midnight approached, 120 American "pathfinders" dropped from the air to mark the zones where the paratroopers of the 82nd and 101st Airborne divisions were to land before daylight behind enemy lines. Pvt. Leonard Devorchak, an 82nd pathfinder, became the first American killed in the invasion. Only 38 of the 120 pathfinders actually found their targets, so brisk was the wind and so murderous the enemy flak.

In 1942, a Canadian-British-American raiding force had tested the German defenses by landing at Dieppe, France, with heavy casualties. When Hermann Goering was captured in 1945, he related that his huge victory at Dieppe lulled the Germans into overconfidence that their "Atlantic Wall" was impregnable. American paratroopers quipped that "the Atlantic Wall has no roof."

Gen. Dwight D. Eisenhower, supreme Allied commander, gave the order of the day to paratroopers of the 101st Airborne in England just before they boarded for the wee-hours assault on Normandy in darkness to start the invasion of the European continent on June 6, 1944: "Full victory, nothing else!" U.S. Army

Sgt. Thomas B. Buff of the 101st Airborne Division noted that "during my descent I saw cows placidly standing around in fields below me. This was a welcome sight as presence of those 'milk dispensaries' meant but one thing to me — at least my landing would not be made in a mined area. It wasn't a bad landing at all, save for coming in backward and coming down right smack in the latrine for every cow in France. I must have been an awesome apparition when I finally reached cover, and how I *smelled*. What a stench. I had cow dung all over me."

Some of the glider troops weren't as lucky. The lead glider of the 101st was co-piloted by Brig. Gen. Don Pratt, assistant division commander. His glider landed in a sloping pasture and at a speed of 100 miles an hour it crashed into a hedgerow (a dike-like mound topped by thick underbrush which enclosed most fields in Normandy.) Pratt was killed instantly, the first general officer to perish at Normandy.

About 13,000 U.S. paratroopers in 822 planes landed at

SUPREME HEADQUARTERS
ALLIED EXPEDITIONARY FORCE

Soldiers, Sailors and Airman of the Allied Expeditionary Force!

You are about to embark upon the Great Crusade, toward which we have striven these many months. The eyes of the world are upon you. The hopes and prayers of liberty-loving people everywhere march with you. In company with our brave Allies and brothers-in-arms on other Fronts, you will bring about the destruction of the German war machine, the elimination of Nazi tyranny over the oppressed peoples of Europe, and security for ourselves in a free world.

Your task will not be an easy one. Your enemy is well trained, well equipped and battle-hardened. He will fight savagely.

But this is the year 1944 ! Much has happened since the Nazi triumphs of 1940-41. The United Nations have inflicted upon the Germans great defeats, in open battle, man-to-man. Our air offensive has seriously reduced their strength in the air and their capacity to wage war on the ground. Our Home Fronts have given us an overwhelming superiority in weapons and munitions of war, and placed at our disposal great reserves of trained fighting men. The tide has turned ! The free men of the world are marching together to Victory !

I have full confidence in your courage, devotion to duty and skill in battle. We will accept nothing less than full Victory !

Good Luck ! And let us all beseech the blessing of Almighty God upon this great and noble undertaking.

Dwight Eisenhower

Letter sent by General Eisenhower
to all troops just prior to the Invasion
of Normandy.

Exercise Tiger

On April 28, 1944, eight LSTs — mockingly referred to as "Large Slow Targets" — were off the coast of England for *Exercise Tiger* (337 ships carrying 25,000 troops) when the "General Quarters" horn sounded shortly after 1 a.m. The LSTs fired their 40mm guns into the night, but many thought it was just part of the exercise.

Even when *LST 507* — the "tail end Charlie" in the convoy — was hit by a torpedo fired by an enemy patrol boat lurking somewhere in the darkness, soldiers and sailors on the other LSTs assumed it was simply a simulated attack.

Also, because the convoy maintained radio silence, it was not aware that the men on *LST 507* had abandoned ship and hundreds clung to life rafts and floating debris: 13 died.

German *E-boats* stalked closer and fired two torpedos at *LST 531*, which sank in six minutes, taking 504 lives. The other LSTs picked up the enemy intruders on radar and fired their deck guns to ward them off.

But more torpedoes zeroed in on the convoy, hitting another LST.

Louis Seibel was on one of the LSTs and heard scraping on the keel that night. "We had a real shallow draft and the torpedoes went right under us, scraping but not exploding. Three torpedoes. Three!" Other LSTs weren't as fortunate.

When the carnage ended, *LSTs 507, 531* and *289* sustained 749 dead — 531 soldiers and 218 sailors — one of the most tragic incidents of WWII.

Survivors and medical personnel who treated them were sworn to secrecy, primarily because of the impending D-Day operation. The dead were granted no formal burial services, nor were their families given any details. Thus little was known about *Exercise Tiger* until revealed in 1987.

Normandy in the pre-dawn darkness with the mission of securing bridges and bridgeheads along the Douve and Merderet rivers. The Germans had flooded many of the landing areas, and numerous paratroopers drowned in marshes when they could not cut their weighty parachutes away. Over two-thirds of those who dropped were lost, killed or wounded at the end of D-Day. A number reassembled with their units, thanks to a crackerjack box toy called a "cricket" which operated with a "click-clack" and was answered by two of the same.

Despite being outnumbered 3 to 1 by German troops in the area, the airborne battalions somehow coalesced and made do with what they had. This led the 101st commander, Gen. Maxwell Taylor, to observe that "never in the history of military operations have so few been commanded by so many." They fought doggedly, paving the way for the supporting invasion forces to join up and capture the vital port city of Cherbourg several weeks later.

Perhaps the widely dispersed landings of the paratroopers fooled many German defenders into concluding, in the early hours of D-Day at least, that these were isolated raids rather than the major invasion. German radar and communication lines had been thoroughly disrupted by repeated bombings and the effective work of the French underground.

Also, the Germans had been tricked into believing that the main invasion force would strike across the narrow 18-mile channel between Dover and Calais. Gen. George Patton helped stimulate this deception by tank maneuvers around Dover, where hundreds of fake, inflatable tanks and landing craft made it appear that the invasion would be launched from that area.

German meteorologists convinced higher commanders that the bad weather would make it impossible for an attack on the French coast. Rommel left for a German vacation on June 4, and most of the German commanders left the next day for a "map exercise" in Rennes on June 6. The *Luftwaffe* even withdrew many of its bombers and fighters from Normandy to the interior.

But the beach defenses were awesome: the crack German 352nd Division had been moved up to the front, the concrete pillboxes, mines, flamethrowers, deadly 88s and a huge collection of beach obstacles were poised for action at Omaha Beach and to a lesser extent at Utah. The full fury of the German defenses was unleashed on the U.S. 1st and 29th Infantry divisions when they tried to land on Omaha.

"The water was deep, our equipment was heavy, waves were four feet high, many of our guys drowned, and we were all pinned down on the

beach," recalled Cpl. Vincent Ciccarello of Hurricane, W.Va., as he landed at H-plus-50 on D-Day. "Our big guns were shelling the shore, and the Germans were answering from the bluffs above the beach, and the whole sky lit up like fireworks," Ciccarello remembered. A mortarman with the 16th Regiment of the 1st Division, he was right in the middle of the withering fire which criss-crossed the beach Easy Red.

Army and Navy demolition teams desperately tried to blow holes in the concertina barbed wire and other beach obstacles. Sgt. Barton Davis of the 299th Engineer Combat Battalion was sickened by the explosion of an assault boat filled with "Big Red One" invaders. "A headless torso flew a good 50 feet through the air and landed with a sickening thud," he said. Combat engineer Sgt. Barnett Hoffner observed that "it seemed we had entered hell itself. The whole beach was a burning fury. All around were burning vehicles, piled-up bodies."

Planners hoped that amphibious, swimming tanks would support the infantry, but of 32 tanks launched, only five reached shore. The others sank, providing steel coffins for their crews. Most of the artillery howitzers were sunk offshore. Fierce fighting erupted on the front of the 29th Division, cut to pieces by the crossfire from the bluffs and both ends of the beach. "If you want to live, keep moving," yelled one soldier, and the cry was taken up by those pinned down on the sand.

Towering over Omaha Beach was a Gibraltar-like cliff, Pointe du Hoc,

Rangers at Dieppe

"At Dieppe, the Rangers made America proud of its sons, and America cheered."

— ROBERT BLACK
author of *Rangers in WWII*

Two years before the momentous invasion at Normandy, GIs died on the beaches of France.

Code-named *Jubilee*, the Dieppe raid on the French "Iron Coast" got under way just before dawn on Aug. 19, 1942. It included a contingent of 50 U.S. Rangers from the 1st Ranger Battalion among the 6,086 participants. Thirty-six enlisted men and four officers from the Rangers were attached to Number 3 Commando, four more went to Number 4 Commando, and the remaining six linked up with Canadian units.

Seven miles from shore, the transports carrying Number 3 Commando crossed paths with enemy warships escorting a German tanker. The unarmed and unarmored transports were riddled by the German E-boats. Four Rangers were wounded in this encounter.

American Lt. Joseph Randall, attached to Canada's Royal Hamilton Light Infantry, was killed on White Beach at the water's edge, the first of America's ground troops to die in Europe during WWII.

Lt. Edward Loustalot, along with three other Rangers from Number 3 Commando, made it ashore, but he was killed while racing across a field of poppies.

Ranger Cpl. Frank Koons, attached to the British Commandos, was credited with being the first U.S. infantryman to kill a German in WWII, firing on an enemy gun emplacement.

Randall and Loustalot were the only Rangers to die in the fighting at Dieppe, though Tech. 4 Howard Henry, attached to the Essex Scottish Regiment, was critically wounded and later died in a hospital in England.

Ten Rangers were wounded: four at sea, and six of the 12 who had made it ashore with the Canadians.

Four Rangers were taken prisoner. Sgt. Lloyd Church was withdrawing with other Rangers attached to the Cameron Highlanders when he was shot in the head. Captured, Church never fully recovered from his wounds and died in 1950.

Of the 4,963 Canadians of the 2nd Canadian Division, 68 percent became casualties at Dieppe. Some 913 of these were killed in action.

A Canadian historian wrote: "The casualties sustained in the raid at Dieppe were part of the price for the knowledge that enabled the great operation of 1944 (the D-Day landings of June 6) to be carried out at a cost in blood smaller than even the most optimistic had ventured to hope."

Back home, the press played up the U.S. role in the battle at Dieppe, eager to rally the American public to support a war that had already been raging in Europe for three years.

According to Col. William O. Darby, "The Rangers at Dieppe learned the meaning of discipline in overcoming fear and in making an assault through flying lead. They felt the first hint of hate against the Germans, for they had lost friends and had seen valiant Commando comrades cut down."

A contingent of 50 U.S. Rangers participated in the disastrous raid on Dieppe in August 1942. This early attack on the French coast cost the lives of six Rangers — the first Americans KIA on the ground in the ETO. Signal Corps

which stretched upward as high as a 10-story building. It was thought that the Germans had six powerful, long-range guns atop the cliffs. Two U.S. Army Ranger battalions, equipped with rope ladders and grappling hooks, were assigned to scale the cliffs to silence the guns which they had been told were there — but really weren't. The suicide mission cost more than 100 lives out of an elite force of 225 men.

Over at Utah Beach, the U.S. 4th Infantry Division assault had its dangerous moments, as landing craft exploded, men drowned as they tried to wade ashore in neck-deep water and were cut down by enemy machine guns, and mines took a terrible toll. A lucky mistake saved many lives at Utah: smoke from the naval bombardment and a strong cross-current caused the first wave to land a mile south of the planned spot.

Meeting lighter resistance, the 4th Division moved inland instead of trying to carry out its original plan. Assistant Division Commander Theodore Roosevelt, Jr., although a brigadier general, was down among the infantry, spurring, inspiring and leading by example. His heroism on Utah Beach won him the Medal of Honor. Due to be promoted to two-star rank on July 12, he died that evening of a heart attack.

D-Day had been an elaborately planned operation — strategically and

Above: Under cover of darkness just after midnight of June 5, 1944, the U.S. 101st Airborne drops into Normandy to begin the invasion of France. Artist Jim Dietz, Seattle

Top: Brig. Gen. Anthony C. McAuliffe, artillery commander of the 101st Airborne Division, gives last-minute encouragement to glider pilots before they take off from England on D-plus-1, June 7, 1944 — the famous invasion of Normandy. U.S. Signal Corps

logistically. The British performed miracles in their sector. Yet despite all the careful advance plans, D-Day was a success because GIs on the beaches, thrust into unpredictable and leaderless chaos, took matters into their own hands and displayed the courage, discipline and initiative characteristic of the best qualities of U.S. fighting men.

Battles at the beaches cost the U.S. Navy 1,102 KIA. On Omaha Beach, the 1st and 29th Infantry divisions along with non-divisional units lost 552 KIA, 2,766 WIA and 1,896 MIA. Making their assault by parachute, the 82nd and 101st Airborne divisions suffered 226 KIA and 1,418 WIA. Thousands more were missing.

With a slender toehold as a beachhead, U.S. troops spent a restless night after the initial assault landings on D-Day. They huddled in slit trenches, without blankets. German artillery and snipers pestered them. Although an occasional German plane, nicknamed "bed-check Charlie," dropped a few errant bombs, American air supremacy was one of the keys to holding the beachhead.

Hitler traveled to a concrete bunker in Soissons, northeast of Paris, but would go no farther toward Normandy. So he immediately ordered that the port of Cherbourg on the Cotentin Peninsula be held "to the last man, at all costs." It was another of Hitler's senseless orders which sacrificed thousands of his troops who eventually surrendered a few weeks later. The

Left: American soldiers stand at the ready aboard a Coast Guard LCI(L) — landing craft infantry, large — on an overcast D-Day with Normandy as their destination. Notice the balloon barges following the parade of LCIs, and the GIs' weapons wrapped in plastic to protect against the salty sea on the windswept journey. U.S. Coast Guard

Below: Infantrymen cram onto Navy landing craft for the crossing of the English Channel on D-Day, June 6, 1944. The troops smiled for photographers, but the smiles would soon give way to the consternation of tossing seas, LCIs blowing up, machine gun and mortar fire, and beaches filled with mines. Many men became seasick, hampering their battle effectiveness. Some jumped overboard too soon and drowned where the water ran deep from shell craters. U.S. Navy

When the front ramp of the LST dropped into the surf, troops caught their first glimpse of the scene at Normandy on D-Day — gray skies further darkened at dawn by the smoke of artillery, mine-infested beachheads, and enemy coastal fortifications. National Archives

Many invading troops died in the sea before reaching Omaha Beach — either drowning in deep water or because their boat was blown up. But those whose landing craft sank made it ashore with rubber life rafts. U.S. Army

Roadways appeared magically on a secured beachhead, and long lines of soldiers and materials streamed ashore in northern France at the outset of the Normandy campaign. With the beachheads under control, an unceasing flow of men and supplies became commonplace to reinforce the units already in combat. U.S. Army

Soldiers of the 8th Inf. Regt., 4th Inf. Div., slosh through an enemy-induced swamp on June 6, 1944, bearing full combat gear and keeping their life belts inflated in case of deep water on the trek to the interior of France.
U.S. Army

(The Germans flooded the land on the French coast, mostly to make landings improbable for gliders. It also severely affected paratroopers, some of whom drowned when they became entangled in their chutes.)

overwhelming U.S. sea and air power, bolstered by hundreds of thousand of foot troops, tanks and vehicles helped swing the balance.

War correspondent Ernie Pyle walked along the Normandy coast on D plus-1 and reported that "men were sleeping on the sand, some were sleeping forever. Men were floating in the water, but they did not know the were in the water, for they were dead.

"For a mile out from the beach there were scores of tanks and trucks and boats that you could no longer see, for they were at the bottom of the wate — swamped by overloading, or hit by shells, or sunk by mines. Most o their crews were lost — and yet we could afford it.

"We could afford it, because we were on, we had our toehold, and be hind us there were such enormous replacements for this wreckage on the beach that you could hardly conceive of their sum total. Men and equip ment were flowing from England in such a gigantic stream that it made the waste on the beachhead seem like nothing at all, really nothing at all."

Troops on the Omaha beachhead pressed slowly southward to the out skirts of St. Lo. The 101st Airborne Division muscled its way to Carentan at the base of the Cotentin Peninsula. Then the 9th Division raced west ward to reach the coast of the peninsula by the morning of June 18. This meant that three German infantry divisions were cut off from the rest o the German Seventh Army. By June 20, the relentless push of U.S. force had reached the outskirts of Cherbourg itself.

'Flak Bait' and 'Suicide Jockeys'

". . . Men who flew through curtains of flak and small-arms fire at less than 1,000 feet, both day and night, to land behind enemy lines in some of the riskiest missions of WWII."

— JOHN L. LOWDEN
author of Silent Wings at War

A WWII recruitment poster enticed young men: "Join the Glider Troops! No Flight Pay; No Jump Pay; But — Never a dull moment!" Few stepped forward, though 7,500 were picked to pilot these silent transport planes. They were commonly known as "suicide jockeys." Those aboard were called "towed target" infantry, or "flak bait."

Casualty rates for Allied glider pilots ranged from 17.5 to 60 percent. Hence the title "suicide jockeys."

According to a 101st Airborne Division history, these pilots were "the most uninhibited individualists in the Army. There seemed to be something about

flying a glider, or being selected for that job, that freed a man from the ordinary restraints of Army life."

During WWII, gliders were used by Allied forces on Sicily in July 1943, and played a key role in the D-Day invasion of Fortress Europe.

At 4 a.m. on June 6, 1944, U.S. glider planes carrying troops and equipment from the 82nd and 101st Airborne divisions began landing at Hiesville, along the Normandy coast of France.

Tragically, the lead glider crashed, killing the 101st's assistant commander, Brig. Gen. Donald Pratt, and the co-pilot. Fifty-two Waco gliders, which could carry 15 men each and were made of wood and metal with a canvas skin, touched down in the same vicinity near Normandy.

Two earlier flights of Horsa gliders were already on the ground, allowing British paratroopers to quickly secure bridges over the Orne River and Caen Canal.

A total of 850 British and American gliders spanned the English Channel and landed at Normandy, mostly at night to protect them from enemy ground fire. Fifty-nine "suicide jockeys" were killed 65 wounded and 162 hurt during crash landings on D-Day and D+1.

Gliders were also employed for Operation Dragoon in southern France in August 1944; in Holland a month later: during Operation Repulse at Bastogne in December 1944 and January 1945, and for Operation Varsity — the Rhine River assault — in March. This final airborne operation involved the largest contingent of glider planes ever used during WWII — some 1,300.

More than 20 years after WWII, in 1966, the National World War II Glider Pilot's Association was formed. Their toast says it all: "To the glider pilots — conceived in error, suffering a long and painful period of gestation, and finally, delivered at the wrong place at the wrong time."

Soldiers from the 79th Infantry Division ham it up with a local woman, a typical street scene during the liberation of Cherbourg, France, during June 1944. Cherbourg marked the first giant step for the invasion troops on the march through France.
National Archives

Once again, Hitler stepped in with an order to the German commander at Cherbourg: "Even if worse comes to worst, it is your duty to defend to the last bunker and leave to the enemy not a harbor but a field of ruins." Cherbourg was ringed by streams which made excellent anti-tank barriers, and the enemy was holed up in concrete bunkers and a maze of underground tunnels. Three U.S. battleships, four cruisers and destroyers bombarded the city. On the afternoon of June 25, the Germans blew up piers and jetties with 35 tons of dynamite.

Finally, on the afternoon of June 26, the German army and naval commanders surrendered, but it took three weeks before the harbor could be de-mined to land cargo.

Although the lightning strikes against the Cotentin and Brittany peninsulas produced quick results by the end of June, both the British fighting toward Caen and the Americans slogging toward St. Lo found the advances were agonizingly slow during June and nearly all of July. The reason for the slow going can be summarized in one word: hedgerows.

Operation Neptune

"It wasn't too bad for us sailors, but I think one of the main reasons why Normandy was such a great success was that the soldiers would rather have fought thousands of Germans than go back into those boats and be seasick again."

— R. McKinlay
Anvil of Victory

Operation Neptune — the naval phase of the invasion of France — was initially designed to get the troops to the coast of Normandy. Secondly, though, the operation helped secure the supply line, which was vital to funneling additional troops and equipment from England until airfields and supply points could be established in France.

On June 5, 1944, the invasion fleet headed out into the English Channel. The Western Task Force, manned mostly by Americans and commanded by U.S. Rear Adm. Alan G. Kirk, was assigned to hit Omaha and Utah beaches at Normandy.

The *USS Arkansas*, oldest battleship in the U.S. Navy's fleet, was one of several warships charged with pounding enemy gun emplacements. Others included the *Nevada*, resurrected from the mud at Pearl Harbor, and the *Texas*.

"Those of our troops who were not wax-grey with seasickness, fighting it off, trying to hold on to themselves before they had to grab the steel side of the boat, were watching the *Texas* with looks of surprise and happiness. Under the steel helmets they looked like pikemen of the Middle Ages to whose aid in battle had suddenly come some strange and unbelievable monster," wrote Ernest Hemingway, for *Collier's* magazine on July 22, 1944.

On board the destroyer *Corry*, deck hands sprayed streams of water on the guns to cool them down and keep the rapid fire barrels from collapsing. Seven Allied battleships, two monitors and 23 cruisers lobbed shells at German gun batteries just prior to the troops landing.

Combined Allied losses at Normandy amounted to 24 warships and 59 damaged. Another 35 merchant and auxiliary vessels were lost; 61 damaged. Coming under the heaviest fire, Allied landing craft absorbed the largest toll — more than 700 sunk or damaged. Some 60 U.S. Coast Guard cutters, through D-Day+10, rescued more than 220 men; by the end of June 1944, 350 had been saved.

Early on June 6, 1944, troops swarmed, ant-like, onto landing ships in England to mount the largest amphibious operation in world history. They crossed the English Channel in a fleet of more than 5,300 various ships and craft, including some 1,200 warships, and landed on five beaches (Omaha, Utah, Sword, Gold and Juneau). The Army stormed the beaches, but couldn't have arrived without the Navy's outstanding support, both in transporting troops and in laying down accurate naval gunfire on enemy gun placements. National Archives

The 83-foot cutters of the U.S. Coast Guard, originally built as "sub killers" and dispatched into the Atlantic to track German U-boats, tested their mettle as rescue vessels in aiding the waves of landing troops during the invasion of Normandy during June 1944. The CGCs saved many lives in a grim setting of enemy gunfire raining down on the invasion armada.

The battleship *USS Augusta* patrols off the Normandy coast on June 12, 1944, surrounded by landing craft that it will help protect as troops continue to mount the offensive to push into France and across Europe. The American sector of beaches totaled 10,000 yards in length. Landing craft met fierce resistance as Field Marshall Rommel tried unsuccessfully to roll up the beach-head. The U.S. Navy played a vital role at Normandy.
National Archives

U.S. Coast Guard cutters cruised up and down the coastal beaches on rescue missions during the Normandy invasion of June 1944. Several landing craft sank from German shelling and mines before troops disembarked. The CGC-1, one of the 83-footers on patrol, picked up 47 soldiers and sailors from a sinking LCI just minutes after H-Hour on D-Day, after dawn on June 6, 1944. U.S. Coast Guard

Father William Dempsey from New York City conducts a mass for troops of the 56th Signal Battalion in the middle of an apple orchard near St. Laurent, France, on the first Sunday after D-Day, June 1944. U.S. Army

U.S. paratroopers of the 101st Airborne Division, among the first on French soil, led an assault on St. Marouf. They produced this "souvenir" Nazi flag as a symbol of their triumph. U.S. Army

Virtually every farming field was surrounded by solid mounds of earth several feet high, topped by thick underbrush and even small trees. Tenacious German defenders behind a hedgerow had excellent protection, good observation of attacking forces, and superb fields of fire into the open field across which attackers had to advance. Furthermore, communication between adjoining units was not easy. The unseen enemy exacted demoralizingly high casualties on advancing GIs.

Higher commanders stormed and raved from division down to regiment, and from regiment to battalion, company, platoon and squad with the cry: "What's holding you up? Why aren't you at your objective? Either get there by 1800 or get relieved of command." During June and July, there were many officers who were cashiered for failing to reach seemingly impossible objectives.

There were a few rewards amid all the carnage. Sgt. William Richard Ogden reported: "Normandy was all apple orchards and hard cider that was delicious and powerful. The *Calvados* came out 120 proof. It worked well in a Zippo lighter. A completely sober GI was hard to find in this area. We also captured a distillery. In the warehouse was enough five-star Hennessey cognac to give four bottles to every man in the 29th Division."

Pvt. Jesse Butler of the battle-hardened 9th Division had spent the night in a corner where two hedgerows intersected. He was awakened when a Tiger tank and several German soldiers started firing just across from his hedgerow. Butler reported that "a bazooka team hopped over another hedgerow about 30 yards from the tank and began to fire on it.

"The first two shells bounced off the armor, but the third shell tore away

the ammunition trailer hauled by the tank. Then the tank commander saw the bazooka team, turned the turret around, and fired one 88mm shell into the hedgerow where the team was.

"The bazooka leader was hit; his left arm, shoulder and head just disappeared. The gunner was very badly wounded and out of action. . . . Soon the riflemen of the company had killed all the German infantrymen, leaving the Tiger without support. So the tank moved out, leaving the dead German soldiers behind."

Carpet bombing of Caen and St. Lo finally produced results. Caen fell to the British on July 9.

Capturing St. Lo was a prolonged affair that cost the U.S. 2nd, 29th, 30th, 35th and 3rd Armored divisions 11,000 casualties. The 35th Division seized Hill 122 overlooking the town while the 29th battered it from the northeast near the end.

Three days after taking command of the 3rd Bn., 116th Inf. Regt., 29th Division, Maj. Thomas D. Howie was killed by a German shell. But he had the honor of leading his battalion into St. Lo on July 18, as his body was borne into the city by jeep, then was draped in an American flag and placed among the ruins of the Cathedral of Notre Dame.

The Normandy Campaign was complete by July 24, 1944. It would prove to be the fourth most costly for the U.S. Army in Europe: 16,293 killed in action and 41,051 wounded since June 6.

Above: A GI maneuvers his bazooka to the top of a hedgerow to fire on an enemy position as another soldier uses the barrier as shelter. Hedgerows presented a constant problem for troops advancing across France during the summer of 1944.
National Archives

Top: Constant bombardment from Army artillery and Air Forces bomb runs reduced the village of St. Lo to rubble. This enabled the Allies to capture it on July 18, 1944, providing high ground for a suitable start of the breakthrough that would follow. St. Lo was one of the war's most bitterly contested battles.
National Archives

Barrage balloons shelter a harbor at Nisida, Italy, filled with LSTs loading equipment for *Operation Dragoon* — the U.S. Seventh Army's invasion of southern France. Three divisions of VI Corps formed the assault force between Toulon and Cannes on Aug. 15, 1944. Winston Churchill observed the action, which originally was called Anvil, but changed because the Germans learned of the code name and its significance. U.S. Navy

Operation Dragoon: Clearing the Rhone Valley

On Aug. 15, 1944, after numerous postponements, the U.S. Seventh Army, commanded by Lt. Gen. Alexander Patch, made an amphibious landing and air drop on the French Riviera's Cote d'Azur between Hyeres and Cannes. "A new Allied army," read an Aug. 16 *New York Times* editorial, "stormed ashore on the beaches of southern France to establish the fourth major front in Europe."

Operation Dragoon involved 300,000 men. The 10,000-man 1st Airborne Task Force led the assault; it consisted of the 517th Parachute Regt., 460th Parachute Field Artillery Bn., 550th Glider, 509th and 551st Parachute Infantry battalions, the 463rd Parachute Field Artillery Bn., the 596th Airborne Engineer Co., and the British 2nd Independent Parachute Brigade. Under *Operation Rugby*, paratroopers air-assaulted into the Argens River Valley near Le Muy. Their mission was to seize and hold a key intersection 13 miles from the coast until assistance arrived from the beachhead.

Despite high casualties, Lt. Col. William Yarborough, commander of the 509th, still believed the invasion was "the most successful Allied airborne assault of WWII."

The inland airborne operation was coupled with a seaborne raid staged by the elite U.S.-Canadian First Special Service Force, code-named the *Sitka Force*, on Aug. 14. Landing on the tiny offshore islands of Port-Cros and Levant, members subsequently destroyed the coastal battery farthest east. This high-risk mission facilitated the safe passage of the main force as it approached the coast from the West.

The predawn assault by the paratroopers made way for Adm. H. Kent Hewitt's Western Task Force, consisting of 880 ships and 1,370 smaller vessels. The U.S. battleships *Arkansas*, *Nevada* and *Texas*, nine escort carriers, 24 cruisers, 111 destroyers and 100 minesweepers joined this massive armada.

As the paratroopers made their way inland to seize the five vital cross-roads from Fayence to Le Muy, 959 planes, including 12 groups of B-17 and B-24 bombers and 163 B-25s from the 12th and 15th Air Forces and the XII Tactical Air Command — with 2,400 planes flying from Corsica and another 1,700 from airfields in Italy — began saturation-bombing the beaches. B-26 Marauders also played a key role in the attack.

This phase of the campaign, code-named *Operation Yokum*, ended at 7:30 a.m. to allow the troops to come ashore. A flotilla of LCT (R) Rocket craft also moved in to secure specific coastal fortifications.

A half hour later, the first wave of Landing Craft Infantry (LCI) — under the direction of the flagship *USS Catoctin* — loaded with 86,000 men, 12,000 vehicles and 46,000 tons of supplies, churned toward the three assault beaches: Alpha in the west, Delta in the center and Camel in the east near St. Raphael. A German bomber hit the *Catoctin*, killing six and wounding 40. "It sounded like buckets of marbles thrown against the ship's sides," said Eugene Carlson, a radioman aboard the ship.

The three U.S. divisions (3rd, 36th and 45th) of Maj. Gen. Lucian K. Truscott's U.S. VI Corps — supported by seven French divisions — stormed ashore "like a man-made hurricane," as William Breuer described it in his book *Operation Dragoon*.

Seaman Douglas Bailey participated in the amphibious landing along France's southern coast and recalled, "I once asked an old salt what to do when and if the ship got hit and we were sinking? He said, just go to the bottom with it then simply walk ashore!"

The first wave of 7th Regimental Combat Team (RCT) of the 3rd Division met only scattered resistance on Alpha Beach. The second wave was not so fortunate; it was quickly pinned down. One patrol made it ashore and headed toward the town of Cavalaire-sur-Mer.

Operation Dragoon, code name for the invasion of southern France more than two months after D-Day, fills the sky with thousands of paratroopers of the 1st Airborne Task Force who dropped ahead of the amphibious landing in mid-August 1944.

66

. . . They called it the 'Champagne Campaign,' this war in the Maritime Alps, because of the way the champagne flowed in the celebrations of the liberated people at Antibes and Cannes and Nice. . . . But when they went back into the mountains, to their foxholes on the terraced hillsides under the shelter of the olive trees, they returned to a full-fledged war.

99

— *Yank* staff correspondent

An LCVP loaded with American troops approaches the ramparts of Fort St. Jean overlooking the French Riviera. The GIs stormed ashore, as part of *Operation Dragoon,* on Aug. 15, 1944. U.S. Army

Struck by flak, this B-24 Liberator of the 15th Air Force flies with its right wing badly damaged, but was still able to release its bombs over Toulon, France, Aug. 6, 1944. The famous port was a prime target because of the German submarine pens harbored there. Mediterranean Allied Air Forces

The platoon leader, Lt. John Creigh, was killed by a mine. Then Sgt. James Connor Jr., wounded four times, ignored his wounds and led his men to capture the key town of Cavalaire — a vital link to controlling the unloading of troops and supplies on Alpha Beach.

At St. Maxime, "Thunderbirds" of the 45th Infantry Division — the fulcrum of the Allied 45-mile invasion line — used heavy wire cutters and Bangalore torpedoes to cut paths through mined, barbed-wire fences, metal stakes — referred to as Rommel's Asparagus — and partially mined railways along Delta Beach. Within minutes, the 157th Regiment reached a 10-foot high fortified wall. Under heavy fire, teams led by Pvt. Walter Ahrens secured demolitions and blew a 12-foot gap in the wall. Men, tanks and vehicles poured through and secured the beach by 7 a.m.

The situation on the far right at Camel Beach was decidedly different. The 36th "Texas" Division headed for the rocky coves and sheer cliffs. As the landing craft emerged, murderously accurate German gunners found their marks. Braving machine gun fire, however, the Texans charged one machine gun nest and then overran the beach and swarmed up onto the Cannes-St. Raphael road.

By shortly after 9 a.m., they took the Green zone of Camel Beach, leaving only the assault on Camel Red where the Germans made their strongest stand. After heavy bombing runs and numerous naval gunfire missions, the division's 142nd Infantry Regiment took the remainder of the beach.

By D-Day's end, as German resistance crumbled, the Riviera landings were complete. In the greatest one-day effort of the Mediterranean war, 60,150 Allied combat troops and 6,737 vehicles had been put ashore. U.S. losses that first day: 198 KIA and 399 WIA. Numerous Germans were killed and wounded and 2,091 captured.

The Allies along the Riviera met opposition from three *Wehrmacht* divisions: the 244th protected the Marseilles sector, the 242nd covered the coastline from Toulon to Agay, and the 148th secured the stretch from Agay to the Italian border. The 11th Panzer and the 198th Infantry divisions were west of the Rhone River and could not reinforce quickly. The landing of the French divisions on Aug. 16 and their ensuing two-week attacks on Toulon and Marseilles, coupled with the rapid advance of U.S. forces north, forced the Germans to withdraw.

Three days later *Task Force Butler,* commanded by Brig. Gen. Fred Butler, was formed to pursue and destroy the Germans before they could escape through the Rhone Valley. The main U.S. forces continued to press

west and then north along Highway 7 to drive the Germans into the waiting blocks at the gorges in the mountain passes east of the highway.

The 11th Panzers had finally bridged the Rhone and linked up with the 198th and 338th Infantry divisions that crossed earlier. The U.S. 3rd Division raced 30 miles in the first 24 hours of its movement toward the Rhone. But by noon of Aug. 20, the 30th Infantry Regiment had run smack into heavy German artillery.

The XII Tactical Air Command, based on Corsica, provided air support for the 7th Army and followed its advance up the Rhone River Valley.

The battle for Montelimar took eight days of fighting that left thousands of casualties on both sides. *TF Butler* reached Grenoble some 30 miles northeast of Montelimar, and Gen. Truscott ordered the unit to "move at first light with all possible speed to Montelimar and block all routes of withdrawal up the Rhone Valley." As the 36th and 45th divisions converged on the village of Montelimar, French resistance fighters harassed the Germans ahead of the Americans and kept the roads intact. The Americans, however, were running out of gasoline.

Meanwhile, the Battle of Montelimar was well under way. As U.S. units attempted to close the trap and block the Germans in a narrow defile along Highway 7, GIs hit fierce resistance from German Panther tanks. Early on the afternoon of Aug. 23, the 36th Infantry's 141st Regiment attempted to take the village, but was thrown back. For three days, the Allies had difficulty blocking the German escape route north through the town of La

Paratroopers of the 509th Parachute Infantry Battalion advance shortly after landing in southern France as part of *Operation Dragoon,* which kicked off on Aug. 15, 1944 with a combined amphibious landing and parachute drop. U.S. Army

"

We climbed down rope ladders into Higgins boats under fire from German planes. Once ashore at St. Tropez on the Riviera, me and a buddy sat by a tree to rest. A bullet from a German sniper hit right between us and splattered bark into our faces. We captured the sniper; he was about 16 or 17 years old; I was 19, an old veteran already.

"

— BERNARD A. ZYLKA
Seventh Army Car Co.

Coucorde. Starting on the 26th, the Americans made one last, two-day attempt to trap the Germans before they could escape north.

The final battle took place along the Drome River, the northern boundary of the quadrilateral making up the battlefield. The 143rd, 157th and *TF Butler* had cleared the valley west from Crest, and on the 28th the 141st gained control of the high ground overlooking Montelimar.

The battle ended with the German Nineteenth Army paying a high price. The Allies took thousands of prisoners, and destroyed some 4,000 pieces of equipment and weapons.

"Over tens of kilometers there was nothing but an inextricable tangle of twisted steel frames and charred corpses — the apocalyptic cemetery of all the equipment of the Nineteenth Army, through which only bulldozers would be able to make a way," said French commander Marshal Jean de Lattre de Tassigny.

Yet, the bulk of the German Nineteenth Army made a 350-mile fighting retreat through the Belfort Gap into Germany. Nevertheless, the Rhone Valley campaign served as a shining example of boldness and initiative. In 14 days of incessant drive, GIs captured 32,211 prisoners and advanced about 175 miles. The French component of the Seventh Army captured Toulon and Marseilles on Aug. 28.

From Aug. 29 to Sept. 14, the Allies moved toward the Vosges Mountains. The Seventh Army moved north, with the U.S. VI Corps leading, and the French I and II Corps followed respectively on the right and left flanks. Seventh Army units made contact with the U.S. Third Army west of Dijon on Sept. 11. Three days later the campaign officialy ended.

Southern France did not come cheap: 7,301 Americans were killed in action — 4,524 of them in the air — and 5,361 wounded during the month-long "Champagne Campaign."

Still, according to U.S. Chief of Staff Gen. George C. Marshall Jr., "[*Operation Dragoon* was] one of the most successful things we did."

After the war, General of the Army Dwight D. Eisenhower declared: "There was no development of that period which added more decisively to our advantage or aided us more in accomplishing the final and complete defeat of German forces than did this attack coming up the Rhone Valley."

Cobra Breakout: Hot Pursuit in Northern France

Operation Cobra launched the major breakout from the Normandy area with tragic results. A massive air strike scheduled for July 24 was called off because of bad visibility, but some planes left before they received word. Their bombs fell short on GIs of the 30th Division, killing 25 men.

Next day, thousands of heavy, medium and fighter-bombers dropped 500-pound bombs, napalm and lighter explosives, killing another 64 soldiers from the 30th Division and wounding 374, when the wind and smoke obscured their targets. One soldier said he saw the B-24s come overhead, and cried "Oh, no, that poor pilot just dropped an engine," but then dived into a trench when he realized a bomb was falling.

Cobra was the beginning of the massive breakthrough which enabled Gen. Patton and the rest of the Allied forces to make their victorious sweep across France to the Seine River and the gates of Paris.

At the end of July, the breakout from the Normandy beachhead enabled U.S. forces to rush west into Brittany toward the four ports of St. Malo, Brest, Lorient and St. Nazaire. Hitler ordered these fortresses to be held "to the last man, to the last cartridge."

Now commanding the U.S. Third Army's VIII, XII, XV and XX Corps, Patton looked on the Brittany campaign as an opportunity to wind up quickly and rush eastward toward Paris.

The German commander in Brittany, Col. Andreas von Aulock, had his headquarters in a casemated fort dug into a rocky promontory. U.S. intelligence estimated between 3,000 and 6,000 Germans in St. Malo, when in fact about 12,000 defended the city, and they vowed to "fight to the last stone."

It would take two weeks of street fighting to raze the town. Frank A. Reichmann of the 1st Bn., 331st Regt., 83rd Inf. Div., recalled: "A platoon of (captured) Germans started to sing farewell to their commander and, in defeat, tried to raise their spirits. Most of them were in tears."

The dispirited enemy flocked to St. Malo's safe haven, rather than surrender in open country. The U.S. 4th Armored Division had captured 1,000 prisoners as it dashed across Brittany, leading to an overly optimistic comment by Americans about scattered German forces: "They've got us surrounded again, the poor bastards."

On Aug. 6, von Aulock demolished all the quays, locks, breakwaters and harbor machinery in St. Malo and set fire to most of the city. From underground pillboxes and camouflaged strongpoints, the Germans held GIs at bay.

After days of house-to-house fighting and advancing under cover of the pall of smoke caused by raging fire, the 83rd Infantry Division finally entered the walled town of St. Malo. But 10 artillery battalions and fighter-bombers still could not persuade von Aulock to surrender. Direct hits by 8-inch guns finally destroyed many of the artillery pieces and machine gun emplacements and forced the enemy capitulation.

St. Malo and the Brittany ports seemed important at first, but they lost strategic significance because they were too far west to supply the fast-moving armored forces streaking eastward across France.

Lorient and St. Nazaire would be cordoned off for the remainder of the war, but Brest was besieged for six weeks.

Whereas the infantry won the battle of the Normandy hedgerows, armor, artillery and tremendous U.S. air power delivered crushing blows to the enemy during the month of August. The Canadians started an attack from Caen southeastward toward Falaise. Patton darted eastward with his armor some 75 miles to the French auto-racing city of Le Mans.

A series of disasters struck the German command. On July 17, Field Marshal Rommel had suffered a serious fractured skull when a 20mm shell

This American infantry mortar unit pummeled the enemy's fortification at the vital port of St. Malo, leading to its liberation in August 1944.
U.S. Army

66

Operation Cobra, *the breakout from Normandy launched July 25, 1944, was 'the most decisive battle of our war in western Europe.'*

99

— GEN. OMAR N. BRADLEY
Commander, U.S. First Army
and later 12th Army Group

An American 57mm anti-tank gun crew shells a German bunker along France's Brittany port of St. Malo. The battle for the walled city lasted several days during August 1944, and Americans moved in under cover of smoke. St. Malo and other Brittany ports to the west lost strategic significance as the front lines moved rapidly eastward across the ETO.

National Archives

from a British plane crashed into his car. Three days later, a bomb exploded at one of Hitler's staff meetings, killing several generals and shattering the *Fuhrer's* ear drums.

Still, Hitler insisted on directing the war on the Western Front. He ordered a suicidal counterattack from Mortain toward Avranches, on the slim hope of splitting Patton's forces.

During the Battle of Mortain, from Aug. 6–12, Hill 317 was held by 600 soldiers of the 2nd Battalion, 120th Infantry, 30th Division. The "Lost Battalion" withstood repeated attacks, suffering 300 casualties before being relieved on Aug. 12.

Hitler's plan to split Patton's forces actually had the opposite effect: U.S. forces encircled and trapped the flower of the German *panzer* armies. The plan was simple: Patton turned north from Le Mans toward Alencon and Argentan to meet the Canadians and spring the jaws of a giant trap.

Swarms of fighter-bombers pummeled the German armor, now out in the open. A veritable turkey shoot ensued in the cloudless August skies. Meanwhile, Patton's forces raced northward, their flanks protected not by infantry but by the 9th Tactical Air Force. Hitler insisted that the Mortain counterattack must continue, but he finally relented and allowed the Germans to fight their way out of the gap between Falaise and Argentan.

American and Canadian forces tried desperately to seal the escape route, but German forces fought just as hard to keep it open.

GIs on the scene asked over and over again: Why didn't we close the trap between Argentan and Falaise, which was approximately 20 miles apart? And why did we let so many Germans — 19 divisions — slip through our fingers as they retreated eastward?

Scores of excuses and explanations have been offered, ranging from guarding against the Canadians and Americans shooting at each other, to the suggestion that time bombs dropped by Allied airplanes might go off if Americans or Canadians tried to join up.

Gen. Omar Bradley said he preferred "a solid shoulder at Argentan to a broken neck at Falaise." Patton was more blunt: "The Germans can't stop us, only these !!! phase lines."

The Falaise Gap was finally closed on Aug. 19, trapping units of the Nazi Fifth Panzer and Seventh armies, for a total of 50,000 POWs. Thousands of Germans were killed. Of the carnage around Chambois and Trun, a U.S. officer reported that it was "beyond the wildest dreams of man . . . the stench is insufferable."

GIs with XV Corps hustle past a bombed-out cathedral during the capture of Mantes, a city on the Seine just 25 miles northwest of Paris. Between Aug. 9–15, 1944, XV Corps moved through LeMans, Alencon, Argentan and Mantes — rendering German forces in north-central France hopeless in their defense.
U.S. Army

66

The Germans can't stop us, only these !!!! phase lines.

99

— GEN. GEORGE PATTON
U.S. Third Army

American infantrymen of the 28th Division step tall around the Arch of Triumph as Eisenhower parades them through Paris on Aug. 29, 1944. Dressed for battle, not display, they had assembled just before noon and strode down the Champs Elysees.
Real Photo, Paris

Opposite: An M-8 light armored car of the 4th Infantry Division rumbles down the Champs Elysees past the Arch of Triumph. This was the same route taken just four years earlier by the Nazi army when it occupied Paris. One of the American tankers said of the liberation, "We couldn't stick around long. The Jerries were on the run and we wanted to keep them that way. The Tricolor flying from the Arch looked pretty good as we went through." Office of War Information, England

Rommel's successor, Field Marshall Hans Gunther von Kluge, was removed by Hitler in mid-August and committed suicide by taking a capsule of potassium cyanide. Southern France was under attack and once again, the Germans discovered that the greatest practitioner of the art of *blitzkrieg* — which they had perfected four years earlier — was a U.S. general nicknamed "Blood and Guts."

On Aug. 19, a five-day cease-fire, requested by the Germans to evacuate their troops from Paris, was granted.

Some 5,000 Germans were in the city, while 20,000 occupied the outskirts. French Resistance forces quickly trumpeted their role in the "liberation of Paris."

That same night, during a torrential rain, a spearhead of the 79th Infantry Division (with a blue "Cross of Lorraine" patch) reached the Seine River at Mantes-Gassicourt, 30 miles northwest of Paris and secured a bridgehead. Amazingly, no German defenders were nearby. Even more surprisingly, the infantry found a dam which allowed the troops to cross single file. In the darkness and rain, each man held onto the belt of the man in front. One soldier lost his helmet, but everybody crossed the 800-foot-wide river safely.

The next morning, additional units of the 79th crossed in boats, and the 151st Engineer Combat Battalion quickly finished a treadway bridge over the river. As the Germans continued their pell-mell retreat, the engineers completed more bridges and U.S. and French forces eagerly looked forward to entering Paris — the "City of Light."

Hitler vowed that if Paris had to be given up, it should be reduced to ruins. Therefore, the U.S. planned to bypass the city and not get involved in house-to-house street fighting. The freeing of Paris, to the French people, was the greatest symbol of the liberation of France. So the French 2nd Armored Division under Gen. Jacques Leclerc was granted the honor of entering the city first, along with the U.S. 4th Division, which marched into Paris from the east.

On the morning of Aug. 25, 1944, the 38th Cavalry Reconnaissance Squadron and the U.S. 12th Infantry Regiment advanced to Notre Dame Cathedral and the eastern part of the city, while the French 2nd Armored occupied the western half. Sporadic gunfire sounded around the city, even after Gen. Charles deGaulle arrived to lead a parade on Aug. 26. Within a few days, combat-ready GIs made their public appearance in the French capital.

Eisenhower paraded the 28th Division through Paris dressed for battle. Members strode around the Arc de Triomphe and down the Champs Elysees. That afternoon the division made a holding attack against German positions east of the city.

Paris may have been jubilant over its liberation, but much of France still remained in the clutches of Nazism.

Brest to Nancy

Well to the rear of Paris, there remained a bit of unfinished business to be taken care of. To the far west, Brest was a thorn in the American side. The 15,500 Germans from the 2nd Paratroop Division — and 20,000 *Organisation Todt* workers (civilian combat engineers) — there held out against the Third Army's VIII Corps.

The main assault on Brest took place on Aug. 25, with the British battleship H.M.S. *Warspite* and medium bombers and 150 Flying Fortresses pounding the coastal defenses. The 2nd, 8th and 29th divisions — *Task Force A* — pressed forward, taking out 75 enemy strongpoints in six weeks of intense fighting. A final push, beginning on Sept. 15, lasted for three days before the garrison at Brest finally caved in; more than 30,000 Germans surrendered.

The U.S. 2nd Division incurred 2,314 casualties; the 29th Division counted 329 killed and 2,317 wounded; and the 8th Division had approximately 1,500 casualties as the price of taking the coastal enclave.

All along 200 miles of front in northern France, GIs in hot pursuit of Germans retreating eastward shouted "End of the war in forty-four!" A U.S. First Army operations officer later wrote: "There was a quality of madness about the whole debacle of Germany's forces in the West. Isolated garrisons fought as viciously as before, but the central planning and coordination was missing. It looked very much as though Adolph Hitler might be forced to surrender long before the American and British units reached the Rhine. That was the avowed opinion of Allied soldiers on the Western Front, and German prisoners were of the same mind."

The Allied headlong thrust had two prongs — Belgium/Aachen Gap and Lorraine/Metz Gap. Patton's Third Army's 450-mile dash from Avranches to Metz in northeast France was the longest ever made by the U.S. Army. Along the way, armed reconnaissance units "isolated the battlefield." That meant, in practice, killing everything German that moved on the roads. Lorraine Province, an ancient battleground, soon took the center stage of combat.

GIs poured across the Seine and Marne rivers. By Aug. 25, 1944, the Third Army had taken Chateau-Thierry; then Soissons. The 5th Armored Division swung toward Compiegne, while other U.S. units breached the Maginot Line. But American armor had gotten ahead of its lifeline: Eisenhower ordered a halt until fuel was brought to the front.

In his journal, Patton wrote: "If I could only steal some gas, I could win this war." Later, pleading with Gen. Omar Bradley, head of the Twelfth Army Group, Patton said: Damn it, Brad, just give me 400,000 gallons of gasoline (one day's supply) and I'll put you inside Germany in two days." The Third Army remained at Verdun along the Meuse River awaiting further orders.

Six days before Patton ran out of gas, the famed "Red Ball Express" began rolling round-the-clock out of St. Lo to Chartres. Most of the truck drivers hauling the fuel were black — they earned an enviable reputation for their performance. But they also paid a price: accidents put one-third of the trucks off the road.

Resuming offensive action, XII Corps was stopped at the Moselle River by stiff German resistance. Elements of the 3rd and 9th Armored divisions, however, crossed the river on Sept. 7. Five days later, bridgeheads were established near Nancy, which fell on the 15th: the 35th Division entered the city unopposed after the Germans had been driven out.

The campaign for northern France was officially over. It had cost the lives of 17,844 Americans and wounded another 47,469.

Battle of Metz

Fighting in France entered a new phase with the encirclement of Metz — part of the Rhineland Campaign — a city near the German border and one made for defending. The fortress city of Metz boasted the forbidding fortifications of Fort Driant.

The fort had concrete walls seven feet thick, connected by underground tunnels with a central fortress. Huge quantities of barbed wire added to the problems facing attackers. The German garrison of 10,000 had ample supplies of food and water. Other forts in the Metz area were similarly equipped. In the early days of November, the 5th, 90th and 95th Infantry and 10th Armored divisions of XX Corps were slowed by the heavy rains which plagued the entire theater.

Hitler took a very personal interest in the defense of Metz, reiterating his order that it must be held "to the last man." The new garrison commander, Heinrich Kittel, pledged to carry out that order.

Many individual feats of heroism surfaced as U.S. forces slowly closed the jaws of the trap around Metz between Nov. 18–22. Pfc. Elmer A. Eggert of L Co., 379th Inf. Regt., 95th Div., advanced alone against a machine gun, killing five of the enemy and capturing four, and earned a Distinguished Service Cross. After his tank received a direct hit, Cpl. C.J. Smith of the 778th Tank Bn. dismounted the .30-caliber machine gun and fought on alone until help arrived; he was also awarded a DSC.

Despite Hitler's own order to defend to the death, he allowed an SS regiment — which he planned to use in the Ardennes offensive — to slip out of Metz in the last stages of the U.S. offensive. Gen. Kittel surrendered Metz on Nov. 21, 1944, although several of the forts, including Driant, held out well into December before giving up.

The 5th Division's November losses were 172 KIA, 1,005 WIA and 143 MIA. The 95th Division estimated 281 KIA, 1,503 WIA and 405 MIA. Records of casualties of other units involved in the Metz operation are incomplete.

Hugh M. Cole, official Army historian of the Metz operation, concluded

Above: An MP directs traffic on the renowned roadway linkage that handled a transport system known as the Red Ball Express — the high-speed delivery day and night of food, ammunition and gasoline essentials to the armored spearheads at the front. The Red Ball route traversed France from St. Lo to Chartres, open only to supply convoys, beginning Aug. 25, 1944. U.S. Army

Top: Infantrymen of XV Corps stride past a battered sign at the entrance to the ancient French town Argentan on Aug. 20, 1944. This came after they drove the defiant Germans out of this very strategic village in a drawn-out fight that lasted eight days. Armored units had infiltrated on Aug. 12. U.S. Army

American infantrymen of the Third Army advance cautiously as they enter Metz, France, on Nov. 19, 1944.
U.S. Army

> "
>
> *It was a weird battle. One time you were surrounded, the next you weren't. Often we took refuge in villages where the Germans were upstairs in the same house.*
>
> "
>
> — Sgt. Pat Reilly
> 313th Inf. Regt.
> 79th Div.

that the capture of Metz was "skillfully planned and marked by thorough execution," and "may long remain an outstanding example of a prepared battle for the reduction of a fortified position."

Beginning in October 1944, four divisions of the U.S. Seventh Army waged a campaign in the Vosges Mountains of eastern France, the scene of bitter fighting for the next four months.

France would undergo one more invasion by the German army before the French people's agony ended. Alsace Province, long a bone of contention between the two countries, adsorbed the full weight of the final Nazi thrust in the West in January 1945.

Operation Northwind in Alsace

All along the frozen, snowbound front in northeastern France during the last days of December 1944, troops of Lt. Gen. Alexander Patch's U.S. Seventh Army braced for an attack. Air reconnaissance, patrols and intelligence reports indicated the Seventh as a target.

The Germans needed a diversion to relieve pressure on their divisions in the Ardennes where the U.S. First Army had regained its balance in the Battle of the Bulge (covered in the next chapter). Patton's Third Army had relinquished ground to the adjacent Seventh as the Third dispatched divisions to the Bulge, leaving Patch's units stretched perilously thin. One veteran recalled manning 1,000 yards of front with only a squad.

The geography of the front also rendered the Seventh vulnerable. The line formed a V-shaped salient, dubbed the Lauterbourg Bulge. The salient's northern edge stretched more than 84 miles, west to east, from a point near Saarbrucken to Lauterbourg. The front then ran south, hugging the west bank of the Rhine River for another 42 miles to a point below Strasbourg, France.

Eventually, 15 U.S. divisions fought along that front — 3rd, 28th, 36th, 42nd, 44th, 45th, 63rd, 70th, 75th, 79th, 100th and 103rd Infantry, 101st Airborne and 12th and 14th Armored. Some 250,000 GIs participated in the defense of the French province of Alsace. Bitter battles would be waged at Wingen, Philippsbourg, Herrlisheim and Rittershoffen.

To Hitler, the Lauterbourg Bulge appeared like a ripe fruit waiting to be plucked and he directed his generals to take it out.

Operation Northwind began in the northwest sector of the salient just after midnight, New Year's Day, 1945, when elements of the German XIII SS and LXXXIX Corps attacked southward.

"They were drunk and marched toward us in columns of two with their rifles slung over their shoulders," recalls Dick Atkinson, a 100th Division veteran. Silhouetted against the deep snow, the enemy troops were easy targets. Atkinson opened up with his machine gun as the enemy formed skirmish lines and attacked over open fields. "I probably killed 150 to 200," he claims.

The two corps of the German First Army attacked south from Sarreguemines and Bitche over the Sarre River valley, at the base of the Lauterbourg salient. Their objective was to reach the Saverne Gap, split the U.S. XV and VI Corps and bottle up the VI, commanded by Maj. Gen. Albert Brooks, on the Alsatian plain with its back to the Rhine.

But the Germans hadn't counted on the determination of the infantrymen from the 100th and 44th divisions and two regiments of the 63rd Division organized into *Task Force Harris*, one of several hastily assembled commands that shifted back and forth to meet new onslaughts. The German XIII Corps attack faltered.

The LXXXIX Corps assault from the Bitche area, employing the German 559th, 257th, 361st and 256th *Volksgrenadier* divisions, and later the 6th SS Mountain Division, proved more successful. They surprised the Americans by attacking through the rough, frozen landscape of the Low Vosges and swept aside an ad hoc command of the 94th and 117th Cavalry squadrons dubbed *Task Force Hudelson*, and the 62nd Armored Infantry Battalion. The fight continued intermittently for three weeks.

The 100th Division hastily blocked the western flank of the LXXXIX Corps attack. To contain the eastern flank of the attack, the Americans threw in *TF Harris*, *Task Force Herren* (regiments from 70th Division), elements from the 79th, 45th and 36th divisions and the 36th Combat Engineer Regiment, to prevent the enemy from controlling vital mountain exits that would have put the Germans behind VI Corps. Patch also deployed the entire 103rd Division eastward.

The snow banked knee-deep and the conditions were so bitterly cold that Howard P. Schreiver, a sergeant with the 45th Division, never dug a foxhole — the ground was frozen solid — and his canteen popped. Pat Reilly, a sergeant with the 313th Regt., 79th Division, recalls infantrymen urinating into their M-1s to unfreeze the firing mechanisms.

By Jan. 5, the initial attacks of *Operation Northwind* waned. But these assaults were only the first of a series of concentric attacks launched in Alsace — most against the Seventh Army. Troops of the French First Army, under Gen. Jean de Latre de Tassigney, also participated farther south, but to a limited degree. Lt. Gen. Jacob Devers commanded both armies as head of Sixth Army Group.

Hitler had more up his sleeve — *Operation Sonnenwende* (Winter Solstice). On Jan. 5, Heinrich Himmler, head of the *Waffen SS* and commanding Army Group *Oberrhein*, launched an attack across the Rhine at

> **"**
>
> *A midnight Mass in the Roman Catholic Church was packed with U.S. soldiers. It was a tense time. We could still lose the war. The soldiers in the church were all armed to the teeth and ready for anything. The enemy was just over the hill. A week later these same soldiers engaged in action which in a very short time changed entirely the course of the war. The Germans had counted on surprise [intelligence forewarned Seventh Army of an attack] and on the belief that our soldiers would be celebrating New Year's Eve and not be in the best of condition. At midnight our artillery went into action. By 3 a.m. firing stopped and Germans surrendered in large numbers. We turned what could have been another Bastogne into the final decisive battle of the war for the U.S.*
>
> **"**
>
> — Staff Sgt. Nelson "V.N." Dungan 12th Armored Division on Christmas Eve 1944 in Niederbronn

Gambsheim, 10 miles north of Strasbourg, into VI Corps' right flank. Two days later, the German Nineteenth Army crossed the Rhine south of Strasbourg at Rhinau. *Task Force Linden,* another ad hoc unit comprising green troops from the 42nd "Rainbow" Division, tried but failed to contain the two bridgeheads. Elements of 14th Armored Division, a few battalions from the 79th Division, and the green 12th Armored Division deployed against the bridgeheads.

South of Strasbourg, Gen. de Latre threw in elements of his French 5th Armored and 1st Infantry divisions against the German bridgehead at Rhinau. *Operation Sonnewende* made few gains, but highlighted the importance of Strasbourg to the Allied and French cause.

Even before the New Year's attacks, Eisenhower ordered Devers to straighten the Seventh's front line and withdraw to more defensible positions in the foothills of the Low Vosges Mountains. The entire Western Front, from the North Sea to Switzerland, adopted a defensive posture as the lines were stripped of troops to help defend the Ardennes.

Devers was reluctant to give up ground won with his troops' blood. He also knew withdrawal meant giving up Strasbourg. Gen. Charles de Gaulle, leader of the Free French, also opposed Eisenhower's plan to abandon the city and threatened to remove French forces from the Allied command and use them to defend the city. Strasbourg symbolized French rule in an area often claimed or annexed by Germany. De Gaulle also feared horrible retribution by the Gestapo against the citizens of Strasbourg.

Eisenhower relented and agreed to protect Strasbourg, and Devers agreed to prepare for a series of staged withdrawals, if necessary.

A fifth attack against the Americans came Jan. 5 by the German XXXIX Panzer Corps made up of the 21st Panzer and 25th Panzer Grenadier divisions striking south toward the towns of Hatten and Rittershoffen. Holding them off were the "orphan regiments" of *Task Force Linden.*

"Two battalions of the 242nd Infantry, 42nd Division, held off those Panzers for three days," noted Ken Carpenter. "When relieved by the 315th Infantry, the 242nd had lost 60 percent of its strength."

Pat Reilly recalls the 313th Infantry Regiment falling back through the Haguenau Forest to the town of Haguenau. Fighting raged in small pockets and villages as the Americans withdrew. "It was a weird battle," Reilly recalls. "One time you were surrounded, the next you weren't. Often we took refuge in villages where the Germans were upstairs in the same house. We heard them and could see them and vice versa. If they didn't make a move we left and if we didn't make a move they left."

The melee reached westward as fighting between the 45th Division and 6th SS Mountain Division picked up around Baerenthal and Mouterhouse and continued until Jan. 21.

On Jan. 16, the German army in Alsace struck. The 10th SS and 7th Parachute divisions, the core of XXXIX Corps' reserve, spearheaded a drive south from Lauterbourg, down the west bank of the Rhine, to link with German forces in the Gambsheim bridgehead.

Winter camouflaged tanks and troops cross the French countryside near Haguenau in January 1945. Heavy snowfall in late January hampered combat operations, allowing the enemy to regroup and muster one final attack before being driven across the Moder River on Jan. 26.

U.S. Army

"The 232nd Infantry was responsible for 33 miles of front along the Rhine and had to man many of the little towns with platoons or squads," added Carpenter. "They held off the 7th Parachute and 10th Panzer divisions for 12 days." Carpenter served with the "Rainbow Division."

To counter the pressing Germans, Brooks pulled his lines back southwest to the Moder River. The move greatly reduced the frontage of VI Corps' units and left the Germans confused and swinging at air.

Reilly recalls a tremendous, nighttime artillery barrage when the enemy pulled abreast of U.S. lines and seemed ready to attack. The next morning, however, there was only an eery silence.

A final lunge over the Moder River line took place the night of Jan. 24-25. Six German divisions struck in three prongs. "The Germans had shot their last bolt in France," as Charles Whiting put in his book *Operation Northwind*. The Seventh Army, no matter how tired and extended, remained intact and operational. In early February, 125,000 GIs — at the cost of 6,400 casualties — played a part in reducing the Colmar Pocket. The last German fortress on the western bank of the Rhine to fall was at Neuf-Brisach ("Waffle City").

Northwind cost both sides dearly, although the figures vary. Seventh

A crew from a 4.2-inch chemical mortar battalion prepares a barrage of white phosphorous shells during *Operation Northwind.* Twelve such battalions saw action in Europe during WWII, firing 2 million rounds of phosphorous in support of the infantry. U.S. Army

"

Memories . . . A child sitting on a

pile of rubble, crying and saying,

'This used to be my house.'

Some things we never forget.

"

— STAFF SGT. BERNARD A. MCALPINE
Recon Section,
165th Engineer Combat

Opposite: During the fierce fights of *Operation Northwind* in Alsace Province in January 1945, GIs often found themselves in small combat actions. Here Lt. Edwyn Cookes demonstrates how he "played possum" behind enemy lines for 18 hours. Unfortunately, his comrades in the background are not pretending. National Archives

Army after action reports listed 11,609 battle casualties for the period of the offensive plus 2,836 cases of trench foot and 380 cases of frostbite. But VI Corps' losses for the same period numbered 14,716 with 773 killed, 4,838 wounded, 3,657 missing and 5,448 non-battle casualties.

German forces sustained 23,000 men killed, wounded or missing. The U.S. processed some 5,985 German POWs.

Northwind engagements speak well for American arms and the GI. Reilly, a student of *Northwind* history, attributed much of the victory to overwhelming U.S. artillery. But many GIs, such as Howard Schreiver, were fresh off the troopships and met the test of battle with small arms. Often outnumbered, they fought the venerable German army to a standstill.

The *Wehrmacht*, four months before its total collapse in May 1945, was not what it once was. Nor was its leadership. Attacks to split VI Corps from the Seventh Army were uncoordinated. The Americans were often surprised by the enemy's inability to control the battlefield.

U.S. leadership, on the other hand, usually was excellent. Devers gave much of the credit for victory — or survival — to Brooks, whom he said, "fought one of the greatest defensive battles of all times with very little."

Devers, too, must receive credit. As overall commander, he held off full-scale German attacks with little or no reinforcement. Today, he is all but forgotten, lost in the shadow of the more popular Patton and Bradley and the controversial Montgomery.

Yet it was Sixth Army Group, the orphan of the Allied armies, that first reached the Rhine in November 1944. The Sixth was prepared to immediately cross the river, against virtually no opposition, and strike into the industrial heart of Germany. But Eisenhower overruled Devers. He ordered him instead to wheel northward in support of the Third Army, which bogged down in an abortive offensive.

Historians can only speculate about the outcome of the war in Europe had Devers been allowed to attack across the Rhine in early December 1944. The possibilities are endless. For one, *Operation Northwind* might have remained on Hitler's drawing board.

★ ★ ★

-1945

Date	Place	Event
June 6	France	**Normandy Invasion.** D-Day: Allies land. *(Operation Overlord).* 2,500 Americans fall at Omaha Beach; 2,499 lost in airborne assault.
June 6–July 24	France	**Normandy Campaign.** U.S.: 16,293 KIA; 41,051 WIA.
June 13–29	France	**Battle of Cherbourg.** U.S. VII Corps captures; 22,000 U.S. casualties.
June 22	Ukraine	53 U.S. B-17s are totally destroyed at Poltava by German bombers.
July 3	France	U.S. VIII Corps opens "Battle of the Hedgerows" on Cotentin Peninsula.
July 7–19	France	**Battle of St.-Lo.** U.S. XIX Corps captures, ending Battle of the Hedgerows. U.S. casualties: 11,000.
July 25	France	**Operation Cobra.** U.S. Third Army breaks out at St.-Lo.
July 25–Sept. 14	France	**Northern France Campaign.** U.S.: 17,844 KIA; 47,469 WIA.
July 31	France	Americans liberate Avranches.
Aug. 4–17	France	**Battle of St.-Malo.** U.S. 83rd ID razes town in two-week street battle.
Aug. 7–12	France	**Battle of Mortain.** U.S. 30th ID withstands German attacks for five days; 2nd Bn., 120th Inf. on Hill 317.
Aug. 13–19	France	**Falaise-Argentan Gap.** U.S. First Army closes, suffering 19,000 casualties.
Aug.15–Sept. 14	France, S.	**Southern France Campaign.** *Operation Dragoon* in Rhone Valley. U.S.: 7,301 KIA; 5,361 WIA.
Aug. 19	France	U.S. Third Army reaches Seine River.
Aug. 22	Italy	Allies liberate Florence.
Aug. 23–28	France	**Battle of Montelimar.** U.S. Seventh Army battles Germans for five days.
Aug. 25	France	**Liberation of Paris.** 38th Recon. Sqd., 4th ID, first to enter.
Aug. 25–Sept. 18	France	**Siege of Brest.** Final assaults by 2nd, 8th and 29th divisions. 30,000 Germans captured. U.S. casualties: 9,831.
Sept. 1–3	Belgium	**Battle of Mons Pocket.** 1st ID and 3rd AD clear pocket and capture 25,000 Germans from 20 divisions.
Sept. 2	Belgium	U.S. First Army elements cross into Belgium; liberate Liege week later.
Sept. 9	Netherlands	U.S. 30th ID enters near Maastricht and liberates city.
Sept. 10	Luxembourg	U.S. 5th AD liberates Luxembourg City.
Sept. 10–April 4, 1945	Italy	**North Apennines Campaign.** U.S.: 8,486 KIA; 20,945 WIA.
Sept. 11	France	Allied Normandy and southern France invasion forces meet near Dijon.
Sept. 11	Germany	Troop B, 85th Cav Recon Sqdn., 5th AD crosses border near Stalzenburg.
Sept. 13–21	Italy	**Battles of Il Giogo and Futa Passes.** Three U.S. divisions capture: 524 KIA; 2,207 WIA.
Sept. 15–March 21, 1945	Germany	**Rhineland Campaign.** U.S.: 50,410 KIA and 165,965 WIA.
Sept. 17–Nov. 28	Netherlands	**Operation Market-Garden.** U.S. 82nd and 101st Airborne divs. drop on Holland: 909 KIA and 3,899 WIA.
Sept. 18	Poland	8th AF flies mission over Warsaw.
Oct. 2	Germany	U.S. First Army penetrates West Wall.
Oct. 4–21	Germany	**Battle of Aachen.** U.S. First Army captures after bitter struggle. U.S. casualties: 8,000.
Oct. 27–Nov. 5	Netherlands	U.S. V Corps and 7th Armored Div. counter Germans in Holland.
Nov. 2–Dec. 15	Germany	**Battle of Huertgen Forest.** Involves 120,000 U.S. troops who sustain 24,000 battle casualties plus 5,000 losses to disease.
Nov. 16	Germany	**Operation Queen.** Largest air attack (2,807 planes) in support of ground forces ever. U.S. First and Ninth Armies open offensive to clear Roer plain.
Nov. 18	Norway	Raid by 44th Bomb Group over Oslo.
Nov. 19–23	France	**Battle of Metz.** U.S. Third Army captures old capital of Lorraine.
Dec. 3	Germany	379th Regt., 95th Div., crosses Saar River, and captures first bunkers on the Siegfried Line.
Dec. 16–Jan. 25, 1945	Luxembourg/Belgium	**Battle of Bulge/Ardennes Campaign.** Largest battle in American history: 600,000 GIs involved.
Dec. 16–Jan. 25, 1945		**Ardennes-Alsace Campaign.** U.S.: 19,246 KIA; 60,050 WIA.
Dec. 17	Belgium	**Malmedy Massacre.** 86 U.S. POWs are machine-gunned by Nazis.
Dec. 24	Belgium	Largest number of aircraft — 2,046 bombers — flown in a single mission during Battle of the Bulge.
Dec. 24	Germany	2,034 8th Air Force heavy bombers hit various centers, losing 31 bombers and 12 fighters.
Dec. 25	English Channel	*Leopoldville* troopship is torpedoed while carrying 66th ID: 762 killed.
Dec. 26	Belgium	**Bastogne.** U.S. Third Army armored relief column reaches besieged town.

1945

Date	Place	Event
Jan. 1–31	France	**Operation Northwind.** Final German offensive in the West, fought in Alsace.
Jan. 23	Belgium	U.S. 7th Armored Div. takes St.-Vith.
Jan. 30	Germany	Three U.S. divisions attack West Wall.
Feb. 9	France	**Colmar Pocket.** U.S. 21st Corps liquidates. Allied casualties: 18,000.
Feb. 13	Germany	U.S. First Army crosses Rhine.
Feb. 14	Germany	U.S. 8th Air Force B-17s (311) drop 771 tons of bombs on Dresden.
Feb. 23–March 10	Germany	**Operation Grenade.** U.S. Ninth Army attacks across the Roer River and captures 300,000 Germans and kills 6,000 while suffering 7,300 casualties.
March 1	Germany	**Operation Lumberjack.** Combined First, Third Army offensive to clear the west bank of the Rhine between Cologne and Koblenz.
March 1–6	Germany	Americans take Muenchen-Gladbach, Krefeld, Treves and Cologne.
March 7	Germany	**Remagen Crossing.** Co. A, 27th Armored Inf. Bn., CCB, 9th AD, crosses Rhine on Ludendorff Bridge.
March 9	Germany	U.S. First and Third Armies meet up to encircle some 10 German divisions.
March 10–13	Germany	U.S. Third and Seventh Armies maneuver to encircle Palatinate, trapping German armies.
March 13–24	Germany	**Saar-Palatinate Campaign.** U.S. Third and Seventh Armies rupture West Wall; take 90,000 German POWs while sustaining 17,220 casualties.
March 15–20	Germany	**Operation Undertone.** U.S. Seventh Army breaks through West Wall.
March 17–21	Germany	Americans take Koblenz, Worms, Saarbruecken and Ludwigshafen.
March 22	Germany	Troops of U.S. Third Army cross Rhine at Oppenheim.
March 22–May 11	Germany	**Central Europe Campaign.** U.S.: 15,009 KIA and 42,568 WIA.
March 23–26	Germany	**Operation Plunder.** Northern crossing of the Rhine by the British includes U.S. 30th and 79th divisions.
March 24	Germany	**Operation Varsity.** U.S. 17th and British 6th Airborne Divisions parachute near Wesel in largest Allied airborne operation (21,680 men) of WWII. U.S.: 159 KIA; 522 WIA. IX TCC: 41 KIA.

A GI's Combat Chronology: Europe, 1941

Date	Battleground	Action
1940		
April 21	Norway	**First U.S. KIA of WWII.** Capt. Robert M. Losey, Air Corps Weather Service, is killed in a German air raid near Oslo.
1941		
Jan. 29	Canada	U.S. Army troops arrive St. John's, Newfoundland.
April 10	Off Iceland	**First U.S. Shot in Anger.** *USS Niblack* drops three depth-charges, initiating undeclared naval war against Germany.
July 7	Iceland	First U.S. troops in European Theater: 1st Marine Brigade (Provisional).
Sept. 4	Off Iceland	First clash between U.S. and Germany: *USS Greer* is attacked by a U-boat.
Oct. 17	North Atlantic	**First U.S. combat casualties in WWII.** *USS Kearny* torpedoed; loses 11 sailors KIA and 24 WIA.
Oct. 31	Iceland	*USS Reuben James* is torpedoed by a German U-boat: 115 sailors are KIA.
1942		
Jan. 26	N. Ireland	First U.S. troops — members of the 34th ID — arrive in Ulster.
May 12	England	First major contingent of U.S. 8th Air Force arrives in East Anglia.
June 12	Romania	**First U.S. Air Combat Mission.** Twelve B-24s of the Halpro Detachment, based in Egypt, raid Ploesti oil fields.
June 15	Malta	Halpro Detachment hits an Italian fleet near the island.
July 4	Netherlands	Six planes of the 15th Bombardment Squadron launch U.S. air offensive over Europe. One is shot down.
Aug. 14	Iceland	First U.S. aerial victory in the ETO. Pilots of the 27th and 33rd Pursuit Squadrons down a German plane.
Aug. 17	France	U.S. 8th Air Force makes first independent raid on a European target — Rouen-Sotteville.
Aug. 19	France	**First U.S. KIA on European Soil.** Three U.S. Rangers are KIA in the British/Canadian raid on Dieppe.
Nov. 8–11	North Africa	**Operation Torch.** Allies land in Algeria and Morocco. Vichy French cease resistance three days later. U.S. Army: 479 KIA; 696 WIA; Navy: 493 KIA.
Nov. 17– May 13, 1943	Tunisia	**Tunisia Campaign.** U.S.: 2,838 KIA and 8,279 WIA. Air campaign began Nov. 12.
1943		
Jan. 27	Germany	U.S. bombs Wilhelmshaven in first all-American attack on Germany.
Feb. 3	Off Greenland	*SS Dorchester* sinks after being torpedoed; 605 soldiers and crewmen of the 904 aboard die, including 4 chaplains.
Feb. 9	Off Iceland	Troopship *Henry R. Mallory* torpedoed and sunk: 300 U.S. servicemen die.
Feb. 19–28	Tunisia	**Battle of Kasserine Pass.** Axis force attacks. U.S. casualties: 6,500.
March 16–20	North Atlantic	Convoy battle is climax of Battle of the Atlantic.
April 7	Tunisia	U.S. II Corps links up with British Eighth Army in Tunisia.
May 6–13	Tunisia	Tunis and Bizerte fall; remaining Axis forces surrender.
May 22	Atlantic	**Battle of the Atlantic.** U-boat withdrawal signals Allied victory. U.S. Atlantic Fleet loses total of 16 ships.
June 13	Germany	U.S. 8th Air Force loses 26 bombers over Kiel and Bremen.
July	Germany	**Operation Pointblank.** Combined Bomber Offensive against German industry begins.
July 9– Aug. 17	Sicily	**Sicily Campaign.** U.S. Army: 2,572 KIA; 5,746 WIA. Navy: 546 KIA. Air campaign began May 14.
Aug. 1	Romania	**Ploesti** *(Operation Tidal Wave).* U.S. B-24s (177) bomb, losing 54 planes downed and 55 seriously damaged.
Aug. 17	Germany	U.S. B-17s (376) raid Schweinfurt and Regensburg; 60 are shot down and 47 totally damaged on Mission 84.
Sept. 3	Italy	Allies land on mainland; Italian army surrenders.
Sept. 6	Germany	45 U.S. bombers lost over Stuttgart.
Sept. 9–19	Italy	**Battle of Salerno.** *Operation Avalanche.* U.S. Fifth Army: 1,084 KIA; 3,525 WIA.
Sept. 9– Jan. 21, 1944	Italy	**Naples-Foggia Campaign.** U.S.: 6,266 KIA; 14,642 WIA. Air campaign began Aug. 18.
Sept. 10	Off Italy	*USS Rowan* torpedoed: 202 KIA.
Oct. 1	Italy	Allies enter Naples.
Oct. 10	Germany	236 B-17s bomb Munster: 39 lost.
Oct. 12	Italy	U.S. Fifth Army attacks across the Volturno River.
Oct. 14	Germany	**Schweinfurt.** Of 229 B-17s, 60 are lost.
Nov. 26	Mediterranean Sea	**SS Rohna.** 1,015 U.S. troops are killed aboard this British troopship when it is hit by a German guided missile.
Dec. 1	Italy	Allies begin assaults on Winter Line.
1944		
Jan. 20–21	Italy	**Rapido River.** U.S. 36th Div. is bloodily checked in its attempt to cross. U.S.: 518 KIA; 663 WIA; and 500 POW.
Jan. 22– May 24	Italy	**Battle of Anzio.** U.S. Fifth Army wages. U.S.: 5,538 KIA; 14,838 WIA.
Jan. 22– Sept. 9	Italy	**Rome-Arno Campaign.** U.S.: 11,393 KIA; 28,124 WIA.
Feb. 20–25	Germany	**Operation Argument.** "Big Week": 3,800 U.S. bombers drop 10,000 tons of bombs, losing 226 planes plus 28 fighters. Casualties: 2,600.
March 4	Germany	U.S. conducts first day-time air raid on Berlin.
March 6	Germany	**Berlin Raid.** Most costly U.S. raid: 69 bombers and 11 fighters.
March 10	Off Iceland	*USS Leopold* torpedoed: 171 KIA.
April 5– mid-Aug.	Romania	U.S. Fifteenth Air Force bombers raid Ploesti, losing 223 planes total.
April 22	Germany	Raid on Hamm. 631 U.S. 8th A.F. bombers lose 15 heavy bombers and 13 escorting fighters.
April 27	English Channel	**Exercise Tiger.** German E-boats attack LSTs during night landing at Slapton Sands, killing 749 soldiers and sailors.
May 11–13	Italy	Gustav Line Offensive opens.
May 18	Italy	**Monte Cassino.** Falls after bitter four-month struggle. Allies suffer 20,000 KIA; 100,000 WIA. U.S. 34th ID plays a pivotal role.
June 4	Italy	U.S. Fifth Army enters Rome.

Date	Location	Event
March 25	Germany	All organized resistance west of the Rhine ceases.
March 29	Germany	U.S. takes Frankfurt and Mannheim.
April 1–18	Germany	**Battle of the Ruhr Pocket.** 18 divisions fight two-week battle, taking 317,000 POWs in largest surrender of war. U.S. Ninth Army — 341 KIA; 2,000 WIA.
April 5– May 8	Italy	**Po Valley Campaign.** Allies begin major attack on Genghis Khan Line. U.S.: 1,914 KIA; 6,160 WIA.
April 10–11	Germany	U.S. forces take Hanover and Essen; Seventh Army enters Bavaria.
April 11–30	Germany	**Harz Mountains.** GIs root out 70,000 dug-in Germans in bitter fighting.
April 14–24	Germany	Battle for Dessau.
April 16–19	Germany	Battles of Halle and Magdeburg.
April 18	Czechoslovakia	A patrol of 358th Inf. Regt., 90th ID, crosses border.
April 18–19	Germany	U.S. 2nd and 69th IDs take Leipzig.
April 15–20	Germany	**Battle of Nuremberg.** U.S. XV Corps defeats 15,000 German diehards.
April 21	Italy	Allies take Bologna.
April 21	Germany	**Last Bomber Downed Over Germany.** Ten men of the *Black Cat* are killed.
April 22–24	Germany	12th AD crosses the Danube River.
April 24	North Atlantic	*USS F.C. Davis* torpedoed: 119 KIA.
April 25	Germany	**U.S.-Soviet Linkup.** Co. G, 273rd Inf., 69th ID, patrol and Soviet forces meet near Torgau on Elbe River.
April 25	Czechoslovakia Austria	**Last U.S. Bombers Downed Over Europe.** Pilsen (7 KIA) and Linz.
April 27	Italy	U.S. Fifth Army occupies Genoa.
April 29–30	Germany	**Battle of Munich.** U.S. 45th Div. engages in house-to-house fighting.
April 29	Italy	**War in Italy Ends.** Germans surrender. Total U.S.: 36,169 KIA; 90,455 WIA.
	Austria	U.S. divisions capture Fussen and cross into Austria.
May 1–4	Austria	**Battle of Fern Pass.** 3rd Bn., 5th Inf., 71st ID clears Pass. U.S. 44th Div. takes Landeck.
May 4	Austria	U.S. Fifth and Seventh Armies link up at Brenner Pass. U.S. ground casualties in Austria: 118 KIA; 507 WIA.
May 5	Czechoslovakia	Firefight at Zhurt. Co. I, 3rd Bn., 357th Inf. Regt., 90th ID sustains 7 KIA.
May 6	Czechoslovakia	U.S. 16th AD captures Pilsen.
May 7	Czechoslovakia	**Last Shots in ETO.** Pfc. Dominic Mozzetta, a member of Co. B, 1st Bn., 387th Inf. Regt., 97th Div., fires the last round at a German sniper near Klenovice.
May 7–8	France	**V-E Day.** German forces surrender unconditionally at Reims.
May 7	Czechoslovakia	**Last Ground Combat in Europe.** Recon. platoon of the 803rd Tank Destroyer Bn., 5th ID is ambushed near Volary. Pfc. Charles Havlat of 2nd Plt. becomes last U.S. KIA in ETO at 8:20 a.m., after Reims surrender. U.S.: 1 KIA; 3 WIA.
May 8	Germany	9th Air Force loses one F-6 vs. 9 German planes shot down.
May 8	Czechoslovakia	9th A.F.'s 12th TRS downs last German aircraft of WWII four hours before war's end over Danube River.
May 8	Czechoslovakia	**Last Hostile U.S. Deaths in ETO:** German ordnance kills 8 GIs of 101st Inf. Regt., 26th ID, in Pernek.
May 10	France	German garrisons in Lorient and St. Nazaire on Brittany coast surrender to U.S. 66th Division.
May 11	Czechoslovakia	Total U.S. ground casualties in Czechoslovakia: 116 KIA and 353 WIA.
May 15	Czechoslovakia	Last German resistance ceases, ending fighting in Europe.
	Europe	**Total U.S. Casualties in ETO:** Army/Air Forces — 177,549 KIA; 472,742 WIA; and 151,920 evacuated due to combat exhaustion. Navy — 5,793 KIA and 6,077 WIA.

TIME LINE

Sept. 1939
- Germany invades Poland, Sept. 1
- Great Britain & France declare war on Germany, Sept. 3

1940
- Germany invades Denmark & Norway, April 9
- Germany invades Low Countries, May 10
- Italy declares war on Great Britain & France, June 10
- France signs armistice with Germany, June 22
- Battle of Britain, July 10–Oct.
- First peacetime draft law in U.S. history, Sept.

1941
- Wavell's first Libyan offensive, Dec. 9–Feb. 7, 1941
- Rommel's first offensive, March 31
- Germany invades Greece & Yugoslavia, April 6
- German airborne assault on Crete, May 20
- Germany invades U.S.S.R., June 22
- U.S.S.R. & Great Britain sign mutual aid pact, July 13
- Seige of Leningrad begins on Sept. 8, ends Jan. 1944, 700,000 deaths estimated

1942
- U.S. declares war on Japan, 1 day after Pearl Harbor attacked, Dec. 8
- Germany & Italy declare war on U.S., Dec. 11
- Battle of Stalingrad, Aug. 23–Feb. 2, 1943
- Battle of El Alamein, Oct. 23
- Allied troops land in Morocco & Algeria, Nov. 8

1943
- Battle of Tunis, May 7
- Axis forces in N. Africa surrender, May 13
- Battle of Kursk, July 4–Aug. 1
- Allies land in Sicily, July 10
- Italians secretly surrender to Allies, Sept. 3
- Allies land at Salerno, Sept. 9

1944
- Allies land at Anzio, Jan. 22
- Allies invade Normandy, June 6 (D-Day)
- Soviets push Germans into Poland, mid-July
- Paris liberated, Aug. 25
- Polish Resistance revolts against Germans in Warsaw, Aug.–Oct.
- Battle of the Bulge (last significant German offensive), Dec. 16–Feb. 7, 1945

1945
- Yalta Conference, Feb. 4–11
- Soviets launch attack on Berlin, April 16
- Hitler commits suicide, April 30

June 1945
- Germany surrenders, WWII in Europe ends, May 7

ATLANTIC OCEAN

IRELAND

GREAT BRITAIN

English Channel

INVASION OF NORMANDY (D-DAY, JUNE 6, 1944)

Roosevelt and Churchill decide[d] Trident Conference (15–25 Ma[y]) to conduct a major cross-Cha[nnel inva]sion of Europe in June 1944. Eisenhower was designated to [com]mand Operation "Overlord." T[he larg]est amphibious assault yet kn[own in] history began on the Normand[y coast in] complete tactical surprise on [the morning of] 6 June 1944. To protect Eise[nhower's] southern flank, the U.S. Seven[th Army] landed in southern France (Op[eration] "Dragoon") on 15 August 194[4].

PYR[ENEES]

SPAIN

Madrid

The Americans wanted to inv[ade in] 1943, but this idea was dee[med impractical and] cancelled in favor of an Allie[d invasion of North] Africa. Operation "Torch" co[mprised U.S. forces] which landed on 8 November [1942. These] forces linked up with Genera[l ...] in April 1943, becoming 18th [Army Group under] overall command of General [...] this unit had forced the surre[nder of all Axis in] North Africa.

From Great Britain

From U.S.

PATTON (NOV. 1942)

Gibraltar (BR.)

SP. MOROCCO (SP.)

FREDENDALL (NOV. 1942)

RYDER (NOV. 1942)

Casablanca

Port Lyautey

Mazagan

Safi

MOROCCO (FR.)

Oran

AL[GERIA]

THE SECOND WORLD WAR
THE EUROPEAN THEATER, 1942–19[45]

- ⊛ National Capital (1937)
- • City or Town
- ✯ Battle Site
- ← Axis Advance
- ← Allied Advance (Soviet)
- ← Allied Advance (American & British)

- Allies
- Axis Countries
- Axis Controlled (Max[imum])
- Neutral Countries
- — National Boundary (1[937])
- — German Boundary B[efore] Invasion of Poland (1[939])

The breakout from the Normandy beachhead took place in July 1944, and the offensive continued using General Eisenhower's "broad front" strategy. Attempts to breach the German Siegfried Line blunted the Allied offensive. The Germans then launched an offensive - the ensuing fight being the "Battle of the Bulge" - through the thinly-held Ardennes Forest in December 1944.

The Allies halted the German offensive in January 1945 and continued the attack, crossing the Rhine River in March 1945 and encircling the Ruhr area in April 1945. This resulted, along with Soviet pressure from the east, in the German collapse and surrender on 8 May 1945.

WORLD WAR II IN EUROPE

World War II began in Europe on 1 September 1939 with Germany's invasion of Poland. United States' involvement started on 11 December 1941, only four days after Japan's attack on Pearl Harbor, when Germany and Italy unexpectedly declared war on the United States. British Prime Minister Churchill met with President Roosevelt in Washington, D.C. (22 December 1941–14 January 1942), and decided to defeat Germany first.

Operation "Husky," the invasion of Sicily, began on 9 July 1943, and after that island was cleared, the mainland of Italy was assaulted on 3 September 1943. Allied forces continued to slog their way up the Italian peninsula until 2 May 1945. Amphibious operations at Salerno and at Anzio were attempts to outflank the Germans in Italy.

NORWAY

SWEDEN
Oslo
Stockholm

FINLAND
Helsinki
Leningrad

ESTONIA
(JAN.-DEC. 1944)

Riga
LATVIA

DENMARK
Copenhagen

Memel
LITHUANIA

Smolensk

U.S.S.R.

(JUNE 1944–FEB. 1945)

Danzig
(Gdansk)
EAST PRUSSIA
(GER.)

Minsk

NETH.
Hamburg
MONTGOMERY (AUG. 1944–MAY 1945)
Elbe
Berlin
VON RUNDSTEDT
(DEC. 1944–JAN. 1945)

GERMANY
Torgau

Vistula
R.
Warsaw
Brest
(JULY 1943–DEC. 1944)
Gomel

KURSK
1943

London
Amsterdam
SENHOWER
UNE, 1944)

nnel
NDY
944)

BELG.
Remagen
BATTLE OF THE BULGE
1944–1945

Oder
R.
(DEC. 1944–MAY 1945)
POLAND
Lvov
(JULY 1943–JUNE 1944)
Kiev

Kharkov

Paris
BRADLEY
(AUG. 1944–MAY 1945)
Rhine River
Prague
Auschweitz
(JUNE 1944–MAY 1945)

l at the
1943)
el inva-
eneral
com-
great-
wn to
coast in
D-Day,"
ower's
h Army
ration

FRANCE
DEVERS
(SEPT. 1944–MAY 1945)
Munich
CZECHOSLOVAKIA
CARPATHIAN MTS.

Vichy
SWITZ.
Vienna
AUSTRIA
Budapest
HUNGARY
ROMANIA

Sevastopol
Yalta

Lyons
ALPS
CLARK
(JAN.-MAY 1945)
Trieste
(JUNE 1944–MAY 1945)

Rhone
River
Po R.
ANDORRA
NEES

PATCH
(AUG.-SEPT. 1944)

Belgrade
YUGOSLAVIA
Danube R.
Bucharest
(JUNE 1944–MAY 1945)

BLACK SEA

de continental Europe in
ed premature and was
invasion of French North
sisted of three task forces
1942. Moving east, these
Montgomery's Eighth
Army Group under the
lexander. By 12 May 1943
der of all Axis forces in

ST. TROPEZ
1944
ITALY
ADRIATIC SEA
BULGARIA
Sofia

Corsica
Rome
ANZIO
1944
Naples
SALERNO
1943
ALBANIA
Istanbul

From
Oran

Sardinia
Palermo
ALEXANDER
(SEPT. 1943–JAN. 1945)
GREECE
AEGEAN SEA
TURKEY

ALEXANDER
(NOV. 1942–MAY 1943)
Algiers
From
Oran

Bizerte
INVASION
OF SICILY
1943

Operation "Husky," the invasion of Sicily, began on 9
July 1943, and after that island was cleared, the
mainland of Italy was assaulted on 3 September

Bône
TUNIS
1943
MALTA
(BR.)

DODECANESE IS.
(ITALY)
CYPRUS
(BR.)

LGERIA
(FR.)
KASSERINE PASS
1943
Crete

45

TUNISIA
(FR.)
MARETH
1943

MEDITERRANEAN SEA

Extent)

Tripoli

937)

fore
939)

Benghazi
TOBRUK
1942
EL ALAMEIN
1942

Cairo

MONTGOMERY
(NOV. 1942–MAY 1943)

LIBYA
(ITALY)

EGYPT

Nile R.

SAHARA

BALTIC SEA

GREAT
RITAIN

PYRENEES

Relative Sizes of the U.S. and European Theater
(Present-Day Boundaries Shown)

N

0   100   200 Miles
0 100 200 Kilometers

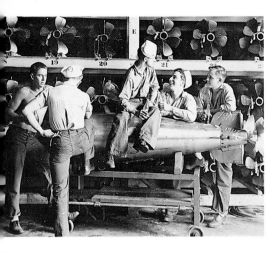

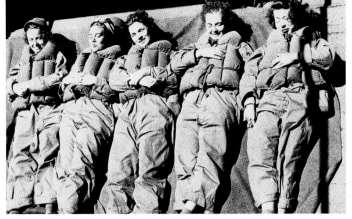

LOW COUNTRIES

Fighting in the Ardennes by Jim Dietz. The Ardennes — commonly known as the Battle of the Bulge — of Belgium and Luxembourg in December 1944 and January 1945 constituted the largest battle in U.S. history. It involved 600,000 GIs and claimed 19,000 of their lives. British Prime Minister Winston Churchill said of the massive engagement: "This is undoubtedly the greatest American battle of the war and will, I believe, be recognized as an ever-famous American victory."

Liberating the Low Countries

First Thrusts: Mons Pocket

66

The enemy is no longer a cohesive force, but a number of fugitive battle groups, disorganized and even demoralized . . .

99

— Allied intelligence assessment

ONCE NORTHEASTERN FRANCE was cleared of major German army concentrations, the way was open to the Low Countries: Belgium, Luxembourg and Netherlands. But as the U.S. First Army pushed into these countries headed for the Siegfried Line in late August 1944, its units confronted the same problem as the Third Army — severe fuel shortages.

In hot pursuit, Combat Command A of the 2nd Armored Division reached Tournai, Belgium, on Sept. 2, 1944. A regiment of the 30th Infantry Division captured the city. The 79th Division eliminated a pocket of resistance at Montdidier, and the 2nd Armored's CCB engaged a German column for 2½ hours. XIX Corps then halted at Tournai because this was a British zone — and the units were out of gasoline.

Meanwhile, VII Corps drove toward Mons, Belgium. Early on Sept. 3, the 3rd Armored Division took the town. The 1st and 9th Infantry closed in behind. The head-on encounter in Mons resulted in a short, impromptu battle. Remnants of 20 German divisions were swept off the field of battle, and 25,000 prisoners taken in three days. The IX Tactical Air Command destroyed hundreds of vehicles of the Fifth Panzer Army.

Typically, bravery was displayed, too. Pfc. Gino J. Merli of Co. H, 2nd Bn., 18th Inf. Regt., 1st Division, "played possum" when his machine gun section was overrun. Yet, he remained at his weapon for the entire night of Sept. 3–4 at Sara-la-Bruyere. When the sun rose, 50 dead Germans were counted in front of his position. Merli was awarded the Medal of Honor for his valiant stand.

By this time, an Allied intelligence report indicated "the enemy is no longer a cohesive force, but a number of fugitive battle groups, disorganized and even demoralized, short of equipment and arms." Yet the fighting divisions were unable to exploit this advantage because they were forced to await fuel for their tanks and vehicles.

Fuel caught up with the advance units, and U.S. V Corps moved along the Meuse River, capturing Liege, Belgium, on Sept. 8. Objectives north of the Meuse were left to the British to liberate. Direct on the U.S. Army's path was the southernmost province of Holland, wedged between Belgium and Germany. The U.S. 30th Infantry Division liberated most of Limburg Province, including its capital of Maastricht (the first Dutch city freed) on Sept. 9.

That same day, U.S. VII Corps entered Luxembourg; Petange was the first town in the Grand Duchy to taste freedom in four years. Next day, the 5th Armored Division had the honor of liberating Luxembourg City, the tiny country's capital, along with other First Army elements.

Due north, the moment the Allies had awaited for five years occurred: the German border was penetrated. The 5th Armored Division's 85th Reconnaissance Squadron, from Luxembourg, crossed over the Our River into Rhineland-Palatinate near Stalzenburg at 6:05 p.m. on Sept. 11. First Army elements advanced five miles farther to Trier within 24 hours. Units of the 3rd Infantry Division pushed to within 1,000 yards of the West Wall or Siegfried Line.

All along the extended front, Allied units were at a virtual standstill, awaiting the order to breach the Siegfried Line — the great man-made barrier Hitler counted on to protect the Third Reich. That order came three days later. But there was also some unfinished business to attend to in central Netherlands. Paratroopers would be needed for this operation.

Infantrymen with tired "dogs" hitch a ride on an M-10 3-inch gun motor carriage as the First Army drives through Belgium toward the Netherlands. By Sept. 14, 1944, German forces had retreated to their own soil. The only thing preventing the Allies from continuing the fight was a lack of fuel. U.S. Army

As the war's tentacles stretched across the continent, the 82nd Airborne Division primed in England for its next jump. On Sept. 17, 1944, the paratroopers lined up to take off for the airborne invasion of Holland, code-named *Operation Market-Garden*. U.S. Army

"

The men knew perfectly well that the impending series of missions into Holland were of grave importance and fraught with danger.

"

— TECH. SGT.
HARRY TINKCOM
82nd Troop Carrier
Squadron

Operation Market-Garden: Drop on Holland

On Sept. 17, 1944, a fair day with light winds and slight haze, pathfinders of the 101st and 82nd Airborne divisions departed from Chalgrove in England, kicking off one of the boldest operations of WWII — *Operation Market-Garden.*

Pvt. Raymond Smith, of the 101st Airborne, described the pathfinder mission: "To mark the drop zone with 4′ × 8′ identifying panels placed in a 'T' shape and to guide the planes in with the Eureka radar set." From his vantage point on Drop Zone C, another 101st pathfinder, 1st Lt. Gordon DeRamus, noted that "the main body of troops came in about 30 minutes later, and it seems as though the Krauts must have known something because I saw around 17 C-47s shot down."

The *Market* part of this audacious operation entailed dropping three airborne divisions — the U.S. 82nd and 101st and the British 1st. These units became stepping stones behind the German right flank in Holland. They cleared the way for a fresh drive by the British Second Army up to and over the lower Rhine — the ground, or *Garden*, phase of the operation.

By dropping the airborne forces in successive layers along a narrow 60-mile belt behind the German front, they gained a foothold on all four of the vital key locations needed for the Allied thrust north — the passage of the Wilhelmina Canal at Eindhoven, the Maas River at Grave and the Waal and Lek rivers at Nijmegen and Arnhem, respectively.

On midday on the 17th, masses of troop carriers and gliders flew in steady stream, oblivious to the intense flak. On the northern route, 1,033 carriers — 408 of them towing gliders — carried the 82nd and British troops toward Nijmegen and Arnhem.

"We were flying at 800 feet below the clouds, bouncing around like a ping-pong ball on a windy ocean," said flight lieutenant Henry McKinley, an American crewman with the Royal Canadian Air Force, flying in a C-47 Dakota. "The glider was twisting and jerking up and down, back and forth at the end of the long stretching tow rope."

The Dakota was flying toward Arnhem when it encountered flak and "all hell broke loose. There was a thunderous explosion and half the cockpit was blasted away," McKinley recalled. The glider was quickly cut loose from its tether and the crippled plane was nursed back to England.

On the southern route another 494 planes — 70 with gliders — dropped the 101st north of Eindhoven.

From a journal kept during the war, 82nd Troop Carrier Squadron Tech. Sgt. Harry Tinkcom wrote: "On the morning of the 17th a tenseness as heavy as the thick haze that covered the ground seemed to pervade. The men knew perfectly well that the impending series of missions into Holland were of grave importance and fraught with danger."

Escorted by aircraft from the Eighth Air Force, 6,000 to 8,000 paratroopers dropped in each division area: 16,500 paratroopers and 3,500 glidermen were on the ground within an hour and 20 minutes.

Farthest south, the 101st, although suffering casualties from the flak encountered over Eindhoven, took four of its five bridges intact. The southern bridge was already destroyed so the paratroopers crossed the water barrier. By dawn they met Nazi tanks near Eindhoven.

To the north, Brig. Gen. James Gavin's 82nd seized the bridge at Grave and critical high ground near Nijmegen, but by the time the troops moved to take the large highway bridge, the Germans had dug in.

Over the next four days, the paratroopers fought bravely for their objectives. The British at Arnhem destroyed a railroad bridge, but could only secure the north end of the critical highway bridge eight miles to the east of their initial drop zone. Meanwhile, the British XXX Corps started heading north along "Hell's Highway" — the road from Eindhoven through Nijmegen to Arnhem.

Early on the 19th, the Guards Armored Division rolled into the 82nd

American troops trudge and motor into the Netherlands on Sept. 18, 1944, and get a warm greeting from a Dutch girl and her father bearing the Stars and Stripes on the roadside.
Signal Corps

A paratrooper from the 82nd Airborne Division in England climbs aboard a transport bound for *Operation Market-Garden* during September 1944. He loads up not only with the usual regalia — four packs, hand weapon and chute — but also a bazooka.
U.S. Army

GIs in Holland salvage a crashed U.S. glider for parts and equipment. The glider went down behind enemy lines in the Netherlands on Sept. 18, 1944, during *Operation Market-Garden,* the massive Allied airborne assault on Holland that month. Signal Corps

Airborne's airhead and linked up with 504th PIR near Grave. George Koskimaki wrote in *Hell's Highway:* "The 101st had completed its main mission . . . it had fought its heart out to keep the corridor open . . . to allow the British to link up with the paratroopers at Arnhem."

With the key bridge over the Waal River blown, the "All-Americans" ferried across the river so simultaneous British-American attacks could launch from both south and north. These assaults, made late on Sept. 20, were successful, but Germans held out until the end of the next day. During the intense fighting, Pvt. John Towle of Co. C, 504th PIR, earned the Medal of Honor, awarded posthumously.

U.S. paratroopers were relieved 71 days after their landing: the 101st on Nov. 11 and the 82nd on Nov. 28. Their casualties ultimately totaled 909 KIA and 3,899 WIA.

First Allied Airborne Army Commander Lt. Gen. Lewis H. Brereton said: "The 82nd and 101st divisions accomplished every one of their objectives. In the years to come everyone will remember Arnhem, but no one will remember that two American divisions fought their hearts out in the Dutch canal country and whipped hell out of the Germans."

Operations in Holland lasted into November, and a relative calm settled over Belgium and Luxembourg after mid-September 1944. The focus of fighting had shifted to the West Wall or Siegfried Line by then. Battles raged from Aachen in the north to Metz farther south in Lorraine. Behind the "Wall," German armies were being mobilized for one last offensive in the West. Belgium and tiny Luxembourg enjoyed their liberation for little more than three months before the *Wehrmacht* once again stormed across their borders.

A Dutch girl with friends receives a stick of chewing gum from men of the 101st Airborne in *Operation Market-Garden* during the jump made famous by *A Bridge Too Far*.

Ardennes: Battle of the Bulge

During the fall of 1944, GIs settled down in recently liberated Luxembourg and parts of Belgium. Despite signs of an impending build up of German forces across the border, U.S. commanders felt confident the Third Reich was on its last leg. They were tragically wrong.

At 5:30 a.m., Dec. 16, 1944, Lt. Charles Braswell awakened to the rumble of sustained artillery fire. That was unusual in this quiet sector of the Ardennes where his 110th Regt., 28th Div., had come to lick its wounds and regroup after the brutal Battle of the Huertgen Forest a month before in Germany.

A short distance to the north, Lt. Ken Mooney, HQ Co., 3rd Bn., 112th Regt., 28th Div., was awakened by the adjutant and informed of a German attack. Mooney had expected some sort of light, retaliatory action ever since the regiment began training replacements in exercises against pillboxes actually manned by Germans. The unwritten rule "live and let live" applied in this rugged, forested terrain where Germany, Belgium and Luxembourg come together and where both armies sent depleted divisions to be restored.

Still farther north, Pfc. Bernard V. O'Hare with the newly arrived 106th Infantry Division buttoned up as shells began to rain down. The "Golden Lions" had been in the line only six days and their ranks were filled with tender 18- and 19-year-olds, an indication that America's manpower resources were stretching thin.

To each American in his bunker or foxhole along this sparsely manned front, the artillery was the typical, local, harassment and interdiction fire. Nothing had indicated an all-out German attack.

In reality, that morning more than 2,000 German guns were pulverizing a 60-mile stretch of front in the Ardennes from Monschau, Germany, in the north, to Echternach, Luxembourg, in the south. When the barrage lifted, three German armies of some 200,000 men crashed against 83,000 unsuspecting GIs in six divisions, four of them — the 4th, 28th, 99th and 106th — either depleted or untested. The Battle of the Bulge had begun with a big bang.

Bulge Order of Battle

Infantry Divisions — 1st, 2nd, 4th, 5th, 9th, 26th, 28th, 30th, 35th, 75th, 76th, 78th, 80th, 83rd, 84th, 87th, 90th, 94th, 95th, 99th and 106th.

Armored Divisions — 2nd, 3rd, 4th, 5th, 6th, 7th, 8th, 9th, 10th and 11th.

Airborne Divisions — 17th, 82nd and 101st.

"

Nuts!

"

— BRIG. GEN. ANTHONY MCAULIFFE

Above: Despite German efforts to seal off Bastogne, American tanks penetrated enemy lines and entered the town. The GIs of the 4th Armored Division, such as the Cobra King crew, suffered some 1,400 casualties along the snowy, windswept road in the Ardennes during December 1944.

Top: In the deep snowdrifts along the German border in January 1945, infantryman Thomas O'Brien of Middlesboro, Mass., a member of the 101st Inf. Regt., 26th Inf. Div., takes time to eat cold C-rations. The conditions sometimes were more severe than what the enemy threw at the advancing soldiers in the Ardennes. Signal Corps

Right: Infantrymen of the 75th Division, guarded by a camouflaged tank of the 750th Tank Battalion, slog through the snow of Belgium and Luxembourg after the German counter-offensive was blunted. U.S. Army

Adolph Hitler conceived this bold attack, code-named *Herbstnebel* — "Autumn Mist" — in a desperate attempt to reverse the fortunes of war for the once invincible *Wehrmacht*. He was convinced he could deliver a crippling blow westward through Luxembourg and Belgium and capture the important Allied port of Antwerp. In theory, the thrust would split the British and Canadian armies from the Americans and force a negotiated settlement.

The German army had used the densely forested Ardennes as an avenue of surprise attack three times in less than a century — 1870, 1914 and 1940. Nevertheless, Gen. Dwight Eisenhower and Lt. Gen. Omar Bradley, commander of the Twelfth Army Group, did not expect an attack to come through this area in 1944. The Germans counted on that thinking when they secretly amassed two armies, Fifth Panzer and Seventh Armies, under cover of the Ardennes. Sixth Panzer Army was formed in full view in hopes the Allies would believe its objective was to defend the Aachen area to the north.

In the forest, the Germans cooked by charcoal fire to reduce smoke, moved only at night, muffled their movement by spreading straw on roads, and sent fighters low over American lines to drown out the sounds of vehicle movement. Commanders communicated by phone, thus depriving the Allies of ULTRA radio intercepts that would have revealed their intentions, and sent the most secretive communications by courier. Only the most loyal German soldiers went on patrol, and units were weeded of all suspect troops.

Hitler painstakingly planned the operation to coincide with inclement

weather. Nature accommodated the Germans that bitter cold, misty morning, December 16, when up to six inches of snow lay on the ground and the sun would remain hidden for days.

In the northern sector, Gen. Sepp Dietrich's Sixth Panzer Army spearheaded the attack against Maj. Gen. Leonard Gerow's V Corps with the objective of reaching the Meuse River at Liege, Belgium, within two days. The Sixth's immediate concern in the opening hours of the attack was to secure its right flank at Monschau so that a panzer corps could sidestep the action and press westward along four major highways leading to the Meuse.

But Dietrich's troops hadn't reckoned with the 99th Division, whose green troops fought back furiously. Driven from their positions, many regrouped around isolated command posts or lone officers and fought on. In the end they were routed and fell back to Elsenborn Ridge, but not before they delayed the delicate German timetable.

The veteran 2nd (Indianhead) Division established positions on the front of Elsenborn Ridge after desperate fighting. Combat was deadly. "From house to house, from wall to wall, along muddy streets and down narrow alleys, the fight eddied . . ." wrote Charles B. MacDonald in *The Mighty*

On Jan. 16, 1945, patrols from the U.S. First and Third Armies hooked up near Houffalize, Belgium, to complete the pincer movement that cut off the Bulge at its waist. The trek to Houffalize tested the patrols to the maximum with frigid conditions and diehard German resistance. The First Army troops needed two weeks to fight 15 miles southward from Garndmenil and Manhay, and the Third Army spent a week covering the seven miles from Bastogne. Most of the German forces escaped before the pincers snapped shut.

Malmedy Massacre

As a convoy from Battery B, 285th Field Artillery Observation Battalion crested a hill near Baugnez, Belgium, on Dec. 17, 1944, it encountered machine gun fire from German Panzer tanks of the *Kampfgruppe Peiper*. Led by SS Lt. Col. Joachim Peiper, the Panzers rushed to break through American lines, desperately trying to regain the offensive during the Battle of the Bulge in the Ardennes.

Overwhelmed, GIs from the 285th who survived the initial barrage surrendered and were herded into a nearby field. With orders from Adolf Hitler to fight "with a wave of terror and fright" and "without regard to humane inhibitions," the Germans committed the worst atrocity against Americans in the European Theater.

Panzer tanks raked the GIs with deadly fire, then foot soldiers walked among the bodies and dispatched the wounded with a bullet to the head. Miraculously, after endless hours of feigning death, about 40 GIs were still alive, though many were badly wounded. When some dashed to nearby trees, however, they were cut down by German soldiers still close by.

Other GIs sought safety in a nearby cafe. A German patrol surrounded and torched it, killing the Americans as they came out of the blazing building.

Of the 150 GIs of the 285th, only 17 straggled back to U.S. lines to tell their harrowing tale of the Malmedy massacre. (Besides those members of the 285th, other victims came from the 575th Ambulance Co., 200th Field Artillery Bn., 32nd Armored Regt., 546th Ambulance Co. and the 197th AAA Aviation Bn.)

The word spread quickly — "No SS troops or paratroopers will be taken prisoner, but will be shot on sight." American units would fight to the last rather than risk surrendering and facing a fate similar to the Malmedy victims.

After the war, 74 Nazis stood trial for the Malmedy massacre. Though 43 were sentenced to death by hanging and 22 were given life in prison, all sentences were eventually commuted.

In 1976, more than 30 years after commanding the Malmedy perpetrators, Joachim Peiper was killed when his home in Traves, France was firebombed. The Avengers, a group of French resistance fighters, were rumored to have carried out the reprisal.

GIs take on the unpleasant task of unloading snow-covered, frozen bodies of fellow Americans who had surrendered, but then were executed by Germans. The massacre took place at Malmedy, Belgium, Dec. 17, 1944 — the worst atrocity committed against Americans in Europe.
U.S. Signal Corps

Endeavor. Outnumbered and with the threat of being overwhelmed, the 2nd withdrew to the ridge and regrouped with remnants of the 99th. But the northern shoulder held against three German divisions.

Immediately to the south, General von Manteuffel's Fifth Panzer Army, aiming for the Meuse around Namur, Belgium, smashed into the 106th Division, which was dug in on the Schnee Eifel, an exposed ridgeline inside the German border.

The 106th was doomed. Maj. Gen. Alan Jones, commanding general, elected to stand pat in the face of an envelopment coming through the Losheim Gap. Three days later on Dec. 19, the 422nd and 423rd regiments held as long as they had the means to fight, costing the enemy valuable time, before surrendering. The 424th Regiment fought throughout the remainder of the battle, including the defense of St. Vith.

South of the 106th, the Fifth Panzer Army also hit the 28th Division, which blocked access to the vital road and to rail junctions at St. Vith and Bastogne. The 28th fought valiantly, but the Germans were too strong. The 112th Regiment peeled northward, while in the center the 110th Regiment disintegrated and survivors scattered.

On the southern flank of the Bulge, Gen. Erich Brandenberger's German Seventh Army pushed the 28th farther south, as the weary Americans prepared for the defense of Bastogne, the town that came to symbolize the Battle of the Bulge.

Von Manteuffel sent his crack 2nd and 116th Panzer divisions racing toward Bastogne, and his troops pushed through hastily assembled Ameri-

66

The Ardennes under overcast skies resembled the dark abode of evil spirits from tales of the Black Forest. Riflemen shivered and crouched in frozen holes waiting for death. It was wonderful to be alive when dawn came, but then, with the realization of what the day would bring, one questioned the very value of life. Our present arrived: a squadron of American fighter planes. I've never seen any artist portray Santa Claus flying a P-47, but he must have been at the controls, for he brought the greatest gift possible — our lives.

99

— Pfc. Ken Roettger
Co. E, 317th Inf.,
80th Div.

can combat commands from the 9th and 10th Armored divisions in their path. The 2nd Panzer Division then halted just three miles from Bastogne because of false intelligence reports of large U.S. concentrations. The German delay proved fatal. Bastogne was there for the taking and the Meuse was only 25 miles distant.

This "bulge within the Bulge" at St. Vith prevented the Germans from reinforcing their Panzer units to the north and south. Though outnumbered almost five to one, the Americans held out for six crucial days, stalling the Nazi push to Antwerp. The 7th Armored Division, sustaining heavy casualties, was awarded the Belgian *Fourragere* and earned the praise of Eisenhower and Churchill alike.

By nightfall, Dec. 21, the situation for the Americans in the Bulge appeared bleak. Peiper's tanks in the north smashed through to Werbomont. In the center, the American defenders at St. Vith withdrew to the west of the Salm River. The bitterly contested village quickly fell to the Fifth Panzer Army.

When Bastogne, Belgium, was besieged in December 1944, infantrymen attached to the U.S. 4th Armored Division were part of the relief force. As the advance across this open field, small arms fire is kept up against the Germans. National Archives

In the south, the Germans were on the outskirts of Bastogne and the Americans desperately plugged the holes in the southern flank of the salient. English-speaking German paratroopers, while few in number but dressed as Americans and dropped behind U.S. lines, also sowed confusion in the chaos. So did 150 men of Otto Skorzeny's Panzer Brigade as part of *Operation Grief*. Everywhere, Americans challenged each other to ensure they were not Germans in disguise.

But the tide had begun to turn for the GIs. As early as Dec. 17, Eisenhower released the 101st and 82nd Airborne divisions, held in reserve in France, for service in the Bulge. Their arrival by the 19th probably saved the battle for the Allies. The 82nd was ordered to Werbomont, 10 miles west of Stavelot, to block the rampaging Peiper.

The 101st was ordered to Bastogne, where it won a place in the annals of military history as "The Battered Bastards of Bastogne." The paratroopers moved into the town in the nick of time, along with a combat command from Third Army's 10th Armd. Div., to deny it to the 2nd Panzer. But they soon were cut off. Von Manteuffel bypassed and surrounded Bastogne, leaving its destruction to a *Panzer Lehr* Division and the 26th

A chow line of American infantrymen braves the elements on their way to LaRoche, Belgium, on Jan. 13, 1945, typifying the hardships that the Bulge imposed on all who battled through it during the very heart of winter. Frostbite was one of the leading causes of casualties among U.S. troops. **National Archives**

Volksgrenadier Division in Gen. Heinrich Luttwitz's XLVII Panzer Corp. Von Manteuffel's panzers rushed toward the Meuse.

Luttwitz, certain he had the 101st in the bag, demanded its surrender. The reply from Brig. Gen. Anthony McAuliffe, assistant division commander, was the now famous and resounding, "Nuts!"

In the south, units of Patton's Third Army, including the 5th Infantry and 4th Armored divisions, arrived along the southern flank to shore up the beleaguered 4th and 28th divisions.

Jack Davis, a medic with the 5th Division, recalled getting the word that the division would wheel north from its positions in France and drive 90 miles through the wintry night to reach Echternach by morning. Trucks, jeeps, tanks, half tracks, all ladened with troops, ignored battlefield regulations to run with "cat eyes" (small parking lights) and streamed northward in a blaze of light. By morning, they were occupying abandoned U.S. foxholes near Echternach and attacking the surprised Germans.

The high water mark of the Battle of the Bulge came around Christmas 1944 when the German 2nd Panzer Division reached Dinant, just four miles from the Meuse and 60 miles from the point of attack. But the division's tanks ran out of gas and came under withering attack by Maj. Gen. Ernest Harmon's veteran 2nd Armored Division. The weather cleared. Like flies, the Jabos pounced on the panzers.

To the north, Peiper's spearhead was trapped and isolated from the rest of the 1st Panzer Division and Deitrich's other SS Panzer divisions could not move forward as the Americans squeezed the bulge. Peiper, too, was running out of gas.

On the southern flank of the Bulge, a combat command of Patton's 4th Armd. Div. under Lt. Col. Creighton Abrams, later a commander in Vietnam, linked with the 101st at Bastogne. The siege was over.

James Cadden was with C Co., 1st Bn., 506th PIR, 101st Airborne Division. After jumping into Holland in mid-September, his platoon sustained casualties at Veghel. By Christmas Day, his unit was just north of Bastogne. "Our activity was limited to patrol probes while other division units fought horrific battles around Bastogne to maintain possession of the town."

But the Battle of the Bulge was far from won. Manteuffel's final attack against Bastogne came Jan. 3, 1945, the same day Lt. Gen. Courtney Hodges

Leopoldville, Christmas 1944

The men of the 66th "Black Panther" Division experienced a miserable Christmas Eve 1944. They had arrived in England only a month before as a "reserve" unit and had hoped to spend the holidays with English families.

But when 28 German divisions plowed through the Allied lines in the Ardennes Forest at dawn Dec. 16, the 66th received orders to depart.

Eight days later, 2,200 men of the division loaded onto two Belgian-crewed transport ships — the *Leopoldville* and the *Cheshire* — for a perilous channel run from Southhampton to Cherbourg, France. The Black Panthers expected to relieve the badly mauled 94th Infantry Division.

German U-boats lurked in the waters surrounding Cherbourg under orders to sink any Allied ships carrying supplies and reinforcements from England. A French frigate and two English destroyers accompanied the two transport ships, infrequently dropping

The Leopoldville, a luxury liner, while transporting 2,200 men of the 66th Division (Black Panthers) from England to Cherbourg, France on Christmas Eve, 1944 was hit by a torpedo fired by a Nazi U-boat. The ship sank within minutes, taking 762 of the soldiers to their deaths.

depth charges to scare off any enemy submarines.

But at 6 p.m., and just five miles from Cherbourg, *U-Boat 486* spotted the *Leopoldville* and fired one torpedo. It struck the defenseless transport on the starboard (right) side, killing 300 soldiers instantly.

In the panic, the Belgian crew lowered a lifeboat and paddled to shore, leaving the inexperienced GIs to fend for themselves. Rescue boats from Cherbourg were delayed because of the holidays, and no one left on board the *Leopoldville* could operate the radio and relay its position.

Rough seas further compounded rescue efforts, preventing Allied ships from maneuvering close enough to the crippled *Leopoldville* to throw transfer lines. Desperate GIs jumped to their deaths, crushed between the ships or sucked under by the churning waters. All told, 762 men from the 66th Division died in this needless disaster.

The division went on to relieve the 94th Division in the Brittany-Loire area on Dec. 29, 1944, containing the Germans in the St. Nazaire and Lorient pockets until the war's end in May 1945.

ordered his First Army to attack. By Jan. 8, Hitler authorized a withdrawal from the tip of the Bulge, an admission the Ardennes offensive had failed.

On Jan. 16, patrols from the First and Third Armies linked up at Houffalize. But it took 12 days to push the Germans back to their original line of departure. From then on, the German army was capable of little more than holding actions against the combined weight of the Allies. As Field Marshal von Rundstedt observed after the war, the Ardennes offensive for the German army was "Stalingrad number two."

The Battle of the Bulge cost the U.S. Army enormously. Some 600,000 Americans were involved — more than on both sides at Gettysburg. Casualties for the combined Ardennes-Alsace Campaign totaled 19,246 GIs killed in action and 60,050 wounded. Another 15,000 soldiers were captured, more than half from the 106th Division. About 90 percent of the First Army's losses were among infantry units. In addition, the U.S. Eighth and Ninth Air Forces lost 414 aircraft and 1,314 airmen killed flying tactical support missions.

Above: Sgt. Ralph Hammond of Alabama, and Tech. 3 Joseph Giellinski of Wisconsin, who fought through the Battle of the Bulge in December 1944 and January 1945, befriend a family in the Bastogne area. Signal Corps

Top: An M-4 Sherman tank, sometimes called "Jumbo," moves through the frosted Ardennes Forest with the 7th Armored Division to enter the Battle of the Bulge in Belgium during the winter of 1944–45. U.S. Army

66

When we arrived in the Ardennes Forest that dark, subfreezing December night, we were almost congealed into a permanent sitting position. Through rain and sleet we barely discerned hills and a dark, pine forest carpeted in layers of ice and snow. This battle already was erupting into spasms of frenzy and bloodshed. . . . We infantrymen were without combat boots, overshoes and waterproof sleeping bags. Sleeping outdoors for weeks, we suffered trenchfoot, colds and pneumonia.

99

— MITCHELL KAIDY
345th Infantry
87th Division

Losses on the German side totaled around 100,000 killed, wounded and captured, including the *Luftwaffe* crews (800 aircraft, or 10 percent of the entire air arm was downed). Among the 81,834 German ground force casualties were 12,652 KIA; 38,600 WIA and 30,582 MIA.

Many lessons were learned in the Bulge. Possibly the most important: never underestimate the enemy. The Americans assumed the Germans were finished after their punishing defeats the summer before. They also ignored intelligence data that pointed to a German attack. Refugees told of massed enemy troops and equipment. Patton criticized the general laxity of the U.S. divisions in the Ardennes. He wrote: "Had V and VIII Corps of the First Army been more aggressive, the Germans could not have prepared this attack; one must never sit still."

Did the Bulge lengthen the war? Some argue that by employing a different strategy Eisenhower might have ended the war before the Bulge began. Others counter that the Germans shot their bolt in the Bulge and thus hastened the end.

Historian MacDonald called the Bulge the "greatest pitched battle ever fought by American arms." It was that and more. It represented the coming of age of the American army in World War II. "The victor in the Ardennes was the American soldier," MacDonald wrote.

Winston Churchill said on Jan. 18, 1945, "This is undoubtedly the greatest American battle of the war and will, I believe, be recognized as an ever-famous American victory."

★ ★ ★

GERMANY

Huertgen Forest by Jim Dietz. "Only the devil himself could have created" the scene that ensued in the horrific Huertgen Forest of western Germany, wrote infantry company commander and author Charles MacDonald. A classic meat-grinder, the battle there between September 1944 and February 1945 chewed up several U.S. Army divisions.

From the Rhine to the Elbe and Danube

Horror in the Huertgen Forest

❝

The Germans had every inch of the forest plotted. They knew the range. The shrapnel came down on you and there was no way of protecting yourself.

❞

— SGT. WALTER LIPINA
83rd Division

HUERTGEN FOREST receives little more than an asterisk in histories of World War II. It wasn't a battle in the traditional sense, with a distinct beginning and ending. And it can hardly be called a victory. Stalemate is a better description.

Huertgen, nevertheless, drew into one of the longest and bloodiest campaigns of the war, a classic meatgrinder that began in September 1944, when the 9th Division attacked elements of the German 353rd Division in this dense, meticulously planted woods. American commanders regarded the Huertgen Forest as a threat to the flank of any thrust into Germany.

Yet areas of the Huertgen remained contested in February 1945 as the Allies began the final drive to bring Nazi Germany to its knees. In five months of brutal fighting, *Huertgenwald* consumed thousands of men and entire divisions, some of the finest in the U.S. Army. And to the men who fought in the Huertgen no other campaign or battle compared during the entire war.

"Well, the hedgerows in Normandy may have been as bad," recalled Foster Gould, a 28th "Bloody Bucket" Division infantryman wounded in the forest.

"Huertgen was indescribable," said Ralph Johnson, a headquarters clerk with the 28th. He recalled his regimental commander receiving a message from Gen. Norman Cota, commander of the 28th, demanding to know why no medal recommendations had been sent to division headquarters. Johnson says regimental replied: "There's nobody left to make recommendations."

The Germans were undaunted and wily. They fought on home ground, from concealed and interlocking bunkers and they infiltrated unseen between American positions to attack from the rear and the flanks. The terrain was hilly and darkened by the nearly impenetrable forest and a

winter sun that set by mid-afternoon. The weather was as much the enemy as the Germans and their incessant shell bursts in the treetops.

The Battle of the Huertgen Forest developed from the Allies' effort to reach the Rhine, a symbolic and real barrier to Germany's heart that had been inviolate since 1805 when Napoleon crossed it. The avenue of attack for the First Army lay through the Aachen Gap where, according to military historian John Keegan, "Eisenhower hoped that a concerted drive on either side of the ancient city of Aachen would allow a breakthrough to Cologne before the winter brought campaigning to an end."

To secure the right flank of the attack, "Gen. Courtney Hodges (First Army commander) had to take the high ground in the vicinity of the Monschau Corridor, a task that involved clearing the German-infested Huertgen Forest," states Charles B. MacDonald in the official U.S. history, *The Siegfried Line Campaign*.

The job fell to Maj. Gen. Lawton Collins' VII Corps. His plan was to drive directly to the Roer River and seal off the forests. While Huertgen was but one of several forests in the area, it represented all surrounding woods and became the name of the furious battle.

The 9th Division arrived first into the Huertgen in mid-September and encountered a taste of what was to come — resolute and brutal defense by small numbers of the enemy.

Infantrymen pushing through the Huertgen Forest near Vossenack, Germany, in mid-December 1944 ran up against wire, pillboxes and mines in the thick foliage. National Archives

"

If I had to decide which battle was worse, I would have to choose the Huertgen Forest over the Bulge.

"

— KARL R. REEMSEN
109th Inf. Regt.
28th Inf. Div.

The 3rd Bn., 47th Regt. was deployed around Schvenhutte on Sept. 18, and was among the first to be hit. Four days later the Germans attacked, but 150 were killed and 45 captured. In other skirmishes, advances were measured in yards. The Americans were stopped by mines, ambushes, bunkers, booby traps — and the shelling.

"The shelling just went on and on," recalled attorney Charles Smith, then an instrument corporal with the 1st Division, whose job was to crawl out in the mud and connect severed communications wires.

"The shrapnel came down on you and there was no way of protecting yourself," said Walter Lipina, a sergeant with the 83rd Division, which was thrown into Huertgen in late December. "The Germans had every inch of the forest plotted. They knew the range. They didn't have to guess where their enemy was."

The tree bursts took out men by the thousands. Foster Gould, a casualty, recalled, "We pushed off Nov. 2. The Germans sucked us in. There was no artillery at first. Then we heard the distant firing and knew we was gonna get it." The shells poured down on Gould's C Company, 109th Infantry. An 88 shell burst on the side of a tree and a piece of shrapnel tore through Gould's right elbow, permanently disabling him.

Fighting often was so close in the dense woods that American infantrymen discarded their wool graycoats, because in the gloom the Yanks looked deceptively like Germans.

On Oct. 6, the 9th Division tried again as part of Collins' advance. The plan was to attack against reinforced German units that included the 275th Division and seize the villages of Germeter and Vossenack, and to continue through the forest to gain the Schmidt-Steckenborn ridge.

The Roer River lay just beyond. The Americans opened the drive with an intense artillery barrage and close-in attacks by P-47s. But once again the 9th was mauled. By Oct. 24, when the division was withdrawn, it had gained only 3,000 yards on a three-mile front and suffered 3,836 casualties.

Despite the resistance and carnage, the top commanders intended to replay the scene in what the troops called the "Death Factory." The 28th Division was thrown into the fray. The Germans countered with a *Kampfgruppe* (battle group) of the 116th Panzer Division and elements of their 89th Division.

The 28th "was to follow the same route as that of the ill-fated 9th Infantry Division: Germeter, Vossenack, across the Kall River Gorge to Kommerscheidt and finally to Schmidt," Charles Whiting wrote in *The Battle of the Huertgen Forest.*

On Nov. 2, behind an artillery barrage of 7,313 rounds, the 28th entered this manmade hell. It fought its way into Schmidt, but was thrown out with staggering losses. The battle resumed once again in the forebod-

Above: GIs spread their rations on a makeshift dining table during the bitter battle of Hurtgen Forest waged in Germany in late 1944. U.S. casualties in this classic "meatgrinder" were horrendous. National Archives

Top: Medics tend to a soldier wounded in fighting during the Huertgen Forest campaign, which began September 1944 and lasted until Feb. 9, 1945. U.S. Army

ing forest. The fighting was so brutal that McDonald called it "one of the most costly division actions in the whole of WWII."

The U.S. high command wasn't yet finished. It readied for *Operation Queen*, an attack into Huertgen in mid-November that would include the 1st, 4th, 8th, 9th and 104th Infantry divisions, and elements of the 3rd and 5th Armored divisions.

The attack opened with 10,000 tons of bombs raining down on German positions from 4,500 Allied warplanes that included heavy bombers from the U.S. Eighth Air Force and the RAF Bomber Command, medium bombers from the U.S. Ninth Air Force, and fighter-bombers from the 9th and 19th Tactical Air Commands.

These new U.S. infantry formations were swallowed in an inferno that consumed thousands of men as they confronted additional German units, including the 12th and 246th divisions and 3rd Panzer Division.

By early December, the Allies had made limited gains. To the north of Huertgen, VII Corps punched the Germans back seven miles. In the south, in the forest itself, gains were about two miles. Once again, on Dec. 10, Collins' VII Corps resumed the offensive, this time joined by the newly arrived 83rd Division. They pushed the Germans back to a narrow belt of forest before the Roer River.

Advancing through the lethal Huertgen Forest of Germany in late 1944, mud-splattered men of the U.S. 4th Division clamber out of a gulch clotted with barbed wire, felled trees and other debris. More than one-fourth of the GIs who fought in Huertgen Forest, rife with booby traps and minefields, became casualties. U.S. Army

For the next two months the lines remained static as the two armies slugged it out a few miles to the south in the Battle of the Bulge. Even as late as February 1945, parts of the Huertgen remained contested with the town of Schmidt still in enemy hands.

Gen. James Gavin, whose 82nd Airborne Division was brought up to join the next offensive, scouted areas of the Huertgen before the division jumped off. Gavin observed a pathetic sight in the vicinity of Schmidt:

"Many, many dead bodies, cadavers that had just emerged from the winter snow. Their gangrenous, broken and torn bodies were rigid and grotesque, some of them with arms skyward, seemingly in supplication."

Those bodies were from the 28th Division. Gavin also found the bodies of wounded Americans still on their stretchers. They had been abandoned during the winter's previous fighting.

Gavin's orders: "Seize the town of Schmidt." On Feb. 5, 1945, the 78th Division, which had been bloodied in the Huertgen in December, jumped off with the 82nd Airborne on the new offensive. The handful of remaining Germans around Schmidt were as dogged as ever, but the battered village finally fell four days later to the 310th and 311th Infantry regiments of the 78th Division.

The Battle of the Huertgen Forest was essentially over, five months after it began and at a terrible cost. According to MacDonald, nearly 30,000 Americans had been killed or wounded. Some 9,000 more were lost to battle fatigue and disease. The 80,000 German troops defending the forest suffered proportionate losses.

"I served with B Co., 330th Inf., 83rd Div. in that terrible battle," wrote Roland Grebinger. "I cannot begin to tell you how bad it really was. But I was one of the fortunate ones, suffering only a bad case of trench foot. I still cry to this day about the American dead there."

To many observers, the battle accomplished nothing. And the sustained combat did little more than save face for the U.S. Army and its commanders from Marshall and Eisenhower on down. They were afraid to admit to their mistake of attacking Huertgen in the first place.

Critics also argue that the Huertgen could have been sealed off, that there was no need to attack a weaker, smaller enemy, sometimes outnumbered 5-to-1, who could enhance their position through brilliant tactics and ideal defensive terrain.

Others claim the top commanders later rationalized the fighting in the Huertgen by arguing the objective was, from the beginning, the Roer dams which had to be captured intact. Yet there was no mention of the importance of the dams until well into the fighting.

MacDonald believes the fighting in the Huertgen was not all in vain. It seriously depleted the German army, diverted up to seven divisions and cost thousands of casualties and prisoners, particularly in those units being readied for the German's upcoming Ardennes offensive.

But, beyond doubt, the Battle of the Huertgen Forest demonstrated the mettle of the U.S. soldier. He had been tested and had bravely persevered.

Rout in the Rhineland

In a Belgian orchard 10 miles from the German border at daybreak on Sept. 10, 1944, a barrage from U.S. 155mm guns of the 991st Field Artillery Battalion thundered into the German frontier town of Bildchen. The church steeple collapsed in a shower of mortar dust and bricks. The German defenders realized that although they were being pulverized from afar, GIs were knocking at the gates of their homeland.

Within five days, U.S. forces assaulted the "West Wall" or Siegfried Line, officially launching the Rhineland Campaign.

GIs joked about the much-vaunted Siegfried Line with its pillboxes and "dragon's teeth" tank obstacles: "All we have to do is to send a couple of dentists to yank out the dragon teeth and we'll tie knots in the Siegfried Line!" The boast came back to haunt its author, as some of the fiercest fighting of the war came as the Americans spent from Oct. 2–21 capturing the first sizeable German city: Aachen.

The day after a Long Tom artillery shell toppled the Bildchen steeple, Staff Sgt. Warner W. Holzinger of the 85th Cavalry Reconnaissance Squadron, 5th Armored Division, had the honor of leading the first patrol across the German border.

Above: Sgt. Carter and Raymond Borge of Portland, Maine, both of the 315th Engineers, 90th Infantry Division, post a welcome sign in front of an array of "dragon's teeth" along the West Wall, or Siegfried Line, breached in September 1944.

Top: U.S. forces advance through the concrete tank obstacles of the "West Wall" of Germany in mid-September 1944. Staff Sgt. Warner W. Holzinger of the 85th Cavalry Reconnaissance Squadron led the first patrol across the German border, starting the Rhineland Campaign.

National Archives

Above: A machine-gun crew with the First U.S. Army covers the streets of Aachen. Soldiers from the 3rd Armored Division, 30th Infantry Division, and the Big Red One — 1st Infantry Division — combined to rout the Germans in bitter house-to-house fighting. On Oct. 20, 1944, Aachen became the first German city to fall to Allied forces. U.S. Army

Top: Under heavy fire, U.S. First Army tanks and infantrymen cross the Rhine into Germany at Remagen. They captured Ludendorff Bridge on March 7, 1945, before Germans could completely destroy it — the only bridge remaining across the Rhine. It held up for 10 days, long enough for GIs to secure the east bank. By then pontoon bridges to the south provided a means across the last natural barrier into Germany. National Archives

But it soon became apparent that the Germans fully intended to use the pyramid-shaped concrete obstacles, plus their string of reinforced pillboxes, to exact a severe toll on the attackers.

Aachen opened the way to the Rhineland and the Cologne plain. To the German garrison — 12,000 strong — defending Aachen, Heinrich Himmler sent this message: "German soldiers! Heroes of Aachen! Our *Fuehrer* calls upon you to defend to the last bullet, the last gasp of breath, Aachen, this jewel city of German *kultur*, this shrine where German emperors and kings have been enthroned!"

Combat engineers, with bangalore torpedoes and TNT, promptly blasted a path through the West Wall fortifications.

1st Lt. Frank Kolb of the 1st Infantry Division led the first platoon to launch the attack toward Aachen. It was rough going. In a five-day period, the 1st Bn., 16th Inf. Regt., lost 300 men out of its 1,300-man strength. Supported by the 3rd Armored Division and the 30th Infantry Division farther north, the "Big Red One" found it slow slogging as the rains churned up the mud and kept the bombers out of the sky.

German SS troops strengthened the enemy lines. Future Medal of Honor recipient Tech. Sgt. Jake Lindsey remarked, "Either those *Krauts* were crazy or else they were the bravest soldiers in the world." House-to-house fighting within Aachen produced murderously high casualties on both sides. (The 30th Inf. Div. lost 3,100 men; the 1st Inf. Div. suffered an equal number of casualties.)

The 238th Engineer Combat Battalion created a humorous diversion by loading up several streetcars on a downgrade into Aachen with time-fused shells and other explosives; swarms of news correspondents covered the bizarre exploit, which actually caused little damage.

Finally, after Aachen was surrounded and his own headquarters came under small arms fire, the German commander surrendered when his ammunition ran out.

"The city is as dead as a Roman ruin," wrote an American observer, "but unlike a ruin it has none of the grace of gradual decay. . . . Burst sewers, broken gas mains and dead animals have raised an almost overpowering smell in many parts of the city." Hitler's prophecy had been realized: "Give me five years and you will not recognize Germany again," he had said.

The U.S. First and Ninth Armies had launched *Operation Queen* in mid-November, with the Ninth clearing the west bank of the Roer River from Brachelen to Altdorf by early December. *Queen* witnessed, incidentally, the largest air-ground cooperative effort to date in the ETO.

Offensive operations resumed Jan. 17, 1945. *Operation Grenade* achieved the Allied assault crossings over the Roer River, followed by a northeastward drive by the U.S. Ninth Army's linkup with the First Canadian Army along the Rhine. The Ninth Army (its dash to the Rhine was dubbed *Operation Flashpoint*) comprised four corps with 13 divisions. In reaching the Rhine, the Ninth Army captured 30,000 German soldiers and killed 6,000, at the cost of 7,300 U.S. casualties.

A sequel to *Grenade* — *Operation Lumberjack* — was a con-

'Black Panthers' Come Out Fighting

Their motto was "Come Out Fighting," and when the 761st Tank Battalion landed in France on Oct. 10, 1944, they were ready, as Gen. George S. Patton said, "to kill those Kraut sonsabitches." But the 761st wasn't just another armored unit. It had yet to be tested in battle, but even more, it had to prove its right to be on the front lines.

Patton reminded them, "Men, you're the first Negro tankers to ever fight in the American Army. I never would have asked for you if you weren't good. I have nothing but the best in my Army. I don't care what color you are, so long as you go up there and kill those kraut SOBs."

Composition of the unit was 6 white and 30 black officers, with 676 NCOs and enlisted men.

On Nov. 7, 1944, the 761st "Black Panthers" began earning their well-deserved reputation in Lorraine, France. For six months, they remained on the frontlines. News of the 761st's exploits spread throughout the Army. Gen. William M. Miley, commanding general of the 17th Airborne Division, wrote: "During the Ardennes operation we had very little armored unit support, but of that we did have the 761st Tank Battalion was by far the most effective and helpful."

From Oct. 31, 1944, to May 6, 1945, the Black Panthers were in action 183 days, serving with the 26th, 87th, 17th Airborne, 71st, 79th, 95th and 103rd divisions. They fought in four campaigns in six countries and lost 71 tanks, incurring a casualty rate approaching 50 percent.

The unit was finally given a Presidential Unit Citation in April 1978 by President Jimmy Carter, who said, ". . . Members of the 'Black Panther' Battalion, coupled with their indomitable fighting spirit and devotion to duty, reflect great credit on the 761st Tank Battalion, the U.S. Army and this nation."

A tank crew of the 761st Tank Battalion, the "Black Panthers," is on the move near Lorraine, France, during November 1944. The 761st later moved into the Ardennes and eventually participated in three more campaigns in six countries. It suffered a casualty rate of almost half of its members and earned a Presidential Unit Citation 33 years after the war ended in Europe. U.S. Signal Corps

Above: Pvt. Alex Drabik of Toledo, Ohio, was the first soldier to cross the Ludendorff Bridge with the 9th Armored Division on March 7, 1945.
National Archives

Right: Ducking enemy fire, American soldiers cross the Rhine at St. Goar in March 1945. One who made the trip said, "Just my luck — I drew an assault boat to cross in. We all tried to crawl under each other because lead was flying around like hail."

"

Either those Krauts were crazy or else they were the bravest soldiers in the world.

"

— TECH. SGT. JAKE W. LINDSEY
Medal of Honor recipient
16th Infantry, 1st Division

verging thrust made by the U.S. First and Third Armies to trap the Germans in the Eifel Mountains during the first week of March. GIs were now poised to "bounce" the Rhine.

Lt. Harold E. Larsen, liaison pilot for the 9th Armored Division, radioed in some amazing intelligence — the Germans had left a bridge still standing across the river.

On the afternoon of March 7, 1945, 34-year-old Sgt. Alex Drabik from Toledo, Ohio, bobbed and weaved his squad across a Rhine River railroad bridge (Ludendorff) at the little town of Remagen, Germany. His company commander, Lt. Karl Timmermann, from A Co., 27th Armored Inf. Bn., 9th Armored Div., who had ordered the crossing, followed close behind. Drabik, Timmermann and a handful of infantrymen, engineers and tankers, performed one of the most incredible feats in the annals of military history.

The Rhine River had not been crossed by an invading army since Napoleon more than a century earlier. Hitler had ordered all the bridges up and down the Rhine to be blown up as the Americans approached. The last bridge, between Cologne and Koblenz, still stood to enable German tanks and artillery to retreat safely. Just as Lt. Timmermann gave the order for Drabik's squad to cross, tremendous explosions shook the bridge and seemed to lift it from its foundations. The structure shuddered, but miraculously remained standing.

Lt. Hugh Mott and two brave armored engineers, Eugene Dorland and John Reynolds, dashed out on the bridge and feverishly cut wires to the remaining explosive charges. The Germans blew a 30-foot crater in the approach to the bridge to prevent tanks from crossing. Sgt. Clemon Knapp

of Rupert, W.Va., and a crew manned a "tank dozer" — a Sherman tank with a bulldozer blade — and filled in the crater. Knapp and his crew received Silver Stars for their actions.

The night of March 7 was one of the darkest of the war. Lt. Windsor Miller gently guided his 35-ton Sherman tanks across the shaky bridge, dodging some gaping holes as he maneuvered between white tapes strung by the engineers. Across the Rhine, Miller's tank platoon beat off several German counter-attacks and helped the armored infantry hang onto their tenuous toehold.

When the bridge was captured, the first troops proudly attached a sign reading: *Cross the Rhine with dry feet — Courtesy 9th Arm'd Div.* The 9th, 78th and 99th Infantry divisions rushed to the scene to reinforce the bridge-head. Military police, tank-destroyer and anti-aircraft units were awarded Presidential Unit Citations for their heroism under fire.

Hitler threw in jet planes, underwater swimmers, giant V-2 rockets and massive reinforcements in attempts to destroy the bridge. The bridge was so severely damaged that it collapsed without warning on March 17, taking the lives of 28 engineers and injuring 63 of the 276th Engineer Com-

A U.S. convoy rolls through Duren, a German town reduced to rubble by 9th Air Force fighter-bombers and ground artillery during the drive to the Rhine River in March 1945. Republic P-47 Thunderbolts in three Tactical Air Commands of the 9th flew thousands of sorties in support of three U.S. armies. Smithsonian Institution

bat Battalion and the 1058th Bridge Construction and Repair Group. But not before a pontoon and treadway bridge had been built under fire on each side of the permanent bridge. The 276th was awarded a Presidential Unit Citation.

By mid-March, U.S. VIII Corps completed mopping up operations west of the Rhine. Within a few days, *Operation Undertone* was under way by the U.S. Seventh Army to clear the Saar-Palatinate triangle.

On March 22, the 90th Inf. Div. cleared Mainz while other GIs achieved a surprise late night crossing of the Rhine at Oppenheim, south of Mainz.

U.S. Navy Unit 2 transported most of the 90th Division across the river aboard LCVPs (Landing Craft Vehicle Personnel) until a pontoon bridge was completed on the 24th. Other naval vessels of *Task Group 122.5* were assigned "depth charge patrol." Strafed by German ME-262s from above, they hunted and killed enemy "gamma swimmers" — frogmen whose mission was to demolish Allied craft and bridges. The task group received the Naval Unit Commendation for its role.

At this point, the U.S. First Army held a bridgehead across the river 20 miles wide and eight miles deep; six divisions were east of the Rhine. The stage was set for the final drive into Germany's heartland.

Routing the Germans in the Rhineland was the most costly U.S. campaign in Europe: 50,410 Americans were killed in action and 165,965 wounded.

Storming the Heartland

Once the Allies had cleared the west bank of the Rhine River, the way was paved to thrust headlong into the heartland of Germany. The Central Europe Campaign was launched by U.S. First Army units near Remagen on March 22, 1945. That night, elements of the U.S. Third Army crossed the Rhine at Oppenheim.

The northern crossing of the Rhine, primarily a British move and dubbed *Operation Plunder*, lasted from March 23–26. The U.S. Ninth Army contributed two divisions — 30th and 79th. The American part was known as *Operation Flashpoint*, and cost the GIs 31 casualties in the actual crossing.

To cross the river, engineer units supplied small landing craft — 38-foot "Sea Mules" (Army tugs hauling bridging equipment).

Air and artillery attacks had pulverized the entire area with massive bombardments. So within a few days, the Germans were stunned into submission.

But an aggressive army of German defenders awaited GIs at Wesel. They had mobilized the "Wesel Division" under *Generalmajor* Friedrich Deutsch from a nucleus of anti-aircraft artillery units, and the presence of strongpoints along a railroad line held up the capture of the city for more than 24 hours.

Still, Lt. Whitney O. Refvem found it a comparative picnic: "There was no real fight to it. The artillery had done the job for us." The 30th and 79th combined lost 41 KIA, 450 WIA and seven MIA.

To support the ground troops of *Plunder*, the Allies launched *Operation Varsity* — the largest single airborne drop made by either side during WWII. Some 21,680 men of the U.S. 17th Airborne and British 6th Airborne divisions jumped March 24 near Wesel. On the way over, 22 C-46s and 12 glider-towing C-47s were shot down. This last airborne operation in Europe proved to be the costliest.

Axis Sally's silky radio voice correctly predicted: "We know you're coming tomorrow and we know where you're coming — at Wesel. Ten crack divisions from the Russia front will be a reception committee." The flak was murderous, and the "reception committee" took its toll.

Fighting in the Diersfordt Forest that first day cost the 17th Airborne 159 KIA, 522 WIA and 40 MIA. Three paratroopers earned the Medal of Honor. In addition to those casualties, the U.S. IX Troop Carrier Command counted 41 KIA, 153 WIA and 163 MIA.

Meanwhile, the U.S. Seventh Army had begun battering the West Wall on March 15 to establish a bridgehead over the Rhine in the Worms area. This assault took place along 40 miles of fortifications from Saarbrucken to Haguenau. *Undertone* was also designed to clear the Saar-Palatinate

Crewmen of a U.S. Third Army M-36 tank destroyer load the hefty shells of a 90mm gun into the turret during a stop near Serrig, Germany, on March 16, 1945. U.S. Army

> ❝
>
> *The time was now April 22, 1945, and our armies were advancing at will . . . full force ahead, annihilating German armies wherever they were found. . . . But over 50 percent of the old battalion members are now wearing the Purple Heart.*
>
> ❞
>
> — History of the 274th Armored Field Artillery Battalion

Two paratroopers of the U.S. 17th Airborne set up a machine gun. Medics conduct rescue operations near Wesel, Germany, in March 1945 using a farmer's wheelbarrow for a stretcher to haul wounded. Code-named *Operation Varsity*, the mission put the 17th across the Rhine in just a six-minute jump out of C-46 transports.

"

After the battle of the Ruhr Pocket, we turned south. We crosed the Altmuhl River at Eichstatt on April 23, 1945. Approaching from the north, I was with the second section of our machine guns. The Germans naturally were on the south side of the river with all avenues of approach zeroed in. I picked a route and we took off on the double. Hadn't gotten 20 yards when an 88 picked us up. By the time I reached the bottom of the hill they had fired 9 rounds at us. I turned around to find I was the only one there. That damn 88 fired 7 more rounds at me coming down the hill. Everytime I would try to back up another round came whistling in. I could not believe they would fire 7 rounds at one man.

"

— TECH. SGT. JOHN
TOKAREWICH
1st Platoon, D Co.,
342nd Inf., 86th Inf. Div.

triangle in conjunction with the U.S. Third Army. U.S. XII Tactical Air Command provided the aerial arm of the operation.

Within five days, the 63rd Division ruptured the main belt of the West Wall, and on March 26 the Seventh Army crossed the Rhine near Worms. Its casualties for the operation totaled 12,000. The Third Army was also successful, capturing large cities like Coblenz, and inflicting 113,000 casualties (including 90,000 prisoners) on the Germans. GIs sustained 5,220 losses in clearing the Saar-Palatinate triangle.

Up and down the Rhine River, the Allies charged across the once-impregnable barrier. Desperate German forces rushed fire brigades to try and prevent the crossings. By ordering his armies to hold their positions to the last man, without retreat, Hitler had stripped away all his reserves and sacrificed them west of the Rhine, exposing the Ruhr River industrial area to invasion.

By April 1, the U.S. Ninth Army in the north and the First Army in the south had snapped the pincers shut around 400,000 German troops defending the Ruhr. Eighteen U.S. divisions fought for two weeks to reduce the pocket. In some towns and cities, such as Hamm and Dortmund, and along ridges and streams, the Germans fought fiercely, especially when SS troops predominated.

Many American heroes emerged from these confrontations. On April 3, Pfc. Walter C. Wetzel threw himself on two enemy grenades to save his fellow 8th Division soldiers; he received the Medal of Honor. Two days later, Cpl. Thomas J. Kelly, a medic, earned an MOH by making 10 trips in the face of heavy enemy fire to rescue and evacuate casualties of his 7th Armored Division.

Attacks on the Ruhr fortress freed thousands of prisoners of war and

Gliders line up by the hundreds in preparation for the largest airborne operation of WWII in the ETO. *Operation Varsity*, the jump around Wesel, Germany, on March 24, 1945, included more than 21,000 paratroopers.

forced laborers. As April progressed, whole German units surrendered, frequently marching into U.S. camps in huge numbers. One 78th Division infantryman started out of the city of Wuppertal with 68 prisoners and was amazed to find when he reached the regimental stockade that he had 1,200! By April 18, 317,000 Germans had been captured.

Mopping up the Ruhr pocket cost the Ninth Army 341 KIA, about 2,000 WIA and 121 MIA. Along the southern and eastern jaws of the trap, the First Army lost about three times that number of men. III Corps units counted 291 KIA, 1,356 WIA and 88 MIA. A single division of the XVIII Airborne Corps — the 8th Infantry Division — sustained 198 KIA, 1,238 WIA and 101 MIA.

U.S. units fanned out across Germany, with some pointing their spearhead toward Berlin. Throughout April, GIs met varying degrees of resistance in their pell-mell drive east. Kassel required house-to-house fighting by the 80th Div.; the 30th Div. was fiercely resisted in Hameln. But other towns submitted meekly to the Americans.

Thrusting northeast, the 3rd Armored Div. fought 10 days to take Dessau. Magdeburg fell in two days to the 2nd Armored and 30th Infantry divisions. After braving "Flak Alley" — the approach to Leipzig guarded by 1,000 anti-aircraft guns — and encountering hard street combat, the 2nd and 69th Infantry divisions secured that city. Stopped at the Elbe River, the U.S. Army would not participate in the brutal battle for Berlin.

Initially, U.S. units bypassed a block of rugged peaks in central Ger-

Members of Co. C, 2nd Ranger Bn., pause during a break in the action after the capture of Rhurberg, Germany, during March 1945. U.S. Army

many, running northeast to southeast for 60 miles to a maximum width of 20 miles. Hitler's fanciful plan was to assemble remnants of the *Wehrmacht* in the forests and fastnesses of the Harz Mountains, then have them counterattack westward to break the jaws of the Ruhr pocket. Some 70,000 enemy troops retreated to this huge enclave. Many of the troops were eager youths from training schools who fought with spirit in their losing cause.

The Ninth Army from the north and the First Army from the south gradually reduced the forest and forced mass surrenders after brisk battles around roadblocks and in wooded areas. In the early stages of the mop-up, VII Corps suffered 80 casualties a day, but in the last five days of increased resistance, U.S. units lost up to 260 men per day in the mountains to diehard fanatics.

Among the units engaged in the semi-guerrilla warfare were the 1st, 9th and 104th Infantry divisions, a regiment of the 83rd Division and a combat command of the 8th Armored Division.

The region's tallest peak, Mt. Bracken, was taken on April 18 after being plastered by the IX Tactical Air Command. Five days later, the last pockets of resistance fell in the Harz Mountains.

Striking south to Hitler's homeland in Bavaria, supposedly the site of the mythical *National Redoubt* where the Nazis would make their last stand, GIs quickly consolidated their gains.

But crossing of the Neckar River was bitterly contested at Konigshafen on April 1. And the 100th Division required nine days of hard fighting to subdue Heilbronn.

The *Stars and Stripes* reported: "For nine deadly days, the Century-men suffered all horrors in a knock-down, drag-out, slugfest for this outer position of the German National Redoubt."

Before daylight on April 4, a battalion of the 398th Inf. Regt. slipped silently across the river a mile north of the town, but was pushed back by an enemy counterattack. Some called the enemy's stand here the toughest encountered east of the Rhine. UP's Eleanor Packard termed it "another Cassino."

Three days later, Pfc. Mike Colalillo of C Company earned the Medal of Honor for single-handedly killing or wounding 25 Germans from the turret of a tank, and on foot with a submachine gun. Also, he assisted a wounded soldier in reaching U.S. Lines.

The 100th Division lost 85 KIA and about three times that number wounded, while capturing 1,500 Germans around Heilbronn. "We knew some of us would die fighting for this cause that we knew was right," Gene P. Riggins wrote 48 years later, who served with the 397th Regiment of the 100th Infantry Division. The winning of Heilbronn opened the way for the drive on Stuttgart.

It took the 42nd Division three days to clear Wuerzburg.

Nuremberg proved to be the biggest single action of the April campaign on the Western Front. The Seventh Army's XV Corps, reinforced by the 42nd Division, ran up against Germans ordered to "defend to the last bullet." And that they did from April 15-20.

Referring to the Battle of Nuremberg, Russell F. Weigley, author of *Eisenhower's Lieutenants*, wrote that a bruising fight for the city was "all the more depressing to the Americans because they saw the war's outcome as assured and such persistently fanatical resistance as absurd. To have to die against such resistance in the final days would be still more absurd."

Yet it happened. "From building to building and floor to floor wily SS panzer grenadiers, mountain troops and the *Luftwaffe* men continually allowed Americans to work past them, only to pounce from the rear," he wrote. They did so with deadly results.

Above: A mortar crew of XX Corps uses a rocket launcher to demolish a fortified German position near Helstroff in the early spring of 1945.

Top: Seventh Army soldiers cross the Danube River in an assault boat in April 1945. During fighting in the Black Forest and Schabisch Alps of Bavaria, Germany, GIs encountered strong opposition from two German armies trapped and eventually destroyed. U.S. Army

Nuremberg. This was once the city of toys, probably the most delightful place in the world for children during the Christmas holidays. It now looks as though some angry story-book giant had strode through it, crashed his fist down on a crumpled tower here, a row of buildings in the dust there, and finally, in his wrath, tumbled great stones from the castle on the hill down upon the populace below.

Out at the Luitpoldhain Stadium, a young German stares moodily at the structure. Off to the right a group of GIs are playing softball in the hallowed grounds of the Nazi Party days. To the left is an ack-ack gun. The youth is bitter. 'Instead of building homes for the workers, Hitler built these monstrosities,' he says. 'Hitler promised us that they would be a monument to the people of Nuremberg. Well, he was right. They still stand, but Nuremberg is no more.'

— CPL. HOWARD KATZANDER
Correspondent, YANK
June 8, 1945

Elements of the famed U.S. 3rd Infantry Division move through Nuremberg in April 1945. Once a Nazi shrine, the city was reduced to rubble during one of the last major battles of WWII on the Western Front. U.S. Army

GIs of the 45th Inf. Div. "mop up" Nuremberg, shrine city of the Nazi Party. They crouch behind a tank and hug the bombed-out buildings to stay out of sniper and machine-gun fire coming from the vicinity of historic, twin-spired St. Lorenz Church (background). U.S. Army

A measure of the intensity of the combat there can be taken from the fact that three GIs from the 15th Regt., 3rd Inf. Div. alone earned the Medal of Honor. One, Pvt. Joe Merrell, killed 23 Germans before he died.

Ringed with anti-aircraft guns, Nuremberg — shrine of the Nazi Party — was only captured after house-to-house fighting amid rubble caused by aerial bombardments. The 3rd and 45th Infantry divisions carried the brunt of the fighting. Late on April 19, the 30th Inf. Regt. entered the heart of the city. At the end of five days, 1,500 Germans were dead or wounded and 17,000 captured.

Four days later, Ulm toppled. And III Corps obliterated a German division near Ingolstadt.

The final major fight in Germany against Americans occurred at Munich, April 29–30. Germany's third largest city and "cradle of the Nazi beast" contained only a modest garrison. Though five divisions were thrown into the fray, only one had a hard go. The 45th Division fought a vicious room-to-room battle before it extinguished resistance in an SS academy on the city's northern outskirts.

On April 30, Hitler committed suicide in his bunker in Berlin. Within a week, at Gen. Eisenhower's headquarters in Reims, France, Gen. Alfred Jodl (later hanged for war crimes) agreed to unconditional surrender terms,

Above: A B-24 "Flying Horseman" from the 449th Bomb Group pummels Osnabruck, Germany, during several strategic missions that helped bring the war to an end in 1945.

Top: After fierce fighting near Munich in late April 1945, German prisoners are ordered to lie prone while U.S. Seventh Army soldiers search for weapons. U.S. Army

Above: A sign marks a spot where the Russian army met U.S. forces on the Elbe River in Germany during April 1945.

Top: GIs from the 82nd Airborne Div., 1st Allied Airborne Army, salute and shake hands with Russian soldiers when they linked up at Grebow, Germany. Both groups await a move to assigned sectors for the campaign to overtake the rest of country.

Army News Features

effective May 8. The war in Germany was finally over. Two other countries, however, remained to be cleared.

Conquering Central Europe, the final U.S. campaign, was an expensive proposition: 15,009 GIs killed in action and 42,568 wounded in battle.

Meeting on the Elbe River

On April 23, 1945, a 6th Armored Division sergeant named Alex Balter decided to send out a message over his radio: "American forces approaching. Listen, Russian forces! This is the voice of your American allies awaiting a meeting with you." About 8:20 a.m., Sgt. Balter repeated the message several times, and suddenly a Russian voice came over his radio: "Bravo, Amerikansky!" Then the Germans tried to jam the transmission by a very loud rendition of *Ach du lieber Augustin.*

Next day at mid-afternoon, 1st Lt. Albert L. Kotzebue of Company G, 273rd Infantry, 69th Division, moved out with a six-jeep patrol and 35 men to probe eastward and "contact the Russians." However, he was warned not to go more than five miles east of the Mulde River. Kotzebue and his men ignored the warning and left his radio jeep behind so his patrol could not be called back.

Just before noon, he and his platoon sergeant, Frederick Johnston, contacted a Russian soldier on horseback. Russian-speaking Tech. 5 Stephen A. Kowalski asked directions to a higher Russian commander, but the horseman became suspicious and galloped off. The patrol made its way to the headquarters of the Russian 175th Rifle Regiment, where members were greeted by Lt. Col. Alexander T. Gardiev.

In the confusion of the moment, Kotzebue radioed the wrong coordinates back to his regimental commander, who by then had sent out three other patrols. When an artillery spotter plane tried to reach those coordinates, it was fired on and forced to return.

Perhaps this is why history records the first Russian-American meeting as taking place at Torgau on the Elbe River, instead of 17 miles southeast where Kotzebue and his men had actually made the first contact.

Maj. Frederick W. Craig and 2nd Lt. William D. Robertson of the 69th Division also headed patrols that contacted the Russians by mid-afternoon on April 25, despite repeated orders by the regimental commander to halt their advance. When the news leaked out that they had violated orders, the division and corps commanders were "irate," according to official records. A court-martial was even considered for Robertson, who after the war became a prominent neurosurgeon in Los Angeles. There was a laconic entry in the journal of the 273rd Infantry: "Something wrong with an officer who cannot tell 5 miles from 25 miles."

Meanwhile, Kotzebue's patrol, drenched in their crossing of the Elbe, took off their soaked shoes and socks and sat at a hastily arranged banquet table in a big farmhouse — the Russian regimental headquarters. Maj. Gen. Vladimir Rusakov, commander of the 58th Russian Guards Division, was somewhat brusque and reserved as he sat down next to the barefoot American lieutenant.

But after the general left, the party developed into a wild celebration with vodka toasts to Roosevelt, Truman, Churchill, Stalin and scores of subordinate civilian and military officials — including a toast to virtually every American and Russian soldier in the party.

Although Maj. Craig and his 47-man patrol had orders to stop, they received such a friendly and boisterous greeting from gratified German civilians that they pressed eastward. By late afternoon, they encountered a column of Russian cavalry galloping across an open field to meet them, throwing their helmets in the air.

Back-slapping and boisterous hugs were followed by enthusiastic testing of each other's weapons. The Russians were quick to criticize the M-1 as too heavy, but expressed thumbs-up on the U.S. carbine and .30

Above: Holding a crude, hand-made flag emblematic of the Stars and Stripes, contrived so Russians on the Elbe River at Torgau would know they are Americans, are (L–R) Lt. William D. Robertson, Sgt. James J. McDonnell, Cpl. Paul Staub and Cpl. Frank B. Huff.

Top: American and Russian soldiers share smokes after joining up at the Elbe River in April 1945. U.S. Army

66

The Russians certainly took their own sweet time in coming those 75 miles from the Oder River.

99

— GEN. OMAR BRADLEY
12th Army Group

Liberating the Death Camps

"There in beds of crude wood I saw men too weak to move dead comrades from their side. It was like stepping into the Dark Ages to walk into one of these cellar-cells and seek out the living."

—Anonymous American Medic at Nordhausen, April 11, 1945

During the waning months of the war, elements of at least 17 U.S. Army divisions liberated 10 major concentration camps. The experience proved heartrending for the GIs involved.

Soon after 4th Armored and 11th Armored Division units converged on Ohrdruf, Germany in late March 1945, patrols from the 4th uncovered the first of many Nazi concentration camps. Though small in comparison to other camps, the horror at Ohrdruf shocked U.S. commanders, including Generals Eisenhower and Patton.

Denying any knowledge of the camp's existence, the local mayor and his wife were forced to tour the site. Afterwards, they went home and killed themselves out of shame.

For the past six months, as Allied forces closed the noose around Nazi Germany, many concentration and POW camps had been evacuated before they could be liberated. Prisoners were moved (often by forced march) to other camps. But in the closing weeks of the war, German guards were more intent on saving themselves and simply abandoned the camps, in some cases for several days before liberation.

To the south, the 2nd Cavalry Group liberated Bad Orb and 6,5000 Allied prisoners interned there. More than 3,000 were Americans.

As XII Corps units pushed toward Meiningen on the Werra River, it uncovered files on all POWs confined throughout the Nazi camp system. This damning information would be invaluable at war crimes trials in later years.

After elements of the 2nd Division captured the university town of Goettingen, they pushed on to Duderstadt due east, freeing another 600 Allied POWs, including about 100 Americans.

By April 11, soldiers of the 4th and 6th Armored divisions were entering Buchenwald, a sprawling concentration

Above: A GI with the Seventh Army gives his cigarettes to inmates leaning over a fence at Dachau, a notorious concentration camp 10 miles northwest of Munich. The Seventh captured Dachau on April 29, 1945, and freed more than 30,000 captives of many nationalities.

Right: Slave laborers lain out in a street at Nordhausen, dead of starvation and beatings. "Rows upon rows of skin-covered skeletons met our eyes," recalled an American medic.

camp in the Thuringia region. Camp guards had fled after inmates there smuggled in weapons and killed or captured other guards. When the GIs arrived, Buchenwald had already been "liberated" by the inmates.

That same day, 3rd Armored Division tanks rolled into Nordhausen. A medic with the 329th Medical Battalion reported the grisly sight at that camp: "Rows upon rows of skin-covered skeletons met our eyes. Men lay as they had starved, discolored, and lying in indescribable human filth. Their striped coats and prison numbers hung to their frames as a last token or symbol of those who enslaved and killed them."

On the outskirts of Nordhausen stood a V-rocket factory which relied on forced labor from the nearby camp.

Five days later, another 1,800 prisoners were liberated at Colditz. A landmark to the Nazi legacy — Landsberg Prison, where Hitler had been imprisoned in 1923 — was seized by soldiers of the 10th Armored and 103rd divisions in late April.

U.S. Army Liberation of Concentration Camps and Prisons	
Division	*Camp/Prison*
3rd Armored	Nordhausen
4th Armored	Buchenwald, Ohrdruf
6th Armored	Buchenwald
10th Armored	Landsberg
11th Armored	Gusen, Mauthausen
12th Armored	Landsberg
14th Armored	Dachau subcamps
20th Armored	Dachau
8th Infantry	Woebbelin
42nd Infantry	Dachau
45th Infantry	Dachau
71st Infantry	Gunskirchen
80th Infantry	Dachau, Ebensee
89th Infantry	Ohrdruf
90th Infantry	Flossenberg
103rd Infantry	Landsberg
104th Infantry	Nordhausen

Note: Other divisions credited with liberating camps include the 4th, 97th and 99th Infantry and the 82nd Airborne.

In mid-April, forces from the 42nd and 45th divisions were closing in on Munich and the nearby concentration camp of Dachau. "The first thing I saw as I went down this road to Dachau were about 40 boxcars on a railroad siding. I looked into these boxcars and they were full of emaciated bodies, loaded all the way to the top. Forty boxcars full of dead people," recalled Walter Rosenbaum, a combat photographer with the Third Army.

During the pitched battle to overpower 300 SS guards, prisoners — in anticipation of being liberated — rushed the wire fences, only to be electrocuted. Hundreds of other prisoners tracked down German guards in hiding and meted out revenge.

"It was turmoil," Rosenbaum continued. "It was quite a scene with the Americans coming in, with these camp prisoners running around crying, going crazy. This was the liberation of Dachau."

Above: Members of the 405th Infantry Regiment, 102nd Infantry Division, put finishing touches on a sign of alliance at a historic meeting with the Russians on the Elbe River, Germany, in April of 1945. Signal Corps

Left: Pfc. John Metzeger, Pfc. Delbert E. Philpott and Pvt. Thomas B. Summers, all from Co. A, 271st Regt., 69th Inf. Div., greet their Russian counterparts near Torgau along the Elbe River on April 25, 1945. Allan Jackson, UPI

"

I was an eyewitness to history in the making. I saw the ranking Russian and American generals embrace, as allied comrades in arms. I also witnessed the free flow of vodka, involving toast upon toast. Then, also at the same place, on the Elbe, I witnessed the surrender of soldiers of the once great German Third Reich.

"

— TECH. SGT.
LEONARD SHUPP
L Co., 406th Inf. Regt.,
102nd Inf. Div.

caliber machine guns. The evening after dinner was spiced with a two-hour serenade of Russian songs, accompanied by a harp, mouth organs and accordions.

Lt. Robertson's three-man patrol made its way toward Torgau with some opposition from Russian mortar, machine gun and small arms fire. He justified his violation of orders with information that some American prisoners were in Torgau. When he was fired upon, Robertson decided he needed a U.S. flag to convince the Russians they were Allies and friends. The Cold War, after all, was still a few months off.

Finding some red and blue paint at an apothecary shop in Torgau, Robertson applied it to a white sheet to fashion a crude flag. (Later, a famous photo depicted Robertson showing Eisenhower the makeshift Stars and Stripes.)

Unfortunately, the flag did not stop the firing. As the Russians later explained, the Germans had tried the same trick before opening fire on them earlier. Finally, the misunderstanding cleared up when Robertson brought one of the Russians who was among the German prisoners to shout across the Elbe River and straighten out the misunderstanding.

Gen. Omar Bradley's response was to the point: "The Russians certainly took their own sweet time in coming those 75 miles from the Oder River."

Pfc. Gardner Hitchcock, from West Memphis, Ark. a 69th Division combat engineer, recalled his assignment to help build a pontoon bridge across the Elbe at Torgau. As he and a fellow engineer were driving a stake to hold one of the cables, "suddenly appeared a scene right out of a Cecil B. DeMille movie," he recalled.

"There were 25 or 30 Cossacks mounted on shaggy ponies. They were short, squat, swarthy men complete with daggers, swords and every other kind of weapon. Almost all had handlebar mustaches.

"They spied us about the same time we saw them. With a great roar they galloped down and surrounded us. Leaping off their ponies, they grabbed us. They began pulling at our uniforms, looking at our insignia. I kept yelling 'Americans-Americans.' Finally, one of the smarter ones asked: 'Amerikanski?' I said, 'Yes.' "

"They all started yelling 'Amerikanski.' They shouted and danced around us. Then we were subjected to much cheek-kissing and bear-hugging (never let a Mongol soldier, who hasn't bathed in a year and is covered with lice and other vermin, kiss you. It's disgusting).

"All this time this is going on our Lt. Peterson, safely on the other side of the river, is screaming at us to come back. Come back — we were captives of our own Allies. Then we were forced to sit down. Four or five of the men ran to their ponies and came back loaded down with about 20 bottles of vodka and red wine. They sat cross-legged and poured water glasses of vodka and wine.

A Third Army armored division column of tanks and trucks, led by a M-4A3 medium tank, fords a stream on its advance into Linz, Austria, on May 5, 1945. U.S. Army

"One by one they would chug-a-lug a glass of vodka and chase it with a glass of wine. After each Russian would down his, there was much shouting and applause. Then with a full glass in each hand, they thrust it at you. If you didn't drink, they were insulted.

"My first time was all right. There was dead silence among the Russians as I downed the first round. They were watching my every move. When I got the last of the wine down, more hugs and kisses. This must have gone on for about an hour. I made it through three rounds. I was only 22. I can remember, after about the second round, thinking about mother and home and how proud Ike would be for holding my own with the Russians."

1st Lt. H.W. Shank of the 104th Mechanized Reconnaisance Troop, 104th Division, used a different technique when he was plied with vodka in meeting the Russians at Torgau. As he recalled the scene: "The Russians took five of us to dinner in a makeshift mess hall with a long table. We and Russian officers filled both sides of the table. The meal was macaroni and meat, salami, small raw fish, raw fat, meat covered with dough, black bread, hard-boiled eggs, hot chocolate and cookies.

"Bottles of vodka had been spaced on the table at regular intervals, and a half of a water glass of vodka set at each place. The waiters wore light blue tunics; every time I took a drink from my glass, the fellow behind me

would refill it. Wishing to appear equal to my Russian hosts, I kept pouring the stuff into my boot, only to have the fellow give me more." U.S.-Russian relations had peaked.

Today, the Torgau Bridge, scene of the famous photograph, is gone. German authorities condemned the aging structure in 1994. When the 50th anniversary of the historic meeting of the Russians and Americans rolled around, only the memories had survived.

Assaulting Alpine Austria

"The war in Austria went on amid an aura of unreality — not really war, yet not quite peace," wrote historian Charles MacDonald. Three main Allied drives penetrated Austria in May 1945: the French into the Vorarlberg, U.S. Seventh Army toward Landeck and Innsbruck, and the U.S. Third Army targeting Linz.

On May 1, the 13th Armored Division reached the Austrian border first in full strength. The next day, as XX Corps bridged the Inn River at three places, capturing both Braunau (Hitler's birthplace) and Passau, the U.S. Third Army altered and broadened its attack. XX Corps, drawing only occasional fire, pressed from its bridgehead over the Inn to the line of the Enns River south of Linz, meeting the Russians there May 4. XII Corps moved along the Danube's north bank; its 11th Armored Division captured Linz. Salzburg surrendered to the 106th Cavalry Group.

Advancing along the Tirol Mountains, the Seventh Army faced an enemy force scattered from Innsbruck to Salzburg. Only a few Germans, however, resisted from the narrow Alpine passes.

On May 2, Austrian partisans seized control of Innsbruck. But the 103rd Infantry Div. still had to fight through occasional German delaying groups to get into the city. Two days later, in a driving snowstorm, the 410th RCT accepted Innsbruck's formal surrender. "The Cactus men could hardly believe their eyes," Ralph Mueller of the 103rd Infantry wrote after the war of the 409th's entrance into Innsbruck. "It was like the liberation of Paris . . . men, women, and children screamed greetings and threw flowers before the advancing troops."

Next objective: Brenner Pass. Without firing a shot, the 411th Infantry Regiment took the town of Brenner just before 2a.m. on May 4, making contact with the Intelligence & Reconnaissance Platoon of the 349th Inf Regt., 88th Inf. Div. at Vipiteno, Italy.

But at Fern Pass, 300 Germans defended a serpentine highway blocked by deep craters. The 3rd Bn., 71st Inf., 44th Inf. Div., attacked this position early on May 1. A reinforced company was sent on a circuitous 40 mile outflanking maneuver, back almost to the Oberjoch Pass. Then i went southwest up the Lech River Valley to another route leading acros

Above: Seventh and Fifth Army troops meet at Nauders, Austria, in the Brenner Pass on May 5, 1945, hours after the Seventh captured the town of Brenner, thus sealing all the passes in and out of Bavaria. The Fifth had fought up the Italian peninsula. U.S. Army

Top: During April 1945, troops of the U.S. Third and Seventh armies surged through the forest of Bavaria to the borders of Austria and Czechoslovakia. U.S. Army

66

We should go together and march on Moscow to end the Communist threat now.

99

— German officer to Lt. William B. Farrell Jr. 65th Infantry Division

a high mountain range to the vicinity of Imst, some eight miles behind Fern Pass.

A second battalion from the 71st Infantry was dispatched on May 2 to help reduce the German position. Following Austrian partisans up a little-known trail, the battalion took the town of Fernstein before dark and seized the pass easily from the rear. On May 3, the 324th Regt., 44th Division, pushed on foot toward Imst and two days later occupied Landeck where the German Nineteenth Army surrendered. Still, a few fanatics fought on for two more days until the official surrender of Germany.

Finally, the 3rd Bn., 5th Inf. Regt., 71st Inf. Div., secured Ernsthofen Dam against stiff opposition on May 6. Part of *Task Force Wooten*, the 3rd Bn. recorded four casualties while inflicting 50 on the enemy at Nieder Gleink near Steyr.

"On May 7, 1945, I led a platoon of 30 men of F Co., 261st Infantry, 65th Inf. Div., near Enns, Austria," recalled former Lt. William B. Farrell, Jr. "To my astonishment, before midnight we had 250,000 German POWs. While waiting for the Russian army to occupy the area east of the Enns River, I met a German officer who said in perfect English, 'We should go together and march on Moscow to end the Communist threat now.'"

By war's end, the 65th Infantry Div. had established contact with the Soviets near Strengberg, and the 71st Division conducted a linkup with a Red army contingent near St. Peters.

"We were the only U.S. troops of the Third Army in combat after the war ended," according to veteran Lawrence B. Rhatican. "Eighteen troopers of the 1st Platoon, 71st Cavalry Reconnaissance Troop, 71st Infantry Division, accepted the surrender of Gen. Lothar von Rendulic and his four armies comprising 800,000 men of German Army Group South at Waidhofen-an-der-Ybbs on May 6, 1945."

Ten U.S. divisions and a dozen cavalry and artillery groups were in Austria when WWII ended. American units lost 118 KIA and 407 WIA in securing Austria's alpine passes.

'On to Czechoslovakia'

"On to Czechoslovakia and fraternization," according to Gen. Omar Bradley, became the battle cry of GIs who liberated Czechoslovakia. Historian Charles MacDonald wrote that "the drive into Czechoslovakia was at first an anticlimax. The fighting was unreal, a comic opera war. . . . "

But to the Czechs, the GIs' arrival was a Godsend. "Thank God, thank God!" exclaimed Dr. Eduard Benes, president of the Czech government-in-exile. "The Americans have just entered Czechoslovakia! Patton is across the border!"

Before the country was free, six infantry divisions — 1st, 2nd, 5th, 26th, 90th and 97th — and two armored divisions (4th and 16th) served there. Also, three groups — 2nd Cavalry, 102nd Cavalry and 3rd Tank Destroyer — helped defeat the Germans there. These outfits were backed by six artillery and engineer groups.

We were as confident as we were ignorant. Sure, war is hell. Men lose their arms, legs, sight, their mind, but certainly none of us. Men would be killed, but not the guy next to you, whom you had known two years and become as close as a brother. Men would die, but it would be 'other' men, not us, not our best friends. . . . Never having heard a German shell fall or having someone trying hard to kill you, we didn't know we should be sober and apprehensive instead of chatting.

99

— PFC. JAMES K. LENIHAN
Co. F., 314th Inf. Regt.
104th Division

GIs take cover in the streets of Pilsen, Czechoslovakia, while eliminating the last hideouts of German snipers in May 1945. U.S. Army

Opposite: Troops of the 94th Infantry Division parade through Pilsen, Czechoslovakia, on the Fourth of July. "I felt we should have gone on to the Moldau (Prague)," Gen. George Patton said. "If the Russians didn't like it, let them go to hell." U.S. Army

The I&R Platoon of C Co., 3rd Bn., 358th Inf. Regt., 90th Inf. Div., entered Czechoslovakia on April 18, 1945. It captured 36 POWs that first day. But Allied units would not be permitted to go beyond Ceske Budejovice (Budweis), Pilsen and Karlsbad to the line of the Elbe and Moldau rivers — the area east would be left to the Soviets. The "Iron Curtain" had already descended.

Advances in western Czechoslovakia were rapid. At Fuchsmuehl, 33 American POWs were found lying in straw beds and in extremely poor condition. In Friedenfelds, more U.S. POWs were liberated — most of whom had been captured in December 1944 during the German counter-offensives in Belgium and Luxemburg.

Flossenburg concentration camp tested the nerves of the most seasoned combat vets. "One who has not seen it cannot visualize it in his mind, and ... one who has not lived through the never-ending days and nights of terror in such a place cannot possibly comprehend a fraction of its misery ..." wrote Capt. John Colby in his book, *War From the Ground Up.*

The city of Cheb was the first liberated by GIs, between April 24-26. At Waldmuenchen, the 359th Regt., 90th Div. encountered heavy resistance. And the 357th Regt. was attacked by a fierce SS unit at Tremlovsky, which was swept aside with heavy losses to the enemy.

Passes at Freyung, Regen and Pegen were then cleared to pave the way for armor units. On May 5 at Zhurt, Co. I, 3rd Bn., 357th Inf. Regt., 90th Div., was raked by a captured U.S. M-8 scout car manned by Germans. One of the company's squads seeking cover in a ditch lost seven killed in action.

Pilsen was seized May 6 by the 16th Armored Division. Staff Sgt. Beverly F. Van Slyke, a squad leader in the Machine Gun Squad of 3rd Plt., Co. A, 64th Armored Inf. Bn., recalled there was little resistance except for snipers.

"After arriving at the town square, snipers opened up on our column and continued for the balance of the day. During the firing, only two men were injured, both slightly, and none were killed. But numerous snipers were killed and a large number captured."

An American advance down the valley of the Vltava River to Prague was not in the cards. Forward elements of the 4th Armored Div. reached as far as Pisek, northwest of Ceske Budejovice, when the order came to a halt. Hostilities ended the next day.

Stopping short of Prague demoralized many GIs. An

Last to Die

GIs of HQ Co., 101st Inf. Regt., 26th Inf. Div., were just counting the hours until the victory announcement as they pulled into the small village of Pernek, Czechoslovakia, just after dawn on May 8, 1945.

At 8 a.m. that day, an announcement came that the war in Europe was over. Even though hostilities stopped, there was still plenty of work to be done.

In front of a stone barn in Pernek, three trucks carried captured and abandoned enemy weapons and munitions. "Sgt. George Guise, the regimental ammo specialist, was supervising the off-loading of those trucks," recalled radio operator Carl DeVasto. Six other soldiers helped Guise.

DeVasto was across the street cleaning his weapon when suddenly an explosion touched off the munitions (possibly when one of the GIs dropped a live round or mine), killing all seven soldiers, plus DeVasto's close friend, Joe Evancho, walking nearby. Artillery shells also exploded, causing the entire village to be evacuated.

Guise, Evancho and the other members of 101st Inf. Regt., died instantly in the blast, the last known soldiers killed by a hostile cause in the European Theatre. Tragically, it all occurred just after the war was declared officially over.

Opposite: Pvt. Forest Darr of Zanesville, Ohio, shows off his souvenir medals to Cpl. Marvin Wells (left) of Bluefield, W. Va., as their field artillery battalion of the 104th Infantry Division pauses during the Rhineland Campaign. Darr collected the German medals in his travels across France, Belgium and Germany in 1944.
Signal Corps

officer of the 16th Armored Division later reported that "hundreds of men in the command wanted and pleaded to go on to Prague, and could not understand why we did not go on."

The only Americans to enter the capital city were members of an Army intelligence team headed by Capt. Eugene Fodor. Arriving May 5, the team had been offered the city by partisans.

As the men of the 2nd and 97th divisions burst across the former western German defensive line known as the "Little Maginot Line" they entered a new world. Driving through the Sudetenland with its apathetic, sometimes sullen German sympathizers, into a riotous land of colorful flags, the Americans were met by cheerful Czechoslovakians with open arms. "It was Paris all over again," MacDonald wrote.

But it was still a war zone. Only hours prior to the effective time of the surrender, GIs sustained casualties in a firefight.

According to Merle Wallace of the Recon Co., 803rd Tank Destroyer Bn., 5th Inf. Div., his outfit was ambushed by a 30-man German unit outside Volary. While evacuating an M-8 light armored car mired in a ditch, German machine gun and small arms fire killed one man from a jeep and wounded three others. That last KIA was Pfc. Charles Havlat of C Co.

On the night of May 7, near Klenovice, the last shot of WWII in Europe was fired by Pfc. Dominic Mozzetta of Co. B, 1st Bn., 387th Inf. Regt., 97th Inf. Div. "Moving back to our line, we saw a sniper in a tree and Mozetta hit him," said Bobby Popejoy, a light machine gunner of Co. B. But the 20-year-old Mozetta, a native of Providence, R.I., in an interview, said: "I don't know whether I hit him, but the sniping stopped. I didn't think anything of it. To me, it was just another shot."

Homer L. Knight of Radcliff, Ky., confirms the claim. "As commander of Co. B, I know Mozetta was identified by patrol members as the individual who fired the last American shot in Europe."

According to Czech Radio, German troops in Prague had "their last wild fling, and behaved like devils." It would be more than three days before the diehards ceased firing. As late as May 10, 30 GIs of a 16th Armored Division tank platoon blocked a 20-mile-long German column near Cimelice in the Russian Zone.

Czechoslovakia, last to be liberated from Nazi occupation, was free, in part, because of the sacrifice made by 116 U.S. soldiers KIA and 408 WIA. In addition, 235 airmen were shot down and killed over that country: seven of them on April 25 during the last U.S. bombing mission in the ETO flown by the 398th Bomb Group. To one Czech citizen, the GIs were "free men who fear nothing on this earth."

★ ★ ★

Behind Barbed Wire

"Für Sie ist der Krieg vorbei!"
(For you the War is over!)

— German soldiers ordering
GIs to surrender

Some 93,941 American servicemen spent a substantial portion of the war as guests of the German prison system. POWs in Germany called themselves "Kriegies" from the German word for POW, *Kriegsgefagener*.

Twenty-five percent of U.S. POWs in the ETO were ground troops, most of whom were captured during the Battle of the Bulge. Another 1,000 had been seized after fighting at Sid-bou-Zid in Tunisia. Most of them were taken to Italy.

The majority of U.S. POWs, however, were airmen shot down carrying out bombing missions. Allied air crews shot down over enemy territory first had to survive bailing out (or the crash landing), then they often faced hostile mobs — the very people they'd been bombing and strafing — who were angry enough to kill them.

Some downed flyers, with the help of local partisans, made it back to friendly lines, but most were captured and turned over to German forces, then transported to POW camps in the Fatherland.

Germany had signed the Geneva Convention in 1929, along with 47 other nations, and abided by it in dealing with American and British prisoners for the most part. Red Cross food parcels and packages from home were generally allowed to supplement meager food rations.

Included in these boxes were dried fruit, canned meat and fish, cigarettes, cheese and crackers, jam, chocolate and soap — many commodities even German families couldn't get, even if they had the money.

Camp guards would often smuggle in other commodities in exchange for what the POWs received. Mail was also delivered regularly at some camps, but prisoners in others might not receive anything at all.

Books, radios and newspapers were permitted, again depending on the camp, so POWs did know how the war was progressing.

As Allied forces approached POW camps near the war's end, many prisoners were relocated, often by forced march. Others were packed aboard stinking freight trains bound for pitiful camps in Poland. These trains became rolling pestholes because so many POWs had dysentery.

Many died as a result of the relocation. "Everyday the Russians were gaining miles. So the Germans decided to evacuate us," recalled Charlie Miller, a B-17 gunner shot down May 15, 1943 and imprisoned. "They put 1,200 of us into the hold of this coal barge. On the way we get caught in an American air raid, cause there were all kind of German battleships there in the Baltic."

It wasn't until April 22, 1945 — just weeks before the end of the war — under the "Standfast" agreement, that Allied POWs could remain behind, with the stipulation that they not take up arms and return to the fight.

At many camps, German guards simply slipped away into the night while there was still time to flee.

Al Gould, a bombadier with the 401st Bomb Group, remembered "looking out through the barricaded window opening of the crude barracks to see nothing but moonlight streaming through the guard tower. No soldier with guns ready. No dogs prowling the compound. The Germans had left."

A chair, bed or table of straw provided a luxury suite to Allied prisoners in this German prison camp at Moosburg where gravel floors were the norm for sleeping. **U.S. Army Air Force**

When U.S. Third Army troops entered the Moosburg camp on April 29, for example, a total of 15,568 American POWs were liberated.

Escape attempts were encouraged, but only 2 percent of all Allied POWs tried to flee. The Brits were especially persistent, though less than 30 airmen — of about 15,000 in captivity — actually made it to friendly lines.

Of the more than 93,900 American POWs held in Europe, only 737 successfully escaped, according to Ronald Bailey, in *Prisoners of War*. One percent, or 1,121, died in the camps.

Above: A tank with the 14th Armored Division enters a prisoner of war camp at Hammelburg in April 1945, liberating hundreds of Allied POWs. Just 737 of upward of 94,000 captured Americans had escaped such camps before V-E Day.

Top: When the war ended in Europe, about 1.7 million Allied participants had been taken prisoner. POWs in the stockade at Bad Orb, Germany, numbering about 6,000, rushed forward with great gusto to greet their liberators from the U.S. Seventh Army in the waning days of the war. U.S. Army

Left: The smiles tell the tale of liberated Allied prisoners of war assembling at the gate to their freedom from a Nazi POW camp at the end of the war in May 1945.
Cpl. Billy A. Newhouse, U.S. Third Army

VICTORY IN EUROPE

Powerful floodlights spread a 'V' for victory across the night sky over Paris, France, in celebration of the end of the war in Europe. Army News Features

Demobilization and Occupation

Coming Home

> "
>
> *Victory in Europe has been attained and the cloud of Nazi oppression lifted forever. The Trident was on the march when the bell rang.*
>
> "
>
> —MAJ. GEN. MILTON B. HALSEY
> Commanding Officer
> 97th Infantry Division

V-E DAY — May 8, 1945 — marked a liberation for the entire Western world. From Times Square in New York to Piccadilly Circus in London, the ending of hostilities also meant an end to the personal sacrifices caused by rationing, blackout restrictions, having a family member in uniform and another working in a local factory to make ends meet.

For the individual GI it was a sigh of relief, and a swig of captured vino, a puff on a cigarette without cupping it to hide the glow of the ash at night, a passionate kiss from an appreciative French girl or a bear hug from an Italian grandfather.

And it was a chance to say a prayer of thanks, for making it through the war alive. In the European Theater of Operations, the U.S. Army, Air Forces' and Navy casualties were immense: some 180,000 men killed in action and approximately 500,000 wounded in action. Their ultimate sacrifice was not forgotten in the V-E Day euphoria.

Since Christmas 1944, the overwhelming request of the American public, according to a Gallup Poll, had been "to have the boys back home again." Yet the cessation of hostilities in the European Theatre did not automatically mean GIs could just toss aside their uniforms and hop on the first boat headed for New York and the "Lady with the Lamp."

When the Germans surrendered there were several million American service personnel in Europe, all anxious to get home. But the knowledge that there was still a war raging in the Pacific tempered many GIs from building up too much hope. A "points" system was developed to stagger the rotation, with those with the most points allowed to leave first. Points were awarded for months overseas — one point for each month between Sept. 16, 1940, and May 12, 1945 — battle stars and for time in service during the same period.

Banner newspaper headlines, street signs, a passionate kiss of joy, the uncorking of a special bottle of champagne — the declaration appeared in many forms across the European continent: Hitler's war machine was vanquished. The war against Germany was over, and on that 8th of May in 1945 the message appeared most clearly on the faces of victory — the masses of troops who were headed home, at last, at the end of a long and bitter struggle. **Photos by U.S. Army, Signal Corps, Stars and Stripes, Army News Features and Smithsonian Institution**

After WWII, the *Honorable Service Lapel Pin* was issued to all armed forces veterans — overseas and stateside — who had served honorably between Sept. 8, 1939, and Dec. 31, 1946.

More than 12 million veterans received the pin — an eagle within a ring with seven white and six red stripes, and a blue arch — affectionately nicknamed the "Ruptured Duck."

Originally designed by Anthony de Francisci in 1925 for all honorably discharged veterans, the gold-plated brass badge was resurrected in 1943.

Due to restrictions on the use of metal, the badge was plastic. After the war, when restrictions were lifted, the pins were again made of gold-plated brass. Veterans who had received the plastic version could trade them in for brass ones.

Soon, though, the pins were forgotten as millions of veterans returned to civilian life and packed their uniforms and memories away.

Mississippi Rep. G.V. "Sonny" Montgomery, who served with the 12th Armored Division in Europe during WWII, best explained the symbolism of the pin:

"While many of the lost Ruptured Duck pins have since been replaced, it's never easy to replace the memories of the friends who never returned to receive their pin. For these and many other veterans, that is what the pin represents now."

An additional five points were given for battle decorations — Distinguished Service Cross and Purple Heart, for instance — including medals awarded by foreign countries, such as Great Britain and France. Plus, an extra 12 points were tacked on for each child under 18 born before May 12, 1945, with three children maximum.

Each individual had a composite point total, and, depending on the service's "critical score" requirement, had to exceed that score to be eligible for rotation. Initially, all enlisted men in the Army and Air Forces required a "critical score" of 85.

The Navy used a separate points system, with 44 points needed for enlisted men to rotate home. But for all of the services the point totals fluctuated. Usually it went up just days before a GI reached the magic number.

The Navy and Coast Guard mustered everything afloat "to bring the boys home," dubbed *Operation Magic Carpet*. But it wasn't quick enough for "the boys" or those waiting for them.

If they didn't have enough points to be discharged, then they would be deployed to the Pacific (as were the 86th and 97th Infantry divisions) or serve as occupation troops. On June 25, the 1st and 4th Armored, 82nd Airborne and 1st, 3rd, 9th, 29th and 36th were designated occupation units for Germany. By December 1945, 60 percent of all Army personnel were still on foreign shores; the Navy had 75 percent of its sailors overseas.

. . .

When GIs finally returned home, they faced an uncertain readjustment period, known as the "furlough syndrome." Troopships took weeks to get from Europe to the East Coast. From there the anxious GIs were sent to disposition centers near the port of entry. Then they boarded trains and buses for another long trip to separation centers near their home.

Here they received a final physical, mustering-out pay, a ruptured duck honorable service lapel pin (see sidebar), separation record, their uniform, travel pay to get home and finally, their discharge.

To make the transition from the military back to civilian life easier, President Roosevelt had promised in 1943 that the nation's fighting men would not be demobilized "to a place on a bread line or on a corner selling apples." Soon after, he signed the Serviceman's Readjustment Act of 1944, more commonly known as the GI Bill of Rights.

This legislation provided for unemployment compensation at the rate of $20 a week for one year (the "52-20 Club"). Low interest business and housing loans were also available to veterans.

But the most popular part of the GI bill was its educational benefits, which allowed millions of veterans to obtain college degrees or vocational-technical training. Overseas service, often measured in years, had earned them that right.

. . .

'ON VICTORY IN EUROPE'
by Ernie Pyle

The following is a rough draft of a column war correspondent Ernie Pyle had been preparing for release upon the end of the war in Europe. It was found on his body the day he was killed — April 18, 1945 — on Ie Shima, near Okinawa, 20 days before the Germans surrendered.

And so it is over. The catastrophe on one side of the world has run its course. The day that it had so long seemed would never come has come at last.

I suppose emotions here in the Pacific are the same as they were among the Allies all over the world. First a shouting of the good news with such joyous surprise that you would think the shouter himself had brought it about.

And then an unspoken sense of gigantic relief — and then a hope that the collapse in Europe would hasten the end in the Pacific. It has been seven months since I heard my last shot in the European war. Now I am as far away from it as it is possible to get on this globe.

This is written on a little ship lying off the coast of the island of Okinawa, just south of Japan, on the other side of the world from Ardennes.

But my heart is still in Europe, and that's why I am writing this column.

It is to the boys who were my friends for so long. My one regret of the war is that I was not with them when it ended.

For the companionship of two and a half years of death and misery is a spouse that tolerates no divorce. Such companionship finally becomes a part of one's soul, and it cannot be obliterated.

True, I am with American boys in the other war not yet ended, but I am old-fashioned and my sentiment runs to old things.

To me the European war is old, and the Pacific war is new.

Last summer I wrote that I hoped the end of the war could be a gigantic relief, but not an elation. In the

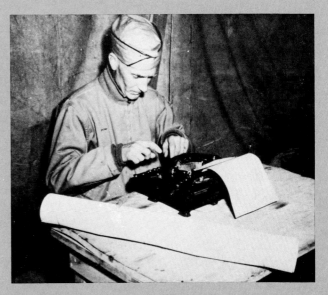

Ernie Pyle, the most respected war correspondent of WWII, at work in Normandy, France, in July 1944, during the bombing of St. Lo.
Courtesy Ernie Pyle State Historic Site

joyousness of high spirits it is easy for us to forget the dead. Those who are gone would not wish themselves to be a millstone of gloom around our necks.

But there are many of the living who have had burned into their brains forever the unnatural sight of cold dead men scattered over the hillsides and in the ditches along the high rows of hedge throughout the world.

Dead men by mass production — in one country after another — month after month and year after year.

Dead men in winter and dead men in summer.

Dead men in such familiar promiscuity that they become monotonous.

Dead men in such monstrous infinity that you come almost to hate them.

These are the things that you at home need not even try to understand. To you at home they are columns of figures, or he is a near one who went away and just didn't come back. You didn't see him lying so grotesque and pasty beside the gravel road in France. We saw him, saw him by the multiple thousands. That's the difference. . . .

Source: Lilly Library

"For the companionship of two and a half years of death and misery is a spouse that tolerates no divorce."

Members of the 106th Division crowd the rails of this troop transport for their glimpse of New York and the U.S.A., in many months.

THE KANSAS CITY STAR.

NOON EDITION

VOL. 65. NO. 232.   KANSAS CITY, MAY 7, 1945—MONDAY—12 PAGES.   PRICE: In Kansas City....3 Cents Elsewhere.........5 Cents

GERMANY SURRENDERS; WAR IN EUROPE ENDS

ON FINAL FRONT

Patton's Third Army and the Russians Converge Upon Nazis in Prague.

TANKS ROAR AT TOP SPEED

Americans in Czechoslovakia Within Fifteen Miles. Reds Sixty Miles of Capital.

THREE HOLDOUT CITIES

Only Dresden and Chemnitz Held in Last Hours by the Germans in South.

Paris, May 7.(AP)—American and Russian armies beat through Czechoslovakia and Austria today in the final mop-up of organized German resistance and embattled patriots in Prague said U. S. Third army tanks were only fifteen miles from that city, largest still in German hands General Patton said Third army troops into the closing campaign. In advances of up to twenty-five miles his tanks and infantry advanced within fifty miles southwest and fifty-two miles south of the Czech capital.

THE WEATHER—SHOWERS.

The Forecast—Kansas City and Vicinity: Occasional showers. Windy; high today, 60; low tonight, 40. Tuesday fair.

JAP SHIPPING HIT

American Bombers Sink 35 and Damage 17 Boats in Land Based Raids.

FOE SMASHES IN CHINA

A Break Through Again Menaces U. S. Air Bases in Pacific War's Only Blight.

By Leonard Milliman,
(Associated Press War Editor.)

American bombers reaching out from the Philippines and Okinawa have sunk thirty-five more Nipponese ships and damaged seventeen others, U. S. "on-to-Tokyo" commanders announced yesterday and today.

A Japanese break through in Central China to within thirty-five miles of the U. S. air base at Chihkiang was the only Night on Allied ground offensives as Washington reports said 4 million Americans would be thrown against Japan after V½-day.

Advance on Okinawa.

The U. S. tenth army resumed its general offensive on Okinawa after killing 3,000 Japanese in last Friday's counterattack.

In the Philippines the 25th division captured the last mill mass controlling the Talavera pass entrance to fertile Cagayan valley of Northern Luzon in a 4-day battle. The 24th and 31st pushed northward on Mindanao still hunting for the main force of some 40,000 Japanese reported to be on the island.

DUTCH NAZI CHIEF CAPTURED.

Anton Mussert Seized by Allied Troops at Utrecht.

UTRECHT, HOLLAND, May 7.(AP)—Anton Mussert, leader of the Dutch Nazi party, was captured by Allied troops at his headquarters in Utrecht today.

LEON BLUM IS RESCUED.

Dr. Hjalmar Schacht Is Also Captured by American Troops.

Los Angeles, May 7.(UP)—Christine Spurr, 22, was recovering today from an overdose of sleeping tablets, which police said she admitted taking because of an unhappy ending to a romance that flowered in Manila's Santo Tomas.

A prisoner of the Japanese for three years, Mrs. Spurr fell in love with another internee who, like

A SUICIDE ATTEMPT FAILS.

Mrs. Christine Sperry Despaired of Internment Camp Romance.

(Delayed)—American troops have captured or rescued Leon Blum, Kurt Schuschnigg, the Rev. Martin Niemoeller and Dr. Hjalmar Schacht.

Unconditional Capitulation of the Nazis in a Historic Meeting at Reims, France, to General Bedell Smith, Acting for General Eisenhower, Is Announced.

JODL SIGNS FOR FOE

Action of the Hitlerite Chief of Staff Follows Broadcast Announcement by Doenitz That Only Choice Left Is to Lay Down Arms.

ENEMY UNDERSTANDS GRIM TERMS

Spokesmen for Reich Make Pledge That Provisions Will Be Carried Out—In an Appeal for Mercy.

London, May 7.(AP)—The greatest war in history ended today with the unconditional surrender of Germany.

The surrender of the Reich to the western allies and Russia was made at General Eisenhower's headquarters at Reims, France, by Col. Gen. Gustaf Jodl, chief of staff for the German army.

This was announced after German broadcasts told the German people that Grand Admiral Karl Doenitz had ordered the capitulation of all fighting forces, and called off the U-boat war.

BULLETINS.

New York, May 7.—C. B. S. correspondent Edward R. Murrow reported from London that both President Truman and Prime Minister Churchill were prepared to broadcast the official news of the German surrender at noon, eastern war time, but that they were delayed because Premier Stalin, who was to speak at the same time, was not ready.

Ottawa, Canada, May 7.(AP)—The Canadian press said today premature announcement of surrender by the German radio disrupted Allied plans for the announcement, believed originally to have been scheduled for tomorrow.

New York, May 7.—C. B. S. reported at 11:38 a. m. an announcement by ABSIE, the official American broadcasting station in Europe, saying "Germany has surrendered unconditionally. The war is officially over in Europe."

Assie said President Truman, Prime Minister Churchill and Premier Stalin are expected to open to the world shortly and announce the official end of the war in Europe."

WAIT ON TRUMAN.

BY ORDER OF DOENITZ

First Word of German Capitulation Comes by High Command Broadcast Over Flensburg Radio.

ASKS WORLD TO DROP ITS HATRED

German Nation Is Urged to Accept Bitter Fate With Unity and Resolution to Heal Its Wounds.

London, May 7.(AP)—German broadcasts said today "all fighting German troops" had surrendered unconditionally.

An announcement on the wave length of the Flensburg radio, which has been carrying German communiques and orders for several days, said:

"German men and women! The high command of the armed forces has today, at the order of Grand Admiral Doenitz, declared the unconditional surrender of all fighting German troops."

The announcement was attributed to the new

Opening Salvo of the Cold War

"I can recall when we focused our concerns…on such things as a tiny patch of the Adriatic. . . . On those bits of geography and the handfuls of people within them in those years, war and peace at times could have hung in the balance."

— PRESIDENT DWIGHT D. EISENHOWER

America almost went to war along the Italian-Yugoslavian frontier in the hectic days of 1945–47.

The partisan forces of Marshal Josip Tito had control of the seaport of Trieste — "Queen City of the Adriatic" — when Allied troops entered the city on April 30, 1945, during the final days of WWII on the southern flank of Europe.

Occupation zones held 5,000 U.S. and British forces facing off against an equal number of Yugoslav army troops, supported by another 65,000 positioned just outside the zone.

Elements of the U.S. Fifth Army, fresh from several gruelling campaigns in Italy, moved into the Allied zone to counterbalance Tito's provocative moves. The 91st Infantry, 10th Mountain and 85th divisions took up positions in May 1945, followed in July by the 34th Division.

By September, the 88th Division "Blue Devils" took over responsibilities for maintaining order in Trieste. They patroled the Morgan Line of demarcation, stretching from Trieste on the Adriatic Sea to the Austrian border.

The last GIs of the 88th departed Trieste Oct. 24, 1947. But one regiment, the 351st Infantry, remained until 1954. By then, perhaps 120,000 GIs had served in Europe's "trigger city" on occupation duty.

An informal changing of the guard takes place April 18, 1947, at Outpost 36 at Montespino, Italy, where occupation troops of Co. E, 349th Inf. Regt. patrol the Morgan Line that separated the Allied zone from Tito's Yugoslavia. National Archives

Pfc. Clifford S. Nelson of the 175th Engineer Company works on a chalkboard with a schoolgirl during his visit to a village elementary school in Weingarten. The 175th was part of the vast Army of Occupation that remained in Germany for reconstruction assistance following the war.
U.S. Army

Left: The U.S. Constabulary, nicknamed the "Circle C Cowboys," formed the equivalent of a light mechanized cavalry division consisting of 35,000 men who policed Germany from 1946–1952. Patton Museum of Cavalry and Armor

Watch on the Rhine

On May 7, 1945, Gen. Dwight "Ike" Eisenhower succinctly summed up the end of WWII in Europe: "Germany surrendered unconditionally its forces on land and sea and in the air. Germany has been thoroughly whipped." But he also wisely anticipated the task ahead.

Referring to the occupation to come, Eisenhower told the press: "The success of this operation will be judged 50 years from now. If at that time Germany is a stable democracy, we will have succeeded."

The effort to revive the economies of West Europe, especially that of Germany, was as important as physically shielding borders from invading armies. Those objectives were assigned to the U.S. Army of Occupation in the Cold War's early years.

U.S. occupation of Germany between 1945 and 1955 had two distinct phases. First came the eradication of the last vestiges of Nazism. Then, with the onset of the Cold War, containing communism became the primary mission. On April 6, 1945, the 69th Infantry Division formally raised the U.S. flag over Germany at Ft. Ehrenbreitstein.

In 1945 the overriding concern of the Western Allies was to ensure that Germany would never again wage war. GIs, like other Allied soldiers, settled down to the often mundane task of helping the former *Reich* become nominally self-sufficient.

Hundreds of U.S. military government units went into action, some within days of the occupation. They found abject poverty and millions of homeless refugees. The Yankee occupiers — the *Amis* — did their best to relieve the suffering of German civilians in many individual ways. But first, there was the matter of demobilization and rotation.

66

West Germany [has been] restored to its full sovereignty as a political and military equal in the Western community of nations.

99

— JOHN DORNBERG
Newsweek

Austrian Sanctuary

"One suddenly becomes a person, with a name, a number, and a paper. One now has a right to move freely in the American zone of Austria."

— Displaced Person

Austria and especially its "City of Dreams" — Vienna — was a hotbed of Cold War international intrigue. "Vienna had everybody spying on everybody else," recalled Glen Gray, an MP with the 796th Military Police Service Battalion.

But it was also a crossroads for the continent's displaced persons (DPs), whom compassionate GIs assisted in the U.S. occupied zone. One had the "right to move freely in the American zone."

Other units in Austria from 1945 to 1955 included the 1st Battalion, 350th Infantry; the 61st, 64th and 6th Military Police companies; the 4th Reconnaissance Battalion; the 510th Field Artillery Battalion; and the 63rd Signal Battalion.

Besides providing security to the U.S. consulate, U.S. servicemen in Vienna were part of the International Patrol. It consisted of four-man military police units, each with U.S., British, French and Russian military policemen, keeping an eye on each other as much as the other countries' clandestine operatives.

Kidnappings, black market activities and plenty of espionage, and occasional brushes with danger, kept the Americans busy in Vienna.

The occupation ended in 1955 — a full 10 years after the war had ended.

When the war ended, 61 U.S. Army divisions and 3 million GIs were in Europe. Within a year of the massive redeployments, however, only three infantry divisions —1st, 3rd, 9th — and 278,000 men remained in Germany. By the end of 1946, even the latter two divisions had departed.

The relative tranquility of the occupation lasted almost three years. New troops rotated with regularity and hundreds of thousands of non-combat forces made the acquaintance of the former enemy from the safe confines of military compounds.

Yet internal security had to be maintained. To achieve that end, the U.S. Zone Constabulary was created as an "instrument of law enforcement" and "a covering force to meet and engage a hostile armed force pending concentration of the major elements of a tactical force." Germans called Constabulary members the *Blitz Polizei* or "lightning police."

In May 1946, most of the 1st Armored and 4th Armored divisions as well as elements of the seven mechanized cavalry groups then in Europe were redesignated Constabulary units. This elite 35,000-man mechanized police force initialy comprised nine regiments, and was responsible for a zone the size of Pennsylvania. Terrain varied from craggy mountain passes to marshy moorland, from river fronts to divided towns and villages.

The Constabulary's 32 squadrons and nine horse platoons (30 horses in each platoon) patroled the U.S. Zone's perimeter and conducted search and seizure operations — known as "swoops" — for hidden arms caches.

Stephen Traynor of Enderlin, N.D., was among the first to join the Constabulary. "As I was a farm boy, I volunteered for the mounted troops and was sent to Sonthofen, Bavaria to train troops in police work of all kinds. Unfortunately, Constabulary service is little known even among fellow veterans of the era."

Reduced in size by one-third within a year of formation, the Constabulary in 1948 was reorganized tactically into the 2nd, 6th and 14th Armored Cavalry regiments (ACRs). The ACRs were deployed along the border to guard against increasingly threatening Communist movements in eastern Europe.

With the activation of the new U.S. Seventh Army, the Constabulary was phased out in November 1950 with the exception of the 15th and 24th Squadrons, which remained on duty until December 1952. (A recon unit of the former 4th Regiment also was stationed in Austria.)

By then, the Allies had helped create a German border guard and custom officer force, numbering 26,700 supported by 1,250 trained police dogs. The longest single border separated West from East Germany, and proved the most troublesome.

The Russians organized East Germans into a 45,000-member border police that kept day-and-night watch over the "Iron Curtain." Ultimately, the fenced-off, booby-trapped border cut off virtually all avenues of escape from the East. But before the barrier was completed in 1952, many refugees found freedom.

GIs stationed along the frontier often unofficially aided many of the

2 million refugees who eventually escaped across the border, including some 3,000 East German Border Guards who deserted.

Meanwhile, GIs helped construct a new Germany literally from the ground up. The *wirtschafswunder* — German economic miracle — was made possible in part by thousands of hard-working Americans, especially members of the U.S. Army Corps of Engineers.

One small example: the 175th Engineer Heavy Equipment Company spent three months clearing land near the village of Weingarten along the Rhine River, earning the people's ever-lasting respect. The town's mayor expressed that gratitude when he said, "Without the help of the American engineers, Weingarten could never have built its community vineyard. We were happy to have American soldiers as our guests."

Such endeavors went a long way toward winning hearts and minds. In villages across Germany, bonds of friendship between former enemies were cemented for generations to come.

While nation-building progressed, tensions with communism mounted. In 1948, two pivotal geopolitical events occurred that affected the Allied occupation of West Europe dramatically.

In February, the coalition government of Czechoslovakia was overthrown in a Communist coup. Soviet leader Josef Stalin's intentions in East

The International Military Tribunal at Nuremberg was unique in judicial history in several ways. In the famous Nazi war crimes trials immediately after WWII, the accusers also were the judges — prosecuting a network of 13 trials for the Allies spanning 1,200 days in court and 330,000 pages of transcripts. The first trial started Nov. 20, 1945, and it lasted until Oct. 15, 1946, with the conviction of 18 Nazi war criminals and three acquittals. Eleven were condemned to death, three to life imprisonment and four to shorter prison terms. Novosti Press Agency

Above: The horse platoon of the 16th Constabulary Squadron marches in Berlin during May 1950. Mounted platoons consisted of 30 horses. The elite U.S. Constabulary served mostly in Germany, some in Austria, for six years after the war. U.S. Army

Right and opposite: The decks of the Queen Elizabeth and Queen Mary are a blur of cheering veterans as they approach New York harbor on June 29, 1945, delivering home thousands of soldiers who survived the war in Europe. National Archives

Europe became clear for the world to see; only Communist regimes would be tolerated there. Western security emphasis quickly shifted from guarding against a scarcely existing Nazi danger to a very real Communist one.

In October 1954, Germany gained admission to NATO and permission to rearm. On May 5, 1955, West Germany became "a full and unconditionally sovereign" nation. The U.S. Army of Occupation became an ally instead of an occupier.

Perhaps John Dornberg, who later became *Newsweek* bureau chief in Bonn, best summed up the American occupation: "After only 10 years, while the physical and spiritual aftermath of war was still everywhere apparent, West Germany was restored to its full sovereignty as a political and military equal in the Western community of nations."

No GI could have asked for a better outcome to a war that tore asunder an entire continent and personally touched the lives of millions of Americans.

A peaceful, prosperous West Europe was the legacy the WWII generation of GIs bequeathed the world.

★ ★ ★

Above: The long and short of it is they're homeward bound: Sgt. Victor Borelli of the 53rd Signal Battalion, 5-feet-2, carries the barracks bag belonging to his buddy, Sgt. Felix Leszyk (right), 6-feet-5, as they head back to the U.S. at war's end.

Right: American troops arrive in England, which was for many a stopover on the way home at the end of WWII. Others stayed in Europe until they accumulated enough points in the discharge system to return to the U.S. National Archives

Bags aloft, running the gauntlet of cheering chums at the Navy Redistribution Center at Lido Beach on Long Island, N.Y., upon being discharged in January 1945 are Mail Clerk 1/C Ernest E. Cochran (left) of Daytona Beach, Fla., and Soundman 3/C Frank E. McCarthy of Somerville, Mass. U.S. Navy

The sign says it all to the men marching beneath it upon returning to the United States in 1945 from the war in Europe. Press Association, Inc.

Discharged soldiers board a bus at Fort Dix, N.J., for their return to civilian life at the end of war in the European Theater. Signal Corps

A troopship overflows with the joy of its passengers — American soldiers who soon will be back with their families as a result of V-E Day in May 1945.

The Brooklyn, N.Y., Army Terminal became the scene of countless joyful family reunions as troopship after troopship took a berth there with anxious overseas veterans aboard, crowding the rails to wave, holler, and disembark from May 1945 on. U.S. Army

Staff Sgt. Arthur Freund leaves a bus at the Separation Center at Fort Dix, N.J., and 48 hours later he steps onto a train back home to Brooklyn, N.Y., after fighting in WWII. Millions of servicemen received their discharge following the war's end in Europe. Like Freund, many required rapid discharges for dependency reasons.
Signal Corps

In Your Own Words

Personal accounts of action on Land, at Sea and in the Air

> "
>
> *It was a wonderful feeling to be alive when dawn came, but then, with the realization of what the day would bring, one questioned the very value of life. . . . As I climbed stiff and frozen from the foxhole to march on aching feet, I wondered if hell wouldn't be welcome as a chance to get warm again.*
>
> "
>
> — KEN ROETTGE
> Rifleman, Co. E, 317th Inf.
> 80th Div., Battle of the Bulge

Czechoslovakia, May 1945

We were given rations at about 5 a.m. on May 5, 1945, and started marching. Scuttlebut soon told us that a number of diehard Germans (SS troopers, etc.) had been able to steal a couple of U.S. armored vehicles during the night. We were on their trail.

There was a U.S. scout plane above, and we did have tank support, but C Company was in the lead.

At about 10:15 or 10:30 a.m., C Company was stopped on a small hill and told to dig in. We could see a small town about a mile ahead. I Company was brought up and sent toward it. The name of the town was Zhurt in Czechoslovakia.

They were within 250 yards of the town when the enemy opened up with machine gun fire. The 3rd Battalion boys hit the ditches on both sides of the road. The tank support was called up and opened fire. In less than 10 minutes the firefight at Zhurt was over.

Within less than an hour jeeps picked up the dead and wounded. I have seen reports of 15 casualties.

I remember vividly saying '. . . and people back home think this damn war is over.' I've thanked God many times for the order that sent I Company into Zhurt instead of C Company. —*Pfc. F. Harmon Furney, C Co., 1st Bn., 357th Inf. Regt., 90th Infantry Division*

A tank destroyer overlooks the shores of Lake Garda in northern Italy. German units in Italy were overwhelmed by the Allied offensive and rushed to make it to the Austrain border before being encircled. The last battle in Italy was fought on Lake Garda on April 30, 1945. U.S. Army

Austria, May 1945

On May 4, 1945, we captured the commander of the concentration camp at Gunskirchen Lager, which was part of Mauthausen.

Under a white flag, he approached us with a young girl. He was dressed in a regular German, not SS, military uniform. The girl said she was Jewish and spoke for the officer, whose last name was Werner. The girl asked us not to harm him, and told us that the prisoners were fed and treated well.

The German guards surrendered while the SS troops exited out the back of the camp. We freed 17,000 prisoners.

While reconnoitering the area east of the Inns River on May 6, 1945, we were halted by an SS officer commanding a platoon. We were taken back to Waidhofen to the German command post in Rothschild Castle. This was the headquarters of German Army Group South, and it directed the last German resistance in Europe of WWII.

We — myself, Lt. Samuell and Cpl. Staudinger — were taken to the office of Gen. Lothar Rendulic, the commanding officer. After asking us light questions concerning rank and other things, he offered to surrender. He wanted us to meet with the Russians and demand that the area we occupied before the war ended would be the area we would occupy after the war. Lt. Samuell turned him down.

After radio contact was made with U.S. forces, the Germans delayed moving out of their headquarters three times. Finally, I was assigned to take the German general and his staff to Ried, Austria. With Gen. George Patton on the phone from Frankfurt, Germany, the formal surrender was planned for May 8, 1945 at Steyr, Austria. Gen.

Willard G. Wyman, commander of the 71st Infantry Division, accepted Rendulic's surrender of four German armies, or a total of 800,000 men. Gen. Rendulic received a 20-year sentence for crimes against humanity at the Nuremburg trials. He served 10. —*Staff Sgt. Lawrence B. Rhatican, 1st Plt., Cavalry Recon. Troop, 71st Infantry Division*

Italy, 1945

With the coming of 1945, the Germans were at work heavily reinforcing a new line of defense along the heights above Bologna called the Genghis Khan Line. Men at the front plunged wearily through snowdrifts, patrolling and probing the enemy lines.

By April, the Allies were ready to attack, which opened on the 5th. In quick succession — Massa, Carrara, Montese, Vergato — fell to the 92nd, 10th, Brazilian and 1st Armored divisions. Other units — U.S. 88th, 6th South African, 91st, 34th and 85th divisions — quickly joined the fray.

Soon the entire German front began to disintegrate. Bologna fell on April 21. Then the Po River was crossed.

Afterward, the Fifth Army fanned out toward the border to cut off all escape routes. The 91st Division pushed east through Vicenza to Treviso and tied in with the British Eighth Army. The 88th swung northeast from Verona to outflank Bolzano while the 10th Mountain fought its way to Lake Garda. The 1st Armored sent flying columns into the great city of Milan. The 92nd Division entered La Spezia and from there sent patrols west to the French border.

On May 2, 1945, all German forces surrendered unconditionally.

As one 88th Division infantryman said, 'We made it!' 'The end of the war,' one 91st Division veteran recalled, 'found us near a tiny village whose name I don't remember. There were no celebrations of any kind and I don't think anyone even muttered, Thank God, it's over. We simply tossed our equipment on the floor of the house we were in, put our heads on our packs, and slept the clock around.'

So ended the long bloody haul up the boot of Italy. Unfortunately, after the fall of Rome, GIs fighting on the peninsula had left the headlines, largely forgotten to history. — *Roy Livengood, 91st Infantry Division*

Czechoslovakia, May 1945

World War II's end was quite unique for me. My unit was the first to enter Pilsen, Czechoslovakia, on May 6, 1945. The three tanks in my outfit engaged in a 2-to 3-hour firefight with the Germans who sniped at us from house windows and church towers. Finally, the order came to cease firing. Enemy snipers came out with their hands up.

Next day, 5,000 Germans of the 11th Panzer Division marched into the town square to surrender. By then, members of the Czech resistance had pulled out their old uniforms and weapons, ready to show their support. The reception in Pilsen was an incredible experience.

But it didn't end there. My platoon was sent to a town called Cimelice on the demarcation line with the Russians on May 10. We were at this outpost until July 1945, facing down Russian tanks. Our orders were to discourage the Russians from going behind U.S. lines, but we were told never to use force to prevent it.

Two of our men were captured by the Russians when they strayed across the demarcation line. Held for two weeks, they were thoroughly interrogated and then released. You might say the Cold War actually began in that little Bohemian village in the summer of 1945. — *Ford Little Jr., Assault Gun Platoon, HQ Company, 64th Armored Infantry Battalion, 16th Armored Division*

Perched atop a tank are members of the 1st Platoon, 71st Cavalry Recon Troop — Sgt. Lawrence Rhatican, Cpl. Charlie Staudinger, Pfc. George Pinc, Pfc. Bruno Kisielewski and Sgt. Dominic Morabito — which ended up in Steyr, Austria, in early May 1945.
Photo courtesy of Lawrence Rhatican

66

A shell landed near the section sergeant and I took over the section. I picked up a route down the hill and we took off on the double. We hadn't gone 20 yards when an 88 (German artillery) picked us up. By the time I reached the bottom, 9 rounds had been fired. I turned around to see if anyone was hit and was surprised to find I was the only one there.

99

—JOHN S. TOKAREWICH
86th Inf. Div., crossing the Altmuhl
River at Eickstalt, Germany

SEA

Crossing the North Atlantic, with German U-Boats lurking nearby, was a perilous journey. Thousands of brave men from the Navy and Coast Guard served aboard transport ships, tankers and destroyer escorts running the gauntlet from the East Coast to Europe.

Greenland, 1943

On June 13, 1943, the USCG cutter *Escanaba* was part of *Task Unit 24.8.2* escorting a convoy from Greenland to Newfoundland. Lord Ha-Ha (a Nazi propagandist) said on the radio that the convoy would never make it to the United States. That's why so many escort ships were assigned.

Suddenly, at approximately 5 a.m., men from the other cutters of the task unit — *Algonquin, Mojave, Raritan, Tampa* and *Storis* — told me they saw a huge cloud of flame and smoke billow from the *Escanaba*. The explosion, most likely caused by an enemy torpedo, was so devastating that we could not send out any distress signals. She sank within three minutes.

There was about 10 or 15 men floating in the bitterly cold water when the *Storis* came to rescue us. Her crewmembers threw a cargo net over the side, but before we could reach it the ship pulled away. Apparently, she had made a contact because her black flag went up. Supposedly, a person could survive only three minutes in that water. It's hard to tell how long I was floating around because I passed out. They told me later that we were in the water for an hour.

When the *Storis* returned, only three of us were left: me, Boatswain's Mate 2nd Class Melvin Baldwin and Lt. R.H. Prause Jr. The lieutenant didn't make it. A total of 101 crewmembers died with only two survivors. Many of the crew were from Grand Haven, Mich., and within four months the townspeople had purchased $2 million in war bonds for the *Escanaba 2*. — *Seaman Roy O'Malley, veteran of the USS Escanaba*

Coast Guard, North Atlantic, 1942–45

I personally made 18 crossings of the North Atlantic on the *USS Camp* (DE 251) and believe me, any person who battled the North Atlantic, the German subs, the weather and seas on a small ship were in harm's way from the time they left port until they returned to the U.S.

Above: The Coast Guard cutter *Escanaba* provided protection to Allied convoys crossing the North Atlantic. Tragically, though, on June 13, 1943, an enemy U-Boat sighted in the Escanaba and fired a torpedo into her side. Within minutes she perished, taking 101 crewmen with her. Only two survived. U.S. Coast Guard

Below: Coast Guardsmen on a convoy patrol watch the explosion of a depth charge. U.S. Coast Guard

❝

The cold North Atlantic shows no trace of the struggle that took place on and beneath its surface more than 50 years ago. Unlike battlefields on land, where the scars of combat can last for centuries, the sea shrouds all traces of the 'Battle of the Atlantic,' which was the longest sustained campaign of World War II.

❞

— SCOTT T. PRICE
The Coast Guard and the North Atlantic Campaign

There were several Coast Guard ships lost in the North Atlantic and Mediterranean that were not identified as such. The Coast Guard was there and most of us who served were proud to have been part of the action. — *Sonarman 2nd Class Tom Taylor, veteran of the USS Camp*

Mediterranean, 1943

The *USS Savannah* (CL-42) participated in the landings at Gela, Sicily, in July 1943 and at Salerno in September 1943. At Sicily, *Savannah* provided fire support and launched scout planes in preparation for the initial invasion. Lt. C.A. Anderson was killed when a German *Messerschmitts* shot down his scout plane. *Savannah* also supported the Seventh Army's advance along the coast of Sicily and in August, the 30th Regimental Combat Team's landing east of Monte Fratello.

On Sept. 8 at Salerno Bay, *Savannah* was the first U.S. ship to open fire against the German shore defenses. She was put out of action at around 0930 on Sept. 11, 1943, after sustaining a direct hit from one of Hitler's radio-contolled bombs. The bomb was one of the first of its kind used.

A total of 197 sailors died, when the bomb exploded in the lower handling room. The ship was saved and, after repairs in Malta, returned to the Philadelphia Navy Yard in December 1943 for further repairs. — *Boatswain's Mate 2nd Class Paul E. Coggins, veteran of the USS Savannah*

The cruiser *Savannah* was shelling Salerno on Sept. 11, 1943, when a radio-controlled guide bomb penetrated the Number 3 gun turret and exploded below decks, killing 197 men and wounding 15. U.S. Navy

“

The spray from the first bomb completely obscured the ship. The British destroyer that was sitting on our starboard quarter signaled to ask 'What damage?' Just as our signalman prepared to answer 'No damage' a second flight of dive bombers came heading for us. The bombs fell so near that the concussion lifted the ship and shook her like a dog shakes a rat. . . . The only casualty aboard the Expositor was a seaman's dungarees. The deck hand, his arms full of 40mm ammunition, was on a ladder in the path of the 4-inch gun's blast. . . . The concussion (when the gun fired) ripped his pants off and I literally mean off. He didn't have a stitch on him. He stood there in a daze for a moment, and then dropped the shells he was carrying and tumbled to the deck after them. Somebody ran to pick him up. There wasn't any more of a scratch or bruise on him than there was pants. He was just dazed, and he couldn't quite figure out why he was mother-naked.

”

—LT. ROBERT B. RICKS
U.S. Naval Reserve, North Atlantic

AIR

Thousands of sorties were flown over Europe during World War II, and every crewman counted how many more missions he would need to reach the magic number before he could return home. Tragically, they also counted the many friends they'd lost.

Above: A Liberator bomber from the 464th Bomb Group passes over a billowing cloud after dropping its payload on the Pardubice oil refinery in Czechoslovakia, Aug. 24, 1944. Missions to Czechoslovakia would continue to the end of the European campaign, with the last mission flown against the Skoda armaments plant near Pilsen on April 25, 1945, by planes from the 398th Bomb Group. U.S. Air Force

Right: The heavy bomber *Judith Ann* from the 459th Bomb Group arrives at Poltava shuttle base in the Ukraine on April 12, 1945. American bombers of the Eastern Command, flying from airbases in England and the Mediterranean, would strike enemy targets deep within Europe then continue on to Poltava and other airbases in the Ukraine. There the planes would be refueled and rearmed for a return mission. The Germans launched a night raid on Poltava June 22, 1944, destroying more than 50 B-17s on the ground. U.S. Air Force

Czechoslovakia, April 1945

Our last mission was also the last American bombing attack in Europe during WWII, and they knew we were coming.

Our assignment was to hit the Skoda Armament Works in Pilsen. The 10-hour mission started early in the morning on April 25, 1945, and the flight was smooth. Of course, we didn't know until about an hour into the flight that Gen. Eisenhower ordered that the factory be notified of the bombing.

We arrived at our destination about 10 a.m. We encountered no fighters and only minimal flak. However, some of us had to make a second run at the target, and by then the Germans had found our range. They concentrated everything they had, and it was very heavy. Our plane got a bunch of holes in it.

Since we started out with four squadrons, we were able to get a lot of bombs on the target. Within about 45 minutes, we blew up most of the factory.

From what I understand, the workers must have taken the warning seriously because only eight of them died.

But the Germans knocked down two of our bombers and killed 12 crewmembers. Some of the men had died in the crashes, but nobody knew for sure what happened to the rest. Supposedly, the Nazis captured and executed them.

In Litice, Czechoslovakia, a town south of the factory, there is a memorial to the 12 who died. We don't begrudge the Czechs their knowledge of the bombing. We must remember that the war was coming to an end, and they weren't our enemies. —*2nd Lt. Charles Hough, navigator, 398th Bomb Group, Eighth Air Force*

Ukraine, 1944

On June 22, 1944, 53 U.S. B-17s were totally destroyed at Poltava during a German night raid in one of the war's worst losses for the U.S. Army Air Forces.

The following day I returned to my base at Mirgorod, and we had another night visit from the Germans. Our aircraft had been dispersed to other bases, but they got the gasoline dump and bomb dump in addition to raising havoc with our pierced plank runway.

I spent that night in a sleeping bag in a corn field a few miles from the base. We had no casualties. —*Warrant Officer Hershell F. Winship, U.S. Army Air Forces, Eastern Command*

Germany, 1945

On April 21, 1945, a B-24, The Black Cat, *became the last U.S. bomber shot down over Germany in WWII. The following two accounts are excerpted from the lone survivors of the 12-man crew. (From the book* Wings of Morning *by Thomas Childers. Used with permission — Addison-Wesley Publishing Company, Reading, Mass.)*

Our plane was hit by flak over Regensburg, and within 10 seconds the plane was on fire and starting into a spin. The left wing was torn off by the shell. All interphone communications failed, and I was unable to determine the disposition of my fellow crew members. Due to the fact that I was seated on the floor with my legs extended into the nose wheel well, I was able to drag myself out.

After escaping from the ship, I dropped several thousand feet in a free fall. I opened my chute at 10,000 feet. I saw the wings and rudders of the ship floating down to earth. I saw the wreckage burning on the ground about three miles from my position.

I saw one chute besides mine; that was the chute of Staff Sgt. Albert Seraydarian, my tail gunner. No other chutes were seen.

Sgt. Seraydarian and I were taken prisoner immediately after reaching the ground. It is my belief that all other crew members were killed in the crash. Sgt. Seraydarian was caught in the spin and remained motionless in the ship. Only when the fuselage broke behind the camera hatch was he able to fall out. He later told me that he had seen Sergeants Brennan and Peterson, the waist gunners, making a futile effort to reach the rear hatch exit. — *Lt. Christ Manners, Bombardier, 466th Bomb Group, Eigth Air Force*

When I came to, I realized that the tail section was torn off from the rest of the airplane. I was terrified.

I had the sense enough to realize that I was floating down in the tail. I put my chute on and in the excitement was only able to hook my left side on. I pulled the ripcord and the chute blossomed out and pulled me free of the tail section. But the chute was badly torn by sliding past the jagged and torn metal of the fuselage and all the other jagged pieces of metal.

When I got about 5,000 or 6,000 feet off the ground I heard whistling noises and looked down behind me and saw two soldiers on a motorcycle shooting at me. I could see flashes from their rifles. I took my .45 and threw it away.

When I hit the ground I was at a very steep angle and hit hard. I hurt my back and ankle. I couldn't move.

The soldiers grabbed me and searched me. I didn't know the language so I pointed to my injuries. They understood and lifted me up and put me in the sidecar of the motorcycle. They let me straddle my arms over their shoulders and they carried me toward this large building.

As I was approaching about the second step I felt a sharp burning pain in my back. I screamed and looked around. This German woman who came from nowhere poked me with a red-hot poker, clear through my flying clothes.

They hurriedly carried me inside, and to my astonishment I saw Lt. Manners there. He was already stripped of his flying clothes. He was soaking wet. I later learned that he had just missed the corner of the building that we were in and landed in the creek. I also learned that he had to put his chute on in midair because he fell through the nose wheel door. He grabbed his chute on the way out. — *Staff Sgt. Albert Seraydarian, Tailgunner, 466th Bomb Group, Eighth Air Force*

For the 12 crew members of *The Black Cat,* the mission of April 21, 1945, was their last. Their bomber was downed over Regensburg, and only two crewmen survived. U.S. Air Force

66

We transported everything from troops and donkeys, to food and gasoline. It was really scary, though, when we were hauling gas cans, knowing just one stray bullet from an enemy soldier on the ground could turn us into a flying bomb. . . . Often we had to land in fields that were mined and there was no way to tell until it was too late. Our planes didn't have engines that would allow us to circle around and find a better landing zone, and we couldn't send one glider in first to check the field while we flew around overhead to see if it blew up. We all landed in a group, and sometimes it wasn't a very pretty sight when those mines blew up.

99

—Capt. Jim Helinger
Glider pilot , 442nd Troop
Carrier Group

CAMPAIGNS AND CASUALTIES
A Concise Reference Section

European Theater Casualties

During WWII, the U.S. Army deployed 68 combat divisions to the European Theater of Operations. Those infantry, armored, airborne and mountain divisions suffered 78% of all Army casualties sustained in the theater.

The infantry, by far, absorbed the greatest percentage of casualties: 80% of Army killed in action. While only 14% of the Army's total overseas strength, the infantry suffered 70% of all battle casualties. Riflemen equaled 68% of an infantry division's man-power, but accounted for 95% of its casualties.

Divisions varied widely as far as time in combat. For instance, the 3rd Infantry Division went into action in November 1942; the 13th Airborne Division arrived in France on Feb. 6, 1945, but was never deployed in combat. Maximum time in combat for the average infantryman was 200 days before he reached the breaking point.

Division	Combat Deaths	Wounded in Action	Division	Combat Deaths	Wounded in Action
3rd Infantry	5,558	18,766	94th Infantry	1,156	4,789
4th Infantry	4,854	17,371	99th Infantry	1,134	4,177
29th Infantry	4,786	15,541	104th Infantry	1,114	3,657
9th Infantry	4,504	17,416	7th Armored	1,098	3,811
1st Infantry	4,280	15,208	102nd Infantry	1,077	3,668
45th Infantry	4,080	14,441	6th Armored	989	3,666
90th Infantry	3,930	14,386	100th Infantry	984	3,539
36th Infantry	3,637	13,191	63rd Infantry	974	3,326
83rd Infantry	3,620	11,807	10th Mountain	953	3,134
30th Infantry	3,516	13,376	75th Infantry	928	3,314
2nd Infantry	3,488	12,785	70th Infantry	834	2,713
80th Infantry	3,480	12,484	103rd Infantry	821	3,329
34th Infantry	3,350	11,545	66th Infantry	800	636
35th Infantry	2,947	11,526	10th Armored	774	3,109
79th Infantry	2,943	10,971	12th Armored	725	2,416
8th Infantry	2,820	10,057	5th Armored	710	2,442
28th Infantry	2,683	9,609	9th Armored	693	2,280
5th Infantry	2,656	9,549	42nd Infantry	638	2,212
88th Infantry	2,556	9,225	92nd Infantry	616	2,187
3rd Armored	2,126	6,963	14th Armored	560	1,955
26th Infantry	2,112	7,886	76th Infantry	523	1,811
101st Airborne	2,090	6,388	11th Armored	522	2,394
82nd Airborne	1,951	6,560	106th Infantry	470	1,278
85th Infantry	1,736	6,314	8th Armored	466	1,572
78th Infantry	1,625	6,103	69th Infantry	383	1,146
91st Infantry	1,575	6,748	89th Infantry	325	692
84th Infantry	1,438	5,098	71st Infantry	278	843
1st Armored	1,428	5,168	65th Infantry	260	927
17th Airborne	1,382	4,904	13th Armored	253	912
95th Infantry	1,372	4,945	97th Infantry	214	721
4th Armored	1,356	4,551	86th Infantry	161	618
87th Infantry	1,295	4,342	20th Armored	59	134
44th Infantry	1,206	4,209	16th Armored	5	28
2nd Armored	1,183	4,557	13th Airborne	0	0

Source: *Order of Battle, U.S. Army World War II* by Shelby L. Stanton (Navato, Calif.: Presidic Press, 1984).

★ U.S. Army ETO Combat Casualties by Campaign

Campaigns are listed in order of highest ground combat deaths.

Campaign	Dates	Ground KIA	Air KIA	Total KIA	% of All KIA
Rhineland	15 Sept. 1944 – 21 March 1945	45,649	4,761	50,410	28.9
Ardennes-Alsace	16 Dec. 1944 – 25 Jan. 1945	17,932	1,314	19,246	11.0
Northern France	25 July – 14 Sept. 1944	15,583	2,261	17,844	10.2
Normandy	6 June – 24 July 1944	13,787	2,506	16,293	9.3
Central Europe	22 March – 11 May 1945	13,376	1,633	15,009	8.6
Rome-Arno	22 Jan. – 9 Sept. 1944	6,585	4,808	11,393	6.5
North Apennines	10 Sept. 1944 – 4 April 1945	5,416	3,070	8,486	4.8
Air Offensive	4 July 1942 – 5 June 1944	0	7,504	7,504	4.3
Southern France	15 Aug. – 14 Sept. 1944	2,777	4,524	7,301	4.1
Naples-Foggia	18 Aug. 1943 – 21 Jan. 1945*	4,667	1,599	6,266	3.5
Anzio	22 Jan. – 24 May 1944	5,538	0	5,538	3.1
Tunisia	12 Nov. 1942 – 13 May 1943*	2,529	309	2,838	1.6
Sicily	14 May – 17 Aug. 1943*	1,819	753	2,572	1.4
Po Valley	5 April – 8 May 1945	1,656	258	1,914	1.0
Egypt-Libya	11 June 1942 – 12 Feb. 1943	0	997	997	.57
Algeria-French Morocco	8 – 11 Nov. 1942	456	23	479	.28
Total		**137,770**	**36,320**	**174,090**	

Source: Computed from Dept. of the Army, *Army Battle Casualties and Non-Battle Deaths in WWII: Final Report.* Washington, D.C., 1953.
*Air campaign beginning dates are earlier.
Note: Designated campaign tally excludes 3,459 KIA not categorized by campaign, which brings the grand total to 177,549 KIA.

★ Select U.S. Navy ETO Ship Fatalities

Listed is a sample of warships that sustained a large death toll in a single incident. All told, the U.S. Navy lost 5,793 men killed in action and 6,077 wounded in the Atlantic Theater: 16% of its total battle losses in WWII.

ATLANTIC

Ship	Cause	Place	Date	Killed
Warrington	Hurricane	Bahamas Islands	9/13/44	251
Leopold	Torpedoed	Iceland	3/10/44	171
Atik	Torpedoed	East Coast	3/27/42	141
Turner	Explosion	Ambrose Light, N.Y.	1/3/44	120
Frederick C. Davis	Torpedoed	North Atlantic	4/24/45	115
Reuben James	Torpedoed	North Atlantic	10/31/41	115
St. Augustine	Collision	Cape May, N.J.	1/6/44	115
LST 531	German MTB	English Channel	4/28/44	112
Truxton	Wrecked in gale	Placentia Bay, N.F.	2/18/42	110
Escanaba	Explosion (?)	Greenland	6/13/43	103
Jacob Jones	Torpedoed	Cape May, N.J.	2/28/42	102
Leary	Torpedoed	North Atlantic	12/24/43	97
LST 507	German MTB	English Channel	4/28/44	72
Plymouth	Torpedoed	North Carolina	8/5/43	70

MEDITERRANEAN

Ship	Cause	Place	Date	Killed
Maddox	Bombed	Sicily	7/10/43	210
Rowan	Torpedoed	Salerno, Italy	9/10/43	202
Savannah	Bombed	Salerno	9/11/43	197
Buck	Torpedoed	Salerno	10/9/43	166

Source: *Seaweed's Ship's History — WWII Losses; Warship Losses of World War II* by David Brown (London: Arms and Armour, 1990); *Dictionary of American Naval Fighting Ships* (Washington, D.C.: Navy History Division, 1963-1991)

In Remembrance of Battle

Campaign Credits Awarded by Service

European-African-Middle Eastern Campaign ★

Army/Army Air Forces

Egypt-Libya	June 11, 1942 – Feb. 12, 1943
Air Offensive, Europe	July 4, 1942 – June 5, 1944
Algeria-French Morocco	Nov. 8–11, 1942
Tunisia[1]	Nov. 17, 1942 – May 13, 1943
Sicily[2]	July 9, 1943 – Aug. 17, 1944
Naples-Foggia[3]	Sept. 9, 1943 – Aug. 17, 1944
Anzio	Jan. 22 – May 24, 1944
Rome-Arno	Jan. 22 – Sept. 9, 1944
Normandy	June 6 – July 24, 1944
Northern France	July 25 – Sept. 14, 1944
Southern France	Aug. 15 – Sept. 14, 1944
North Apennines	Sept. 10, 1944 – April 4, 1945
Rhineland	Sept. 15, 1944 – March 21, 1945
Ardennes-Alsace	Dec. 16, 1944 – Jan. 25, 1945
Central Europe	March 22 – May 11, 1945
Po Valley	April 5 – May 8, 1945
Army Air Forces; air combat	Dec. 7, 1941 – Feb. 2, 1945

and anti-submarine warfare in addition.

[1] Air campaign began Nov. 12
[2] Air campaign began May 14
[3] Air campaign began Aug. 18

Navy/Coast Guard

North African occupation
Sicilian occupation
Salerno landings
West Coast of Italy operations (1944)
Invasion of Normandy
Northeast Greenland operation
Invasion of Southern France
Reinforcement of Malta
Escort, anti-submarine, armed guard
and special operations

Dates for the Navy correspond, in most cases, to those of the other services.

Victory Medal, World War II

Authorized on July 6, 1945, for members of the U.S. armed forces who served on active duty at any time between Dec. 7, 1941, and Dec. 31, 1946. It was also awarded to members of the Philippine armed forces.

American Campaign Medal

Established by executive order on Nov. 6, 1942, and amended by another executive order on March 15, 1946, which set the closing date. It was awarded to all members of the armed forces who, between Dec. 7, 1941, and March 2, 1946, served on land or aboard certain ships, for an aggregate period of one year within the continental limits of the U.S., or for 30 consecutive days or 60 non-consecutive days outside the continental limits but within the American Theater of Operations. Naval personnel who participated in certain specified operations — escort, anti-submarine, Armed Guard, and others — were awarded one bronze star for each operation, to be worn with this medal.

European-African-Middle Eastern Campaign Medal

Established by executive order on Nov. 6, 1942, and amended by another executive order on March 15, 1946, which set the closing date. It was awarded to all members of the U.S. armed forces who served in the prescribed area or aboard certain ships of the Navy between Dec. 7, 1941, and Nov. 8, 1945.

Medal of Honor Recipients: A Select Few

Capt. Jack L. Treadwell of Snyder, Okla., has the Medal of Honor hung around his neck by President Harry Truman in Wurzbach, Germany, in March 1945.

1st. Lt. Audie Murphy (r.) receives the Medal of Honor from Seventh Army Commander Lt. Gen. Alexander Patch on June 2, 1945, near Salzburg, Austria. Murphy returned home with 33 medals and citations, including the Distinguished Service Cross, two Silver Stars, Legion of Merit, three Purple Hearts and two Bronze Stars. He served 28 months with Company B, 15th Infantry Regiment, 3rd Infantry Division.

MEDAL OF HONOR RECIPIENTS BY BATTLEGROUND

Battleground	Medals Awarded	Percentage
France	62	29.0
Italy	48	23.0
Germany	46	22.0
Belgium	18	8.0
Europe (air war)	15	7.0
Romania	7	3.0
Sicily	5	2.0
Holland	3	1.5
Morocco	3	1.5
Tunisia	3	1.5
Luxembourg	2	1.0
South Atlantic	1	.5
Total in ETO	**213**	**100.0**

Lt. Col. Matt Urban (l.) accepts the Medal of Honor from President Jimmy Carter on July 19, 1980 — 36 years after the fact — during a 9th Division reunion in Washington, D.C. Among his 29 medals, Urban earned two Silver Stars, a Legion of Merit, three Bronze Stars, and seven Purple Hearts. He served from North Africa through Germany as a member of Company F, 60th Infantry Regiment, 9th Infantry Division. Congressional Medal of Honor Society

Staff Sgt. Lucian Adams of Port Arthur, Tex., receives congratulations upon presentation of the Medal of Honor by Lt. Gen. Alexander M. Patch Jr., commander of U.S. Seventh Army's 3rd Division, IX Corps. On Oct. 28, 1944, Adams reopened supply lines near St. Die, France, in a lone assault with an automatic rifle against four machine guns, three of which he eliminated. U.S. Army

Tech. Sgt. Robert E. Gerstung from Chicago received the Medal of Honor for action in December of 1944 when he helped temporarily penetrate the Siegfried Line or "West Wall." U.S. Army

Staff Sgt. Herbert H. Burr of Kansas City, Mo., was decorated for action in Germany during March 1945. U.S. Army

The Infantry OCS Hall of Fame at Fort Benning, Ga., is named for Lt. Thomas W. Wigle, an OCS graduate of 1943 from Detroit who was awarded the Medal of Honor posthumously. With the 34th Inf. Div. on Sept. 14, 1944, near Monte Frassino, Italy, Wigle died when his attack against three houses of German soldiers led to the capture of 36 and seizure of a defensive strongpoint. U.S. Army

Sgt. Henry Schauer is credited with killing 17 Nazi soldiers in 17 hours of battle at Anzio, earning him the Medal of Honor and the nickname "German an Hour Schauer."

National Archives

Sgt. James P. Connor of Wilmington, Del., performed "conspicuous gallantry" in leading a platoon after its leader was killed and, while wounded three times, landing his unit of the 3rd Div., Seventh Army on Cape Cavaleire in southern France in August 1944. It earned him the Medal of Honor. Signal Corps

President Harry Truman congratulates Sgt. Charles A. MacGillivary of Charlottetown, Prince Edward Island, one of the few Canadians to receive the Medal of Honor during WWII. MacGillivary earned America's highest military award for action with Co. I, 71st Inf. Regt., 44th Inf. Div., in Woelfling, France, on New Year's Day of 1945.

After 50 years the guns are silenced, but for those Americans who fought in WWII, the memories remain as vivid as if they occurred just yesterday.

Thousands of Americans rest in serene cemeteries overseas, such as the Epinal WWII Cemetery in Vosges, France. American veterans who return to visit WWII battle sites and these gardens of stone ensure that their buddies who didn't make it back are well cared for.

Rocco Telese (inset) of the 339th Infantry Regiment (the "Polar Bears"), 85th Infantry Division, returned to Tremensuoli, Italy, to pay tribute to Medal of Honor recipient Lt. Robert Waugh, who died May 14, 1944, during the assault on the Gustav Line.

Recommended Reading: Books by Battle

Single-Volume History of World War II

Gilbert, Martin. *The Second World War: A Complete History*. N.Y.: Henry Holt & Co., 1989. 846p.

General Histories

Doubler, Michael D. *Closing With the Enemy: How GIs Fought the War in Europe, 1944–1945*. Lawrence: Univ. Press of Kan., 1994. 354p.

Ellis, John. *The Sharp End: The Fighting Man in World War II*. N.Y.: Scribner's, 1980. 372p.

Kennett, Lee. *GI: The American Soldier in World War II*. Warner Books, 1987. 265p.

Perret, Geoffrey. *There's A War To Be Won: The U.S. Army in World War II*. N.Y.: Random House, 1991. 623p.

MacDonald, Charles B. *The Mighty Endeavor: American Armed Forces in the European Theater in WWII*. N.Y.: Oxford Univ. Press, 1969. (Reprint 1994.) 621p.

Aachen

Whiting, Charles P. *Bloody Aachen*. N.Y.: Stein & Day, 1976. 191p.

Air War (General)

Davis, Richard G. *Carl A. Spaatz and the Air War in Europe*. Washington, D.C.: Center for Air Force History, 1993. 808p.

Perret, Geoffrey. *Winged Victory: The Army Air Forces in World War II*. N.Y.: Random House, 1993. 549p.

Hammel, Eric. *Air War Europa: Chronology, 1942–1945*. Pacifica, Calif.: Pacifica Press, 1994. 572p.

Airborne Operations

Devlin, Gerard M. *Paratrooper! The Saga of U.S. Army and Marine and Glider Combat Troops During WWII*. N.Y.: St. Martin's Press, 1979. 717p.

Atlantic Naval War

Abbazia, Patrick. *Mr. Roosevelt's War: The Private War of the U.S. Atlantic Fleet, 1939–1942*. Annapolis: Naval Institute Press, 1975. 520p.

MacIntyre, Donald. *The Naval War Against Hitler*. N.Y.: Charles Scribner's Sons, 1971. 478p.

"Big Week"

Infield, Glenn. *Big Week: The Classic Story of the Crucial Air Battle of WWII*. N.Y.: Brassey's, 1974/1993.

Bulge

Astor, Gerald. *A Blood-Dimmed Tide: The Battle of the Bulge By the Men Who Fought It*. N.Y.: Donald I. Fine, Inc., 1992. 532p.

Dupuy, Trevor N., et al. *Hitler's Last Gamble: The Battle of the Bulge*. N.Y.: Harper Collins Publishers, 1994. 576p.

Cherbourg

Breuer, William B. *Hitler's Fortress Cherbourg: The Conquest of a Bastion*. N.Y.: Stein and Day, 1984. 274p.

Dresden Air Raid

Irving, David. *The Destruction of Dresden*. N.Y.: Holt, Rinehart & Winston, 1983.

Dragoon, Operation (S. France)

Breuer, William B. *Operation Dragoon: The Allied Invasion of the South of France*. Novato, Calif.: Presidio Press, 1987. 261p.

Elbe, Meeting at

Scott, Mark. *Yanks Meet Reds: Recollections of U.S. and Soviet Vets from the Linkup in WWII*. N.Y.: Capra Press, 1988. 300p.

Exercise Tiger

Lewis, Nigel. *Exercise Tiger: The Dramatic, True Story of a Hidden Tragedy of World War II*. N.Y.: Prentice Hall Press, 1990. 271p.

Falaise-Argentan Pocket

Blumenson, Martin. *The Battle of the Generals: The Untold Story of the Falaise Pocket — The Campaign That Should Have Won World War II*. N.Y.: William Morrow & Co., 1994. 288p.

France

Bonn, Keith E. *When the Odds Were Even: The Vosges Mountains Campaign, October 1944-January 1945*. Novato, Calif.: Presidio Press, 1994. 294p.

Maule, Henry. *Normandy Breakout*. N.Y.: Quadrangle/N.Y. Times Book Co., 1977.

Miller, Robert A. *August 1944: The Campaign for France*. Novato, Calif.: Presidio Press, 1988. 280p.

Weigley, Russell F. *Eisenhower's Lieutenants: The Campaign of France and Germany, 1944–1945 (Vol. I)*. Bloomington: Indiana Univ. Press, 1981. 588p.

Whiting, Charles. *'44: In Combat from Normandy to the Ardennes*. N.Y.: Stein and Day, 1984. 219p.

Germany/Central Europe (General)

Simons, Gerald. *Victory in Europe*. Alexandria, Va.: Time-Life Books, 1982. 208p.

Essame, H. *The Battle for Germany*. Bonanza Books, 1969.

Toland, John. *The Last 100 Days*. N.Y.: Random House, 1965.

Weigley, Russell. *Eisenhower's Lieutenants: The Campaigns in France and Germany, 1944–1945 (Vol. II)*. Bloomington: Indiana Univ. Press, 1981. 1,151p.

Hurtgen Forest

Whiting, Charles. *The Battle of Hurtgen Forest: The Untold Story of a Disastrous Campaign*. N.Y.: Pocket Books, 1989. 300p.

Italy

General

D'Este, Carlo. *World War II in the Mediterranean, 1942–1945*. Chapel Hill: Algonquin Books, 1990. 218p.

Morris, Eric. *Circles of Hell: The War in Italy 1943–1945*. N.Y.: Crown Publishers, Inc., 1993. 498p.

Anzio
Blumenson, Martin. *Anzio: The Gamble That Failed*. N.Y.: J.B. Lippincott, 1963.
D'Este, Carlo. *Fatal Decision: Anzio and the Battle for Rome*. N.Y.: Harper Collins, 1991. 566p.

Monte Cassino
Hapgood, David and Richardson, David. *Monte Cassino: The True Story of the Most Controversial Battle of World War II*. N.Y.: Berkley Books, 1986. 286p.

Mountains
Orgill, Douglas. *The Gothic Line*. N.Y.: Zebra Books, 1986.

Rapido River
Blumenson, Martin. *Bloody River: The Real Tragedy of the Rapido*. London: Allen & Unwin, 1970.
Smith, Lee. *A River Swift and Deadly: The 36th Infantry Division at the Rapido River*. Eakin, 1989. 200p.

Salerno
Morris, Eric. *Salerno*. N.Y., 1983.

Sicily
D'Este, Carlo. *Bitter Victory: The Battle for Sicily, 1943*. N.Y.: Harper Perennial, 1991. 666p.

Leopoldville (Ship Sinking)
Sanders, Jacquin. *A Night Before Christmas*. N.Y.: G.P. Putnam's Sons, 1963.

Malmedy Massacre
Bauserman, John M. *The Malmedy Massacre*. Shippensburg, Pa.: White Mane Pub., 1995.
Whiting, Charles. *Massacre at Malmedy*. N.Y.: Stein & Day, 1971.

Market-Garden, Operation
Ryan, Cornelius. *A Bridge Too Far*. N.Y.: Simon & Schuster, 1974. 670p.

Metz
Kemp, Anthony. *The Unknown Battle: Metz, 1944*. N.Y.: Stein & Day, 1980. 250p.

Mortain
Featherston, Alwyn. *Saving the Breakout: The 30th Division's Heroic Stand at Mortain*. Novato, Calif.: Presidio Press, 1993. 304p.

Normandy
Ambrose, Stephen E. *D-Day: June 6, 1944*. N.Y.: Simon & Schuster, 1994. 704p.
D'Este, Carlo. *Decision In Normandy*. N.Y.: Harper Collins, 1991. 555p.

North Africa (Operation Torch)
Gelb, Norman. *Desperate Venture: The Story of Operation Torch, The Allied Invasion of North Africa*. N.Y.: William Morrow & Co., 1992. 366p.

Northwind, Operation (Alsace)
Whiting, Charles. *The Other Battle of the Bulge: Operation Northwind*. Chelsea, Mich.: Scarborough House, 1990. 198p.

Occupation of Germany
Davis, Franklin M. *Come as a Conqueror: The U.S. Army's Occupation of Germany, 1945-1949*. N.Y., 1967.

Ploesti Air Raid
Dugan, James & Carroll Stewart. *Ploesti: The Great Ground-Air Battle of August 1943*. N.Y.: Random House, 1962.

Remagen Bridge
Hechler, Ken. *The Bridge at Remagen: The Amazing Story of March 7, 1945 — The Day the Rhine River was Crossed*. Mont.: Pictorial Histories Publishing Co., Inc., 1993. 232p.

Rhineland Campaign
Allen, Peter. *One More River: The Rhine Crossings of 1945*. N.Y.: Scribner's Sons, 1980. 320p.
Whitaker, W. Denis & Shelagh. *Rhineland: The Battle to End the War*. N.Y.: St. Martin's Press, 1989. 422p.
Whiting, Charles. *Bounce the Rhine: The Battle for the Heart of Germany*. N.Y.: Avon Books, 1992. 240p.

Ruhr Pocket
Kessler, Leo. *The Battle of the Ruhr Pocket: April 1945*. Mich.: Scarborough House, 1990. 224p.
Whiting, Charles. *Battle of the Ruhr Pocket*. N.Y.: Ballantine Books, 1970.

Schweinfurt Air Raid
Coffey, Thomas M. *Decision Over Schweinfurt*. N.Y.: McKay, 1977.
Jablonski, Edward. *Double Strike: The Epic Air Raids on Regensburg/Schweinfurt*. N.Y. Doubleday & Co., 1974. 271p.

St. Lo
St. Lo, 7 July - 19 July 1944. Nashville, Tenn.: The Battery Press, Inc., 1984. 128p.

Tunisia (Kasserine Pass)
Blumenson, Martin. *Rommel's Last Victory*. Boston: Houghton Mifflin, 1967.

 **1st Infantry**

 **2nd Infantry**

 3rd Infantry

 **4th Infantry**

 **5th Infantry**

 **8th Infantry**

 **9th Infantry**

 **10th Mountain**

 **26th Infantry**

 28th Infantry

 29th Infantry

 **30th Infantry**

 34th Infantry

 35th Infantry

 36th Infantry

 42nd Infantry

 **44th Infantry**

 **45th Infantry**

 **63rd Infantry**

 **65th Infantry**

 **66th Infantry**

 69th Infantry

 **70th Infantry**

 **71st Infantry**

 **75th Infantry**

 76th Infantry

 78th Infantry

 79th Infantry

 80th Infantry

 **83rd Infantry**

 **84th Infantry**

 **85th Infantry**

 86th Infantry

 87th Infantry

 88th Infantry

 89th Infantry

90th Infantry **91st Infantry** **92nd Infantry** **94th Infantry** **95th Division** **97th Infantry**

99th Infantry **100th Infantry** **102nd Infantry** **103rd Infantry** **104th Infantry** **106th Infantry**

13th Airborne **17th Airborne** **82nd Airborne** **101st Airborne**

1st Armored **2nd Armored** **3rd Armored** **4th Armored** **5th Armored** **6th Armored**

7th Armored **8th Armored** **9th Armored** **10th Armored** **11th Armored** **12th Armored**

13th Armored **14th Armored** **16th Armored** **20th Armored**

Shoulder patches provided courtesy of
Val Kolesik, Independence, Missouri

Profiles

EDITORS

RICHARD K. KOLB
Editor-in-Chief, *VFW Magazine*

As magazine editor, he conceived the four-year series — "50 Years Ago This Month" — upon which this book was built. He determined the content and edited and created the copy at all stages of development.

Kolb joined the magazine in 1989, and became publisher in 1990. He writes often for the magazine. His 36-part series on the *Saga of America's Overseas Veterans* appeared 1989–94.

Previously, Kolb was a staff writer and editor for corporate and association publications in the petroleum industry. As a free-lance writer, he contributed more than 50 articles, mostly on military history and veterans issues, to 20 national publications.

A Vietnam veteran (4th Infantry and 101st Airborne divisions), he holds a degree in political science (University of Alaska), with emphases in international relations, history and journalism.

Long active in veterans affairs, he chaired the Vietnam Veterans Leadership Program in Houston, Tex., coordinating a public outreach and employment campaign during the 1980s.

He resides in Kearney, Mo., and belongs to VFW Post 5717.

GARY L. BLOOMFIELD
Senior Editor, *Faces of Victory*

He contributed feature articles to the WWII series and was photography editor for the entire project. He also wrote many of the book's sidebars and sections.

He worked on the *VFW Magazine* staff from 1989 to 1995. He was a civilian Army public affairs specialist in Kansas City previously. He holds degrees in English (Avila College) and liberal arts (Baker University).

During his 10 years in the Army, he served two tours in Korea, and in Germany. He earned recognition as Army Journalist of the Year (1977), U.N. Command Best Journalist (1978) and USAREC Best Journalist (1989). Photos he shot have appeared in numerous national and international publications.

He resides in Belton, Mo. and belongs to VFW Post 9879 in San Francisco.

MICHAEL McKENZIE
Consulting Editor, Addax Publishing Group

He served as a copy editor of the manuscript, photograph cutlines and first-person accounts.

Currently a regional correspondent for *Sports Illustrated* and local sports radio commentator, McKenzie has worked since 1965 as an editor, columnist and reporter for newspapers and magazines, including *The Kansas City Star & Times* and *The Atlanta Journal*, as well as a broadcaster.

As part of a reporting team with the *Kansas City Star & Times*, he shared a Pulitzer Prize in 1981. To his credit are one book and two anthologies.

His B.A. degree from Westmar College (Iowa) is in English. He was an information and broadcast specialist with the U.S. Army during 1967–70 at Redstone Arsenal, Ala.

He resides in Shawnee Mission, Kan.

ROBERT WIDENER
Art Director, VFW Magazine

He created the cover of the book, plus lent extensive input into the design and the photo spreads. He was responsible for design and layout of the WWII series. Widener moved from a Kansas City advertising agency to the magazine in 1989.

After earning a degree in English from Emporia State University, he spent several years in advertising, primarily in graphic design. He has more than 10 years' experience as a graphic arts specialist.

He resides in Kansas City, Mo.

DOMINIC J. CARACCILO

Author of the *Ready Brigade of the 82nd Airborne in Desert Storm* (1993), he contributed nine articles to the "50 Years Ago This Month" series on Europe.

Caraccilo teaches systems engineering at the U.S. Military Academy, his alma mater, at West Point.

He commanded HQ Co., 2nd Bde., 82nd Airborne Division — the Ready Brigade of the National Command Authority — during the Persian Gulf War, 1990–91.

A member of the VFW, he resides at West Point, N.Y.

DAVID P. COLLEY

He wrote three articles in the series that formed the foundation of the book.

He has written two books and has another in progress on the *Red Ball Express in WWII*. A free-lance writer, Colley's byline has appeared in a variety of national magazines.

His interest in WWII developed as he grew up in Europe, roaming the battlefields such as the Bulge and Huertgen Forest. He revisited those sites in 1994 to gather material.

Colley was an editor and reporter with several newspapers from 1968–80, including the *Baltimore Evening Sun*, before he turned full-time to free-lance writing.

He resides in Easton, Pa.

KEN HECHLER

Author of the award-winning *The Bridge at Remagen* (1957; revised edition, 1993), from which a movie was made, he wrote four articles for the *VFW Magazine* WWII series.

A U.S. Army combat historian, he landed at Normandy, crossed France, witnessed the attack on Bastogne, and was at Remagen, Germany during the capture of Ludendorff Bridge in March 1945.

Hechler is West Virginia's secretary of state. He previously served nine terms in the U.S. House of Representatives. Also, he was once a White House assistant to President Harry Truman.

He resides in Huntington, W. Va., and is a life member of VFW Post 1064.

OTHER CONTRIBUTORS

Michael Graham wrote "Mobilizing for the War Against the Axis" and **Gustav Berle** wrote much of the section entitled "Watch on the Rhine." VFW Staff Writer **Timothy Dyhouse** researched and edited first-person accounts.

norman rockwell